Women, Girls, and Addiction

Women, Girls, and Addiction

Celebrating the Feminine in Counseling Treatment and Recovery

Cynthia A. Briggs and Jennifer L. Pepperell

Routledge
Taylor & Francis Group
New York London

Routledge
Taylor & Francis Group
711 Third Avenue.
New York, NY 10017

Routledge
Taylor & Francis Group
2 Park Square,
Milton Park, Abingdon,
Oxfordshire OX14 4RN

First issued in paperback 2014

Routledge is an imprint of the Taylor and Francis Group, an informa business

© 2009 by Taylor and Francis Group, LLC

ISBN 978-0-415-99352-4 (hbk)
ISBN 978-1-138-88440-3 (pbk)

Library of Congress Cataloging-in-Publication Data

Briggs, Cynthia A. (Cynthia Ann), 1972-
    Women, girls, and addiction : celebrating the feminine in counseling treatment and recovery / Cynthia A. Briggs and Jennifer L. Pepperell.
        p. cm.
    Includes bibliographical references and index.
    ISBN 978-0-415-99352-4 (hbk. : alk. paper)
    1. Women--Substance use--Prevention. 2. Addicts--Counseling. 3. Women--Counseling. 4. Addicts--Rehabilitation. 5. Feminist theory. I. Pepperell, Jennifer L. II. Title.

HV4999.W65B75 2009
616.86'06082--dc22

2008053196

Visit the Taylor & Francis Web site at
http://www.taylorandfrancis.com

and the Routledge Web site at
http://www.routledgementalhealth.com

To women and girls who suffer silently,
may this book help give you a voice.

CONTENTS

PREFACE

She sits across from me with tears in her eyes. Her skin smells musky, of hard work and hot sun, and her hair is carelessly tossed into a ponytail. She is dressed simply but neatly, in a cotton button-down shirt and blue jeans. She tells me about her five children, and of her struggles to find work, to feed them, to keep them all together in one household. Her devotion as a mother is clear, but her direction is not. She is 35 years old, African American, separated from her junkie husband. She is a cocaine and alcohol addict referred to me by her probation officer for treatment. I am a 26-year-old white woman from the suburbs whose drug use experience is limited to a handful of cigarettes, an occasional beer on a Friday night, and one failed attempt to get high on a secreted joint. She tells me about her struggles: She cannot find work because she doesn't have a permanent address, and she cannot rent an apartment without a paycheck. She is at risk of losing custody of her beloved babies because she cannot stop using cocaine, the drug her former husband introduced her to. I listen to her describe the terrible poverty in her life, and I wonder how to overcome the impossible barriers between her and abstinence.

For counselors and counselor educators alike, addiction counseling presents a unique and difficult challenge. Counseling students are often mystified and intimidated by the process of treating addicted individuals, and experienced counselors can feel unprepared for clients who present with addiction issues. However, preparation for working with addicted clients is critical, necessary, and sorely needed. In 2005, approximately 8% of Americans aged 12 and older used illicit drugs, and about 23% had engaged in binge drinking in the previous 30 days.

Heavy drinking was reported in 6.6% of U.S. citizens aged 12 or older, about 16 million individuals. Approximately 30% of the U.S. population reported tobacco use. Most new drug users and smokers were under age 18 when initiated to use; most alcohol consumers were under age 21 when initiated (National Survey on Drug Use and Health [NSDUH], 2005). Clearly, substance use is prevalent and widespread.

In addition, *process addictions*, or addiction to a behavior such as gambling, Internet gaming, or sexual activity, can confound counselors. Few treatment resources exist. However, the statistics emerging from the research sources available are alarming. For example, both men and women reported high levels of depression and anxiety related to gambling, along with drug and alcohol problems (DATA, 2002). Internet gaming addiction is being considered for inclusion in the next version of the *Diagnostic and Statistical Manual* (Olson, 2007). And finally, sexual addiction is estimated to affect 3% to 6% of the population (Hall, 2006). Clearly, these process addictions present additional clinical challenges.

Unfortunately, much of what we believe we know about addiction, treatment, and recovery evolved from an exclusively male perspective. In the research realm, until the 1990s, the vast majority of studies were conducted on male clientele (Greenfield, 2002). The results from these studies, indicating "best practices" in addictions counseling, were thus generalized to women without evaluating the effectiveness of such practices on this population. Biological, psychological, and sociological discoveries about addiction were assumed to be universal, based on the male experience (Greenfield). However, as we know now, women do in fact experience addiction differently than men. For example, because of their biochemistry, women experience *telescoping* on the road to addiction: Even though women may begin problem use later in life, they become addicted more quickly than comparative male clients (Parks, Hesselbrock, Hesselbrock, & Segal, 2003). Telescoping appears to exist for both substance and process addictions (DATA, 2002). Women also exhibit different psychological components to addiction, including a desire to suppress painful emotions, while men tend to engage in addictive behavior to enhance positive emotions (Haseltine, 2000; Hegamin, Anglin, & Farabee, 2001). And finally, with regard to social factors, women and girls' addictive behavior is inextricably linked to relationships. Women are likely to be introduced to their primary drug of addiction by a male partner, such as a boyfriend or spouse, and are less likely to receive familial support for their recovery (Cook, Epperson, & Gariti, 2005; Gordon, 2002; Nelson-Zlupko, Kauffman, & Dore, 1995). Clearly, the experience of women addicts in treatment is vastly different from that of men, and these differences are crucial to recovery.

Another point to consider: Currently, about 95% of treatment programs in the United States are based on the Minnesota or 12-Step models of treatment (Veach, Remley, Kippers, & Sorg, 2000). The 12-Step movement was founded by Bill Wilson and Dr. Bob, two heterosexual white men of privilege (Matthews & Lorah, 2005). While the 12-Step movement has certainly impacted the recovery movement in profound ways, it is presumptuous to assume it might be applicable to all. For example, the first step requires the addict to admit powerlessness over the substance (or process, in the case of gambling and other compulsive behaviors) of addiction and to acknowledge life has become unmanageable. The underlying assumption of this step implies the addicts' ego and inflated sense of personal power have contributed to downfall. However, consider the case study example presented at the beginning of the preface. A female client, experiencing extreme poverty, at risk of losing her children, with the additional oppression of her race and gender, feels very little sense of personal power. Often, social pressures and discrimination have deeply influenced her addictive process, along with her primary relationships (in this case, her ex-spouse), poverty, unemployment, and low self-esteem. To insist this client admit her powerlessness is moot: She is already well aware of her lack of power.

This book emerged from our work with women and girls who do not fit traditional, male-oriented models. It comes from our own frustration in attempting to counsel women and girls in a treatment system that does not fit their needs. It comes from our passionate belief that these women and girls deserve better. They deserve an understanding of their experience, based on research conducted with women and girls and from a lens that views their socialization in a society where men continue to benefit from their majority status. They deserve to have a book dedicated to them. This book is not just about alcohol use or drug use; it is also about process addictions, including shopping, gambling, sex, and food. We will also examine girls who self-mutilate and what that process means to them. This is a book that sees all addiction as addiction. It is not about what the substance is, but about the process and the needs of each individual woman. This book will examine the biological, sociological, and psychological components of addiction for women and girls. We will discuss what works in counseling and what does not.

Most importantly to us, this book is not about men. We will not spend time in each chapter comparing women to men. This is a book for and about women and girls. Much of the literature on addiction is about men; there is no shortage. This is not a book that will be doing that safe gender dance. We write as women, for women. We write based on our research and clinical experiences. We hope you enjoy it, and that it gets you talking. It certainly did for us.

This book is intended for both practicing counselors and counselor educators. Our mission is threefold. First, we discuss the female experience with addiction broadly, through historical and developmental lenses. Our purpose is to educate the reader about the complex sociological web in which addiction develops and recovery occurs. We will examine these processes from a feminist perspective, offering our critique on traditional norms and assumptions about addictive behavior. Second, we more closely examine the specific barriers and strengths of women experiencing addiction, including the biological, psychological, and sociological factors in contemporary society. Third, we present specific research and practice-based treatment and recovery interventions. We hope to leave practioners and students alike with a toolbox of effective interventions to best serve their female clientele. Throughout this text, multicultural considerations regarding race, ethnicity, ability status, and sexual orientation will be included.

And finally, at the end of Chapter 1, we introduce you to Sheila, our case study subject, whose story is woven throughout the text. Sheila is a fictitious character, a composite of many of the clients we have counseled in the past. Her story is meant to demonstrate the complex nature of women's addiction and to give readers a concrete glimpse into the life of a struggling addict. Discussion questions also help readers reflect on Sheila's case and explore their own opinions and biases.

We hope that you will enjoy reading this book as much as we enjoyed writing it and that you find it challenging and engaging.

ACKNOWLEDGMENTS

I first have to thank my coauthor, Jennifer Pepperell, without whom this book would have never have been written. Jennifer's confidence, pragmatism, and organization lay the foundation for this book to be born and kept us both on track through the "stuck" places of the writing process. Jennifer and her family also welcomed me into their lives after we met on the first day of our doctoral program at Oregon State University. For that I am so grateful. I also must thank Tim Hatfield, Mary Fawcett, Nick Ruiz, and Gaylia Borror at Winona State University for welcoming me into the profession and supporting (putting up with) me during the writing process. I am blessed to work with such fine people who are collaborative and supportive in everything they do. Huge thanks to Sarah Musburger-Garcia and Sara Schiebout, who assisted in editing this document. You are both amazing students, graduate assistants, and future counselors. I am also thankful for Dana Bliss, our editor at Routledge, who remained calm and supportive through all the ups and downs of the writing process. Thank you, Dana, for believing in us. Finally, and most importantly, thank you to my family for raising me so well and for letting me go to find my path. I love you immeasurably.

Cyndi

When I first started thinking about working on a book, Cyndi was the first person I thought of as a coauthor. Her partnership and friendship have meant more than I could ever express in words. This process has been so much fun with her. I thank Walter Roberts for his endless support and constant teasing; I did not have a big brother growing up, but

I have found myself lucky enough to get one as an adult. I am also endlessly thankful for Rick Auger, who has been a constant rock of support and mentorship, who somehow can manage to keep Walter and me in line. To Deb Rubel, thanks for the friendship and honest conversations; you taught me that it is okay to be a strong, opinionated woman in higher education. Thanks, Leah, for your help, and I am looking forward to your final leap into the profession. I am very grateful to Dana Bliss, our editor and external support system, who was so supportive and steady during this process; you really made it as easy as possible. Finally, to my family: my mom and sister, who have always been supportive; my dad, while not with me in body any longer, is always around; my partner, Peter, who puts up with more than any one man should have to (that strong opinionated woman thing); and my two daughters, who are amazing young girls—I cannot wait to see what you do next.

Jennifer

I

An Overview of Women, Girls, and Addiction

1

FEMINIST THEORY AND
ADDICTION COUNSELING

Walk the good road, my daughter, and the buffalo herds wide and
dark as cloud shadows moving over the prairie will follow you....
If the pride and virtue of the women are lost, the spring will come
but the buffalo trails will turn to grass. Be strong, with the warm,
strong heart of the earth. No people goes down until their women
are weak and dishonored... [from the Sioux tradition]. (Zinn,
2003, p. 104)

Upon opening this textbook, one might initially ask why a text on
women and girls struggling with addiction is needed, rather than simply including a chapter or two dedicated to women in a broader text.
Or, while reading this first chapter, one may wonder what is going to
be different about this book, and how will it differ from other addiction counseling texts? This text is written from a critical feminist perspective in that it supports and affirms the development of women and
girls from a female viewpoint. This means women and girls who are
struggling with addiction are first and foremost women and girls. If
gender is not included as a treatment criterion, then treatment is likely
to fail. Drug and alcohol treatment has among the highest recidivism
rate of any counseling treatment in the field, in part because addictions
counseling is often not geared toward individual client needs, especially
with regard to cultural differences, including gender. This text will provide an exploration of the addictions process for women and adolescent girls and treatment recommendations appropriate for them based

on their unique experiences primarily related to their gender, which is biologically, socially, and psychologically constructed.

The purpose of this chapter is to introduce the reader to feminist theory and social justice as they relate to addictions counseling for women, so the reader might better understand the long-standing cultural norms that have shaped the profile of addiction in the 21st century. The need for a feminist counseling perspective emerged because most psychological pathology and treatment frameworks were developed by men for a male clientele. Thus, women came to be seen as "other": Men are the norm, women are "different" (Crawford & Unger, 2004). In most counseling texts, women's issues are considered in a special section for multiculturalism, as are individuals of various races, sexual preferences, ages, and ability statuses. What this implies to the reader is that women are to be considered a special case, where men will be easier to treat within the existing framework.

Before we begin, it is important to define addiction and what that existing framework is. According to the *Diagnostic and Statistical Manual*, 4th Edition, Text Revision (DSM-IV-TR; American Psychiatric Association [APA], 2000), an individual with an addiction problem is experiencing the following in conjunction with the compulsive ingestion of a substance (e.g., alcohol, cocaine, prescription painkillers): tolerance, withdrawal symptoms when attempting to cut back or quit, inability to control use, negative impact on one or more areas of life functioning (e.g., family, work, recreational), and continued use of the substance in spite of physical or psychological problems as a result of the substance use. A lengthier discussion of specific criteria for addiction can be found in the next chapter.

The above criteria apply to substance dependence. However, it is well known that individuals can develop addiction to activities and behaviors as well, including gambling, pornography, food, self-harm, or Internet gaming, to name a few. There are no specific diagnostic criteria for these *process addictions*, aside from gambling, in the DSM-IV-TR (APA, 2000). Thus, we will rely on the above criteria for substance addiction for the discussions in this text. Throughout the text, when we refer to addiction, we include both substance and process addictions because we perceive both to be significant social problems that are worthy of discussion.

FEMINIST THEORY: AN OVERVIEW

On a personal note, we (the authors) often notice that in some circles, it appears social justice endeavors no longer apply to women; women are liberated, and thus further discussion of women's issues is unnecessary. We disagree. Women are still marginalized and oppressed in U.S. society and in addictions counseling research, so we feel it is imperative to maintain focus on the needs of women and girls, both collectively and as individuals. The oppression of women who experience addiction is complex, multifaceted, and systemic. Addiction cannot be treated in isolation (i.e., separated from other mental health issues, from cultural influences, or from biological conditions), and thus the counselor must also become the advocate. The root of social justice is advocacy, as is the root of feminism; the two go hand in hand. We assume since you are reading this book that you, on some level, are open to both.

To understand the philosophical premise of this text, a discussion of feminist theory is necessary. It is also recommended that the reader do additional exploration into feminist theory as needed because the discussion here will simply provide an overview and is not intended to reflect an exhaustive study of feminism. Generally speaking, feminist theory allows gender to be of primary concern when doing research or counseling a client. The socialization and systemic concerns for women and girls include minimization and victimization in the United States and world societies; socialized gender roles, which may inhibit full psychological, social, and spiritual development; and the oppression that results from "feminine" characteristics not being valued among leaders in society. From a feminist theory, these are some of the issues to consider when working with girls and women, particularly in addictions counseling.

In order to describe addictions counseling from a feminist perspective, it first becomes necessary to understand a definition of *feminism*. As with all women, our own perspectives on the meaning of feminism are colored by life experiences and education. The authors are heterosexual women who both identify as Caucasian, of European ancestry. We were raised in middle- to upper-class neighborhoods, one of us from the East coast, the other from the West. We both consider ourselves privileged, by virtue of our race, educational level, and current socioeconomic statuses. Because of this, our perspectives might easily be qualified as part of the dominant Eurocentric culture. However, we claim our feminist stance as valid because we simultaneously attempt to broaden our world views and embrace the perspective of others with cultural values different from our own. As we attempt to define feminism, we draw upon the wisdom of other thinkers and writers but acknowledge that their words are filtered through our own experiences onto this page.

Feminism is, at its simplest, the idea that women are as capable as men. This perspective evolved in the United States in the mid-1800s, birthed in the middle-class arena of white, married women. Since the first wave of feminism that connected to the suffrage and abolitionist movements, feminism has been vilified and glorified and experiences an uneasy relationship, at best, with women in the United States. Today, *feminist*, a term misunderstood and often poorly defined, is not widely embraced by women regardless of political, cultural, or philosophical stance (Freedman, 2002).

DIVERSITY IN FEMINISM

It would be irresponsible of us to talk about feminism without mentioning the growing dissatisfaction of women of color within the feminist movement. Much of this internal debate stems from the mission of the feminist organizations. For example, when the focus of the group is on equal wages or gender equality in a police department, but no focus is on the growing cut in welfare or police brutality, women of color feel that disparity (Hernandez & Leong, 2009). The feminist organizations tend to be run by white women of privilege, and women of color may not be able to find their voice or place in the movement. This clearly has long-term implications for the movement, not only for unifying women, but also for defining a purpose.

It can be asserted that there are as many definitions of feminism as there are feminists (hooks, 2000). On the one hand, this constructivist stance allows for women to own the term on an individual basis. Women are freed from the constraints of a ready-made belief system. Instead, we can identify as feminist in a personally relevant way based on our race, class, sexual orientation, or nationality (Freedman, 2002). On the other hand, endless definitions may ultimately weaken the use of the term and leave feminism as a movement without a supporting theory. In fact, the lack of a consistent definition in the United States may imply a growing apathy toward the feminist movement in general (hooks).

Creating a concise definition is difficult without marginalizing one subgroup of women or another. As most feminist publications arise from the experience and belief system of white, educated, middle-class, heterosexual women, how can their beliefs fully encompass the experience of women of color, lesbian women, or women from developing countries? Popular feminist theory has been criticized for narcissistically focusing on the needs of white women of privilege. As women have been historically relegated into supporting roles for men, so women of color have been relegated into supporting roles for white women (Collins, 2000; hooks, 2000). The "common oppression" asserted by white feminists denies the experience of women outside that world (hooks). How then, can any one definition of feminism suffice? And how can the feminist movement survive without a definition? The problem is a paradox.

For the purpose of this text, a definition of feminism must be in place. Hooks (2000) suggests a movement from individual to collective interests, calling for the eradication of domination in all relationships, resulting in the transformation of society. In that vein, we adopt Freedman's (2002) definition:

> Feminism is a belief that women and men are inherently of equal worth. Because most societies privilege men as a group, social movements are necessary to achieve equality between women and men, with the understanding that gender always intersects with other social hierarchies. (p. 6)

IDENTITY DEVELOPMENT

One critical component to addictions counseling for women is the concept of identity development. Women form their identities in a way that is different than men, and understanding this process helps when determining which treatment models may be best. We will briefly address it here, and then come back to it in other chapters. As an overview, Gilligan and her colleagues (Gilligan, Ward, & Taylor, 1988) were among the first in the field of psychology to recognize that women are not men, girls are not boys, and women do not form identities in the same ways in which men do. This groundbreaking research in the area of moral development led the charge for others. What we now understand is that women and girls form their identity in connection with others (Jordan, Kaplan, Miller, Stiver, & Surrey, 1991). Women and girls are healthier, happier, and can nurture themselves when they do not isolate themselves, but bond and join with others in order to find their voice and purpose. When girls connect with others as they are developing, they learn to see themselves as others see them, and as they would like to be seen. These interactions help them to learn who they are and who they would like to become. As the United States values autonomy and independence more than interdependence, women are often perceived, or perceive themselves, as "weak" when they cannot operate as independently as society dictates. When women don't connect, they lose part of themselves, their sense of identity or self-esteem. Helping women find their identity is done by helping them connect both to others and to the parts of themselves they love.

SOCIAL JUSTICE CONSIDERATIONS

Other issues that arise when looking at women from a traditional frame of reference is that women's relational needs are often pathologized, or in the addictions field, labeled "codependent" (Covington & Surrey, 1997). In addition, addictions counseling for women often stems from a traditional male perspective that fails to acknowledge a woman's need for additional community support. For example, as clinicians, we often found our agencies lacking in specific services for women. Single mothers were required to attend evening group sessions, yet no childcare existed after hours, and the public buses stopped running at 7 p.m. With such barriers, how can a woman be expected to consistently make it on time for treatment? Furthermore, within the current, traditional framework for addictions counseling, lateness or absence to treatment is seen as resistance, so a woman without adequate childcare who misses group treatment to tend to her dependents will be seen as unready or unwilling to engage in counseling. It's a paradox. How can a single mother succeed in such a system?

Thus, a feminist perspective dictates that counselors must be advocates for women clients. Feminist researchers and clinicians advocate for change on the micro (individual) and macro (agency, community) levels. We believe in order for there to be lasting, generational change, there must be systemic change. The way that women and girls are socialized and the way that society views women must shift in order for there to be any real change.

We propose using feminist theory as a lens through which to understand the experience of addicted women and girls in counseling. The women and girls who struggle with addiction do so in part because of gender expectations, pressures from others, and an inability to live up to the systemic pressures. The struggles created for women and girls in the United States as a result of systemic sexism and oppression can make recovery for these addicted clients especially difficult. When one has been victimized, as most women who struggle with any form of addiction have, it can be almost impossible. When women are cut off from the ones they are connected to, or if they are hurt by the ones they love and trust, they begin to lose their identity. When a woman loses her sense of identity, she may seek it elsewhere, through shopping, self-mutilation, or a bottle.

Because it is through connection that women find their identity, women must heal through connection. In counseling women and girls who are suffering from addiction, we must help them find themselves again. This can be done by helping them to reconnect to others and then ultimately to themselves.

CURRENT PRACTICE

Currently, there are three different typical treatment options available to individuals suffering from an addiction: an outpatient treatment program, a brief inpatient treatment program, and community-based support groups. The level of treatment is based on the severity of the addiction and the symptoms that one is demonstrating at the time of the assessment. The American Society of Addiction Medicine (ASAM) provides providers with a guide for the type of treatment that would be most appropriate for the symptoms. Outpatient treatment is for individuals who are not detoxifying and are stable. This level of service includes group work and may include individual counseling, depending on the agency. The length of time and number of groups per week will vary. Inpatient care may be a short 48- to 72-hour stay to detoxify, or a longer 15-day program, depending on insurance and the type of care needed. The longer stay would be considered Level III, Residential/Inpatient Treatment, or Level IV, Medically Managed Intensive Inpatient Treatment (ASAM, 2008), typically then moving to an outpatient program for follow-up. The majority of treatment programs are based on the Minnesota/12-Step model.

The third method is the community-based support groups. These groups are not treatment groups, but are groups run by other members who have had shared experiences. The most common groups are ones based in the anonymous fellowships: Alcoholics Anonymous (AA) and Narcotics Anonymous (NA). The system these groups are based on includes frequent meetings, primarily in a group format, and other members of the group run the meetings. During the meetings, individuals work on their 12 Steps, which includes admitting to powerlessness, making amends to individuals that have been hurt, and turning over the addiction to a higher power. This 12-Step model is at the root of other common treatment methods, which will be discussed in further chapters.

The methods that are most often used to treat addictions do not appear as effective for women and girls. We know, for starters, that women are much less likely to be diagnosed with an addiction problem than men (Velasquez & Stotts, 2003). Much of the misdiagnosis, or ignoring of addiction for women and girls, stems from the difference of how addiction is perceived by many clinicians. Women tend to minimize addictive behaviors, and blame those behaviors on negative emotional states, such as anxiety or depression. If women are not identified or diagnosed with an addiction, they clearly cannot be helped (Velasquez & Stotts). As one can imagine, much of this discrepancy comes from the way in which women are socialized around addiction. This socialization begins in childhood, where girls get the message that addiction is shameful and unsafe, or that it prevents them from being able to perform adequately as a partner and mother (Velasquez & Stotts). Women and girls then tend to hide their addiction, and society is willing to ignore their addiction in favor of something else. When addiction is finally recognized in women and girls, they are often punished rather than helped.

One of the results of this is that women tend to practice their addiction alone, and with that often comes guilt and anger. This isolating feeling works against a woman's need to connect to others, to be part of a group in order to have a strong sense of self. When women are isolated and addicted, it drives them away from much of what would assist them in recovery. Women and girls who are addicted must be viewed "within the context of their relationships to others, recognizing that they are part of a larger relational and multigenerational system" (Velasquez & Stotts, 2003, p. 498). Traditional treatment methods do not view women this way.

From a feminist and relational perspective we must begin to view women and girls as being drawn to their addiction in ways that help them to make connections, help them to feel loved, energized, or supported (Covington & Surrey, 1997). Women and girls often use substances or food or gambling as a way to cope with the hurt from their relationships, or a way to bring those relationships closer. Current treatment must begin to focus on these areas to be successful. It is also why self-help groups like AA so often fail women and girls. While they may be relationally oriented, they do nothing to work with women and girls on the relational or cultural aspects of their addiction. They don't address the abuse or violence that many women addicts face, nor do those programs address any of the concurrent issues that women may face.

SUMMARY

So far, this chapter reviewed feminism, feminist theory, and identity development, and the current addictions counseling practices, but what does this mean for addictions counselors? With regard to addictions counseling, this means the concerns of women clients are every bit as valid, important, and worthy of attention as those of male clients. Furthermore, women clients are disadvantaged when counselors are uneducated about the specific biological, cultural, and social issues they face as they struggle to overcome their addiction. This text is an effort to close that educational gap so that counseling services for addicted women clients can be more effective in meeting their needs.

Case Study

Sheila is a 30-year-old African American woman who has come to you for counseling because of a history of depression and anxiety. She also is concerned that she might be addicted to painkillers that she was given by her doctor after having a Cesarean section six months ago. She says that she is not able to stop taking the medication even though the pain is gone, and that she often falls asleep while caring for her two children, ages 3 and 6 months. In addition, Sheila reports moderate alcohol use, and reveals she drinks more when stressed. She is a stay-at-home parent, and her partner works full-time as a bank manager. He is also concerned about her use of pain medication and alcohol, and her depression.

From a feminist perspective, an addictions counselor would consider the relationships and the social construct of Sheila's world. We would also consider how her race and her experiences with racism contribute to her worldview. Is Sheila experiencing close relationships with her partner? Does she feel she is treated equally in her home? We would also look at the wider social system that Sheila lives in as a stay-at-home mom. Does she feel valued, and does she have support? Very often women who stay home to raise children can feel isolated and minimized, and it will be important to find out what her experience of staying home is. Does she have connections with other women who stay home with their children, and what are their experiences? These may be contributing to the depression and anxiety that she is feeling. It would also be important to determine if she truly does have diagnosable depression and anxiety, or if these are labels that she has ascribed to herself. With the current trend to advertise antidepressant and antianxiety medication in popular magazines (most often targeting women), it will be important to know how she sees these labels and where these diagnoses came from.

Her relationship with her partner will be important to understand, as will how she sees parenting and how that has affected their home. Along with all of this, it will be necessary to learn about her background and to determine if there is any abuse or trauma that may be contributing to the current situation. These would be the issues that would be worked on, along with learning more about the pain medication use, and providing strategies to end that use.

DISCUSSION QUESTIONS

1. From a feminist perspective, how do you begin to see Sheila's relationship with her partner?
2. What role might gender and race play in your understanding of Sheila's current life situation?
3. If you think about being relationally oriented in your work with Sheila, how does that change what you previously thought about what treatment recommendations you would make?

2

WOMEN, GIRLS, AND ADDICTION
A Historical Perspective

Women and girls throughout United States history have shared a complicated relationship with drugs, alcohol, and processes of addiction. It is difficult to overestimate the impact of social norms and stereotypes on women and girls with regard to addiction. Take a moment right now and try this mental exercise: Picture a man in a bar, holding a bottle of beer. Imagine all the details: the pool table in the background, the multicolored lights, and the paper coasters on the bar. Perhaps he's drinking with buddies, or perhaps he's alone. What descriptive words come to mind as you imagine this scene? Most will imagine a typical beer advertisement: rugged, clean-cut, "normal" guys out for a night with the boys. Some will imagine a decent, hard-working man on his way home from work. Others will imagine a tough guy, maybe a little rowdy, but a lot of fun to hang out with. Most descriptors will be positive, or at least framed within the social norms of manhood.

Now try the same experiment imagining a woman at the bar holding the same bottle of beer. How does it change for you? Most of us understand intellectually that it is perfectly normal for a woman to be in a bar, enjoying a beer, but when we imagine this gendered picture, our attitudes shift. Negative words begin to creep in: immoral, low-class, party girl, slut. We tend to judge more harshly the drinking behaviors of women than we do of men. And for most of us, this shift is nearly unconscious, and we are hardly aware it has occurred. Consider this: Until the 1950s, in the United States it was illegal to show a woman drinking alcohol in a movie or advertisement (Covington, 2008). People found it distasteful to see women engaging in alcohol use.

The stereotypes and social constructs run even deeper when we picture boys and girls engaging in addictive behaviors. Typically, a boy sneaking a taste of his dad's beer at age 12 is considered a bit naughty, but normal. A girl doing the same is something shameful: She is on the road to ruin. If upon examination these attitudes seem a bit Victorian to you, they are. In this chapter, the historical foundations of current attitudes about women, girls, and addiction are examined. Alcohol, drugs, and processes of addiction will be individually examined for women and girls. Contemporary issues of addiction, including prevalence and characteristics of addiction for women, are also reviewed. But before we examine addiction from a feminine perspective, it's important to define addiction as it is currently regarded in the mental health community.

WHAT IS ADDICTION?

There are many ways to become addicted to a substance or process. Because the purpose of this text is to conceptualize the uniquely female attributes of addiction and recovery, a clinical description of each possible drug or process of abuse and addiction will not be presented. Rather, we will highlight the primary drugs or processes of concern from a more holistic perspective. Gender considerations with regard to the biological, psychological, and sociological components of addiction tend to be universal across addictions, as do treatment considerations. For a more definitive work on types of drugs, we recommend *Buzzed* (Kuhn, Swartzwelder, and Wilson, 2008), an excellent guide to the full spectrum of drugs of abuse.

So what constitutes a *drug* or *process* of abuse? Drugs can be any chemical substance, legal or illegal, that creates an altered state for the user. Drugs include alcohol, nicotine, prescription medications (such as Oxycontin or Valium), illegal drugs (such as methamphetamine, heroin, or marijuana), as well as common household items that can be abused (inhaling or "huffing" from spray cans or abusing cough and cold medications). Drugs typically fall into two categories, stimulants or depressants. Most people who use drugs do so to either suppress or enhance an emotional state. So while the stressed out, agitated, single mom of three might use alcohol (a depressant) to relax, the shy college freshman might try cocaine (a stimulant) in order to feel more powerful, in charge, and confident.

Process addictions actually work very similarly to drugs in that they either stimulate or suppress certain emotional conditions by triggering the release of certain chemicals in the brain (for more discussion on brain chemistry see Chapter 3). For the purpose of this text, we chose several process addictions currently of most pressing concern for women and girls. However, the range of processes of abuse is broad and includes television, Internet, computer gaming, shopping, sex, pornography, food, self-mutilation, and gambling. The concept of addiction applied to an activity is very much up for debate in the medical and psychiatric communities, but we assert that any activity done compulsively to the detriment of wellness and overall life functioning may constitute abuse or addiction. In order to understand this better, let's examine how addiction is currently defined by the American Psychiatric Association (APA).

The *Diagnostic and Statistical Manual of Mental Disorders*, Fourth Edition (APA, 2000), is considered the essential tool in generating mental health diagnoses for physicians, psychiatrists, psychologists, and counselors. The word *addiction* is not actually used in its diagnostic criteria for substance- and process-related issues. Instead, the DSM-IV refers to *substance abuse* and *substance dependence* and defines the two as follows.

Substance abuse refers to a maladaptive pattern of use that impacts an individual's life functioning in one or more ways: failure to fulfill major responsibilities at work, school, or home; using in ways or situations that may be physically hazardous; legal problems related to substance use; or a pattern of social or interpersonal problems related to substance use. If one or more of these areas have been affected in the past year, and the criteria for substance dependence has not been met, then counselors can assign a diagnosis of substance abuse.

Substance dependence includes diagnostic markers related to failure in life-role functioning (as described above) and also includes criteria related to physiological functioning, for example: tolerance marked by need for more substance to get the same high, or diminished high; withdrawal symptoms; substance taken in larger amounts over a longer time than intended; failure to cut back on use and a desire to reduce amount used; spending considerable time obtaining and using substance; and using when there is clear physiological detriment (e.g., cirrhosis of the liver). Three or more of these criteria must be met in the previous 12 months for a diagnosis of substance dependence.

There are very few diagnostic criteria in the DSM-IV related to process addictions. In fact, the only process addiction noted in the DSM is compulsive gambling. The criteria for this disorder include features very similar to those of substance dependence: preoccupation; a need to gamble more and take greater risks for the same "high" (tolerance); no success in cutting back on use; restlessness or irritability when trying to cut back (withdrawal); significant impairment to one or more areas of life functioning (work, school, home, legal); continuing in spite of tremendous losses; and borrowing money from others to continue gambling. Sound familiar? It is remarkable how similar process addictions look to substance addiction when broken down this way. Even though official diagnoses do not exist for other types of process addictions, including sex, food, and Internet addiction, the symptoms of withdrawal and tolerance, the patterns of maladaptive behavior, the significant impact on areas of life functioning, and the need for more and more to achieve the same (or even a lesser) high are all very similar.

In summary, addiction can be described as:

- A well-established, problematic pattern of appetitive behavior with ...
- Physiological and psychological components to behavior and ...
- Behavior is resistant to change. (DiClemente, 2003)

These are the general criteria we use throughout this text to refer to addiction. Now that we have a general understanding of the clinical features of addiction, let's begin to examine addiction from a gendered perspective.

WOMEN AND ALCOHOL USE

In colonial times, alcohol was used pervasively in day-to-day life and was consumed freely by men, women, and children. Alcohol was perceived as ceremonial, comforting, and restorative. By the early 1800s, a cultural shift was under way. Moralists began criticizing alcohol use among women, citing few reasons why privileged women might imbibe aside from oppression or lack of reasoning ability. Two other reasons were directly related to the medical establishment: Women might drink because of prescription for feminine issues, including problems with pregnancy and premenstrual difficulties; or women were prescribed alcohol as a detoxification tool from other addictions (Straussner & Attia, 2002).

In the Victorian era of high moral values and the ideal of familial peace, inebriation by alcohol was seen as distinctly masculine, while addiction to opium was acceptably female. Thus, it was considered low-class for women of means to engage in excessive alcohol use. This stigma differed for women of color or women in poverty: Because they were already perceived as "lesser than," drinking was simply one more sinful behavior in addition to being born of a particular race or socioeconomic status (Straussner & Attia, 2002; National Center on Addiction and Substance Abuse [NCASA], 2006).

Prohibition in 1919 was a constitutional amendment largely backed and supported by white women of means who perceived alcohol to be the cause of many broken homes because husbands succumbed to the vice. Wives were seen as keepers of morality in the home, calling for temperance and moderation. In fact, one of the most politically influential groups of late 1800s was the Women's Christian Temperance Union (WCTU), powerful in spite of the fact that women were not granted the right to vote until 1920 (Straussner & Attia, 2002; WCTU, n.d.). At this time, it was asserted that godly women did not drink and female drinkers were portrayed as whores and prostitutes (NCASA, 2006). To understand the legacy of this cultural movement, reflect on the alcohol advertising of today. In general, women are portrayed as overtly sexual in media ads for all alcohol types. The link between sex and alcohol has not weakened over the past 150 years.

Interestingly, the same women who advocated for Prohibition also worked for the repeal of Prohibition a decade later, after the crime and murder rates skyrocketed in the presence of bootlegging. White, middle- and upper-class women were perceived as the keepers of morality, the protectors of virtue. Thus, after Prohibition, a woman who abstained from alcohol use was still perceived as virtuous, while men were socially permitted to drink again (Straussner & Attia, 2002).

Historically, alcohol use was perceived as a man's problem. Subsequently, women were generally ignored in all medical and treatment efficacy studies. In fact, only 29 studies on women alcoholics appeared in the English language research literature between 1929 and 1970 (Greenfield, 2002). Until about 15 years ago, men were studied almost exclusively, and the results were generalized to women. As a result, counselors have until only very recently been ignorant about the effects of alcohol on women clients, and counselors know even less about how to help them recover. According to the 2005 National Survey on Drug Use and Health (NSDUH), 45.9% of women over age 12 were current drinkers, compared to 58.1% of men. Over the past three decades, alcohol abuse and addiction has increased for women: In the early 1980s, surveys showed a lifetime prevalence of 5.17 men experiencing alcohol use disorders to each woman. By the early 1990s, the gap narrowed to 2.45 men to each woman (Greenfield, 2002). Currently, approximately 6 million women in the United States either abuse or are dependent on alcohol (NCASA, 2006).

Furthermore, social stigma for women who use alcohol in excess still exists. A drunken man is seen as masculine, normative. A drunken woman is seen as morally degenerate. This gender stereotype produces an additional layer of complexity to the treatment of women alcoholics. On the one hand, women may be more reluctant to enter treatment and may experience greater levels of shame or guilt about their addictive behaviors. On the other hand, women may claim excessive drinking as a sort of liberation from gender stereotypes as they drink in order to "keep up with the boys." For example, college-aged women (18–22) are engaging in more binge drinking behaviors (Gordon, 2002) than women in other age groups, a stereotype often attributed to male students. Thus, these young women are comparing their level and frequency of drinking to male students who may be physiologically more capable of processing larger quantities of alcohol without harm. If women are using these men to gauge what is normal, they are at risk of developing serious physical problems. They may also be longer in realizing their use has become problematic.

WOMEN AND DRUG USE

It is estimated that 7.7% of men abuse illicit drugs, compared to 5% of women (Gordon, 2002). Approximately 7.5 million women and girls misuse or abuse prescription medications, and about 2.5 million women experience dependence on illicit drugs (NCASA, 2006). The current drug crisis for women evolved from a long and complicated history. Late in the 18th century into the early part of the 19th century, Godfrey's Cordial (also called "Mother's Helper") was used among the middle and upper classes to treat colicky or otherwise troublesome infants and children. Because Godfrey's contained a significant amount of opium, death from poisoning quite often occurred when the elixir was overused ("What Were Godfrey's Cordial and Dalby's Carminative?" 1970). For example, women in the 19th century were regularly prescribed laudanum for pain, Coca-Cola syrup (containing cocaine) for energy, or cannabis for feminine problems and headaches (Gordon, 2002). The medical field, like addiction treatment programs, used men as primary research subjects and for resultant treatment modalities, so there was little understanding in the medical community about female reproductive and emotional disorders. If a woman complained of headaches, moodiness, or any similar ailment, the doctor prescribed any one of the highly addictive elixirs guaranteed to soothe an addled woman's nerves. If a woman displayed signs of addiction, she was generally prescribed another addictive medicine to alleviate withdrawal symptoms. So the cycle continued, as these women spent their adult lives unnecessarily overmedicated.

As a result, by the late 1800s most of the estimated 250,000 morphine and opium addicts in the United States were white women of privilege (NCASA, 2006; Straussner & Attia, 2002). Common beliefs held that white women were the least resistant (compared to women of color and men) to the powers of morphine, particularly if they were fair-haired and blue-eyed. The decline of white women into drug addiction was coupled with fears of "losing" white women to Chinese men, believed to be the importers and sellers of opium-related substances. The stereotype emerged of one Chinese man living with multiple white common-law wives, whom he kept in a state of perpetual intoxication with opium (Campbell, 2000). This perception caused panic at the time because it became widely stereotyped that drug use was creeping "up" from those living in poverty (primarily people of color) to higher socioeconomic classes and threatening the quality of life. It was, in part, due to the fear of losing white women to these lower socioeconomic classes that drug policy began to change, and the federal government began to get involved in regulation and control (Campbell). The country rallied to the rescue of its seemingly invaluable white mothers, sisters, and daughters.

This effort to control the behavior of white women extended conversely into the punitive. While legislation and law enforcement focused on salvation, social focus turned to the female, white opium addict as a vampire of sorts, intending to corrupt the lives of those close to her, including her children (Campbell, 2000). What we see here is the foundation for the duality of women's addiction that still exists today. Women are perceived both as victims of drug, alcohol, and process addictions, unable to regulate their behavior, and as corrupt and corrupting. Women's addiction was seen as the result of a rapidly changing society and women's inability to cope; following, addicted women were assumed to spread addiction to the men in their lives. Note this stereotype did not apply to women of color, who were collectively perceived as susceptible to addiction, and whose mental health and addiction issues did not warrant the concern of governing bodies (Campbell, 2000).

The Harrison Act, passed in 1914, intended to regulate narcotics distribution and prescription. The wording of the act was interpreted by law enforcement thusly: Because addiction was not a disease, addicts were not actual patients, and thus, physicians would be in violation of the Harrison Act if they prescribed a narcotic to a known addict. The reaction to this act was similar to that following Prohibition: Crime escalated as addicts entering withdrawal sought relief through the black market, and treatment centers became overwhelmed by those seeking assistance (Brecher, 1972; NCASA, 2006). Because narcotics were no longer regulated by individual physicians, addicted individuals sought relief through illegal means. Once able to manage their addiction privately, addicts now spent time, energy, and money acquiring their substance of addiction through illegal means, threatening both their livelihood and social standing (Gray, 1998). After the passing of the Harrison Act, the number of privileged white women addicted to opiates declined. The face of opiate addiction changed to a man living in poverty in an urban environment, using heroin intravenously (NCASA).

The 1950s brought the dawn of the psychopharmacological revolution (Smart & Fejer, 1972, p. 153), when adults began to value mood alteration for its own sake and began seeking emotional stimulation or suppression through the use of licit and illicit drugs. Also in the 1950s and 1960s, the prescription habits of the medical community shifted to barbiturates (once believed to be safe and nonaddictive) for sleep, and amphetamines for weight loss. Additionally, addictive tranquilizers (i.e., Mother's Little Helper) were often prescribed for nerves (NCASA, 2006). Again, the targets of these prescriptions were mostly white middle- and upper-class women. Among the rural African American community, however, marijuana was for sedative purposes, in the absence of the more expensive alternatives afforded by wealthier women, as described above (Straussner & Attia, 2002). The use of psychoactive drugs at this time was much more prevalent among women than men (Smart & Fejer, 1972).

Interestingly, the trend of overprescribing addictive painkillers and sedatives continues today. In fact, men lead women in numbers of addicts for every substance except prescription medications. It appears that women lead men in prescription drug consumption and addiction regardless of age, geographic location, or socioeconomic status (Nelson-Zlupko, Kauffman, & Dore, 1995). Because of shame and social stigma, women are likely to abuse substances in private as opposed to social, public settings. Because prescription medication appears socially sanctioned, prescribed by a physician, these meds carry less of a stigma than illicit or street drugs. Women obtain them in the proper, sterile environment of a doctor's office or emergency room, rather than on the street or from a dealer. Again, women are culturally defined as the keepers of morality and home life, and drug abuse and addiction do not fit into that neat, tidy image. However, while women of middle and upper socioeconomic classes who become addicted to prescription medication are considered victims of unscrupulous doctors, prostitutes, women of color, or mothers who use are considered criminal and immoral (Campbell, 2000). Again, women are subject to a striking dichotomy: either moral victim or immoral deviant.

A modern example of this stereotype lies in the Showtime network's series *Weeds*. Mary Louise Parker plays a white, upper-class soccer mom whose husband dies suddenly of a heart attack, leaving her as the sole financial supporter of her two sons. Unsure of how to provide for them, she turns to dealing marijuana out of her home. This series is considered groundbreaking and original for two reasons: (1) the seemingly preposterous juxtaposition of the main character's gender, social, and racial status and her occupation; and (2) the fact that viewers will actually sympathize with her, even though she is engaged in such "immoral behavior." If we changed the race, gender, and economic status of the main character to African American, male, and poor, this show would be described not as "creative" and "groundbreaking," but as "gritty" and "real." It would not surprise us to see an African American man selling drugs; seeing a white woman doing the same shakes us to the core. In fact, when Parker's character needs help growing her business, she turns to an African American man for help, reinforcing stereotypes about African American men as drug dealers. Once again, these stereotypes serve no one.

A discussion of women in relation to drugs of addiction would be incomplete without mention of nicotine dependence, primarily through cigarette smoking. Cigarettes are often overlooked as a dangerous drug of addiction, especially in comparison to prescription drug abuse or narcotic use. However, while about 17,000 Americans die each year from causes related to drug abuse, and about 85,000 die from alcohol-related problems, about 435,000 die from tobacco use (Drug War Facts, n.d.). Examining tobacco use through a historical lens, cigarette smoking was considered low-class for both men and women. However, while men were socially permitted to smoke, women were legally and socially prohibited from doing so. Women who smoked were considered deviant (or, interestingly, artistic), low-class, and disreputable (NCASA, 2006). Thus, men made up the majority of smokers until World War II (Gordon, 2002), after cigarette companies capitalized on the suffragette movement by marketing cigarettes as a feminine symbol of liberty from oppression. In 1935, 9% of women smoked, compared to 52% of men. By the late 1940s, 45% of women smoked, and the numbers continued to rise, peaking in the mid-1960s. Increased awareness of the harms of smoking caused a decline in the numbers of smokers overall since the 1960s, and today approximately 23% of women smoke, compared to 27% of men (NCASA, 2006).

WOMEN AND PROCESS ADDICTIONS

Finally, women are susceptible to process addictions, or addictions to an action or behavior rather than a substance. Process addictions are a new area in research literature. Thus, little empirical information exists on their progress and treatment outcomes, especially for women. For example, gambling has long been assumed a male-dominated activity because men gamble at a rate of 2:1 to women. Thus, studies on gambling focused on the experiences of male participants, largely overlooking women as appropriate for study (Potenza et al., 2001). However, recent studies of problem gambling reveal women are more likely to prefer slot machines and other gambling games based on luck rather than skill, experience greater financial difficulty as a result of their gambling, and seek treatment via Gamblers Anonymous (GA) at a dramatically smaller rate than men: 93% to 98% of GA participants are male (Potenza et al.).

Differences exist when examining sexual addiction as well. Estimates of the population who are sexually addicted range from 3 to 11%, and about 20% of clients seeking treatment for sex addiction are women (Ewald, 2003; Hall, 2006). While sex-addicted men tend to prefer sexual experiences involving objectification, sex-addicted women seek experiences involving role playing, fantasy, power, and dominance (Schneider, Sealy, Montgomery, & Irons, 2005). Women who have experienced powerlessness either through societal oppression, or following a history of sexual, physical, or emotional abuse, may attempt to secure a sense of personal power through sexual activity. With regard to gambling and sex addiction even in the 21st century, women are assumed to be morally superior and impervious to such base urges. Subsequently, women often feel a deep sense of shame once they find themselves compulsively seeking out these processes, and are reluctant to seek help. For women with children, this is especially true because mothers who succumb to process addiction (and chemical addiction for that matter) are perceived as bad parents, who are unable to "rise above" their compulsions. For women, addiction is considered a moral failure, and shame complicates recovery significantly.

GIRLS AND ADDICTION

It is clear gender differences exist between women and men with regard to the development of addiction issues, and that our understanding of addiction for adults is based primarily on male-based research. What this creates is a gender gap in our awareness of the progression of addiction.

But for many, addiction begins early, in childhood and adolescence. For example, approximately 80% of cigarette smokers began smoking before the age of 18. Twenty-three percent of high school students are currently smokers (while only 21% of U.S. adults claim the same), and approximately 1,140 individuals under the age of 18 become regular (daily) smokers each day (Centers for Disease Control and Prevention [CDC], n.d.). Alcohol and tobacco have long been perceived as *gateway drugs* for harder substance use later in life. It appears that the younger the age of initiation to tobacco or alcohol (particularly before age 15), the more likely an individual is to progress to marijuana or hard drug use by age 25. If the age of initiation is after 17 years, the likelihood of progression to illicit drug use decreases significantly. This is an important consideration as addictions professionals design and develop drug prevention and treatment programs for adolescents (Golub & Johnson, 2001).

There are few resources to provide a clear picture of the historical evolution of girls' addictive processes. However, there are some clear components of adolescent development that appear to contribute to abuse and addiction regardless of the substance or process of choice. First, boys and girls experience different changes in adolescence. Adolescence is made up of two distinct stages: early adolescence and late adolescence. Early adolescence is marked by significant hormonal changes, moodiness, and changes in family and peer relationships. Late adolescence is a period of consolidation when, in the best cases, boys and girls begin to develop a strong sense of self and identity as they prepare for their roles as adults (Husler & Plancherel, 2006). As most parents are aware, boys and girls enter and leave adolescence at different ages. Typically, girls mature earlier, both physically and emotionally, than boys. What is important about these two stages is that it appears that regardless of addiction, girls who begin abusing substances or processes during early adolescence are more likely to develop full-blown addiction in adulthood than girls who abuse substances or processes in later adolescence. This piece is key to the development of prevention and intervention plans for counselors. Those vulnerable years of early adolescence are when girls develop their personal and communal identity, and an early relationship with addictive substances or processes can derail healthy adult development.

Equally important, girls begin the process of individuating from their families of origin and finding connections with peer groups earlier than boys do. Girls place great value and derive a sense of identity from peer groups more so than boys. Additionally, girls' self-esteem tends to be positively correlated with the quality of their friendships (Crawford & Unger, 2004). Thus, it is important for girls to maintain harmony and cohesion within their friendship groups, including potentially harmful use of substances or processes. In adolescence, girls first begin to use drugs or alcohol when introduced to substances through friends as a way to fit in. Substance use helps girls feel like they belong and are a part of a group. This is critical for girls because it is a crucial part of their individual identity development. With more and more girls experimenting with alcohol and drug use in order to help them fit in socially (Pipher, 1994), more and more girls have become addicted. Girls abuse substances and processes for a variety of reasons, including to cope with psychological issues, social pressure, and familial factors (NCASA, 2006; Pipher, 1994).

Finally, as with women addicts, socially conditioned gender roles influence how and why girls use some substances. In the previous paragraph, we mentioned how girls use substances to identify with a social network and to feel a part of a group, an important developmental consideration for adolescent girls. Similarly, girls will use substances to feel a part of a romantic couple, as well as to fit in with male peers. What is disturbing is that often these male peers and boyfriends introduce and assist in maintaining girls' dependence on alcohol or drugs. For example, for women and girls using heroin, their partner or a male friend is often the first person to introduce them to the drug, to encourage them to use the drug intravenously, and to encourage their continued use of the drug (Eaves, 2004). Thinking of this situation along gender lines, women and girls both seem to have a more difficult time saying no to a male friend than to a female friend. Note how in U.S. culture when a man says no to a request he signals the end of the debate, but when a woman or girl says no she denotes the beginning of negotiations. Thus for girls, pressure from male friends or partners may make it feel difficult to refuse. Also, using with a partner legitimizes their addiction, and removes some of the intrapersonal psychological stigma. With these broad concepts in place, we now turn to a discussion of girls' relationships with alcohol, drugs, and processes.

GIRLS AND ALCOHOL USE

As in all research fields, the attention a particular issue draws is often dependent upon public interest and government funding. In the past century, interest in girls' drinking behaviors has waxed and waned based on public opinion. After a relatively quiet period in the 1950s and 1960s, the medical community again grew interested in women's and girls' drinking behaviors after an increase in diagnoses of alcoholism and cirrhosis of the liver in women (Wilsnack & Wilsnack, 1978).

Public health concerns are often an impetus for greater funding and research attention.

In the 1970s' medical community, an increase of girls' and young women's drinking behaviors was largely attributed to the women's liberation movement. The perception was that changing gender roles and identity created a culture where drinking was more permissible "and may offer girls and women new goals and aspirations, perhaps causing stress that alcohol can reduce ..." (Wilsnack & Wilsnack, 1978, p. 1856). What is obviously flawed in this argument is the idea that opportunity for the fulfillment of dreams might cause stress significant enough to cause an increase in drinking behaviors. Issues such as ongoing and increasingly aggressive sexism and oppressive attitudes were not considered factors for increased drinking behaviors. Socially sanctioned opportunity did indeed increase for girls and women in the 1970s. However, these opportunities were regulated by the traditional system of patriarchy that monitored and controlled the extent of female empowerment and success. Perhaps it was this tension that exacerbated drinking behaviors, not the opportunities themselves.

While Wilsnack and Wilsnack (1978) did not find a significant relationship between attitudes about traditional femininity and drinking behaviors, they did note that girls who seemed to reject traditional femininity were more likely to experience problem drinking earlier in life (particularly in Hispanic, African American, and Caucasian communities), while women who embraced traditional femininity at a younger age were more likely to develop drinking problems later in life. This study, though flawed, gives some sense of the complexity of the impact of gender role on substance abusive behavior.

More contemporary research studies take into account the impact of social conditions on girls' drinking behaviors. Focusing simply on an individual's intrapsychic process without taking into account social and cultural factors can be regarded as a *fundamental attribution error* (Crawford & Unger, 2004). In other words, when counselors place causality of the problem solely on the individual without considering oppressive factors, further damage can be done to that individual's well-being. With regard to girls and alcohol use, Engels, Scholte, van Lieshout, de Kemp, and Overbeek (2006) found that adolescents who engaged in alcohol use were perceived as more social and self-confident and had more friends. This study, even with acknowledged limitations, gives us a glimpse into how adolescents see the use of alcohol as helpful. This is one piece of research that supports what many counselors in practice have heard repeatedly from adolescent girls about alcohol use:

that use is strongly linked to peer support and cohesion, self-esteem, and identity.

Historically, girls have been less likely to engage in addictive behaviors than boys. Today, what we see is a narrowing of the gap with regard to age of first use. In fact, age of initiation to alcohol use has narrowed significantly over the past 40 years: In the 1950s, for every girl who took her first drink of alcohol between the ages of 10 and 14, four boys took their first drinks (a ratio of 4:1). By the early 1990s, this ratio was 1:1 (Greenfield, 2002). Girls and boys are now equivalent in their early drinking behaviors. Most disturbingly, the 2005 NSDUH revealed that contrary to historical trends, 17.2% of females aged 12 to 17 reported current alcohol use, compared to 15.9% of males the same age. For many girls, alcohol is the drug of choice because it is easy to access and inexpensive.

It appears that Asian, Black, and Hispanic girls consistently report lower levels of alcohol use than Native American or Caucasian girls. Also, middle- and upper-income girls were more likely to use alcohol than lower-income girls, contrary to common stereotypes (Lips, 2006). Common characteristics of girls abusing alcohol include affective disorders such as depression and anxiety, delinquency and other rebellious behavior, low academic achievement, low self-esteem, nonconformity, and conflictual relationships with parents (Lips). We encourage counselors to incorporate this knowledge with caution, as labeling behaviors as "delinquent" or "nonconformist" often pigeonholes girls along traditional gender lines, which can exacerbate mental health or substance abuse problems.

GIRLS AND DRUG USE

There is a dearth of information about the history and etiology of addiction among adolescent girls. While earlier in the 20th century it appeared girls trailed boys significantly in their drug-abusing behaviors, by the 1970s, the gap appeared to be closing. In a 1972 survey (Smart & Fejer, 1972), girls trailed boys in all categories of drug use except for prescription meds (including tranquilizers) and inhalants. In a 1972 survey of Youth Corps volunteers (Eisenthal & Udin, 1972) (typically kids with social immaturity and behavioral problems), boys drank alcohol regularly at a higher percentage (41% to 30%), but girls were more likely to be regular users of marijuana and speed (marijuana: 8% to 4.5%; speed: 3.3% to 2.2%). It appears that normative behavior within the group and regular use by the group leader impacted girls' drinking and drug-use behaviors more than direct social pressure (Eisenthal & Udin).

Today, about 5% of adolescents in the United States meet the diagnostic criteria for a substance use disorder (SUD; Tarter, 2002). However, more than half of adolescents (54%) have experimented with an illicit drug. Additionally, it is estimated that by 12th grade, about 80% of adolescents have been exposed to alcohol, 63% to cigarettes, 49% to marijuana, 16% to amphetamines, and 9% to cocaine (Tarter). Among eighth graders, 52% have used alcohol, 41% tobacco, and 21% marijuana (Tarter). The rate of dependence on illicit drugs is about 3.3% among 12- to 17-year-olds, and the rate of alcohol dependence is 3.6% for this same group. Over the past 20 years, heroin use among adolescents has been on the rise as the drug becomes less expensive, easier to obtain, and purer in its potency (Eaves, 2004). There appears to be no difference in the rates of dependence between male and female respondents overall (Tarter, 2002). However, pairing gender with ethnicity did reveal some statistical differences. Rates of dependence were similar for White males and females (2.8% to 2.9%). However, among African American and Hispanic adolescents, the rates of dependence varied based on gender. African American males experience illicit drug dependence at a rate of 3.2% to 1.7% for females. Among Hispanic adolescent males, 4.9% are dependent on illicit drugs compared to 3.0% of Hispanic adolescent females (Tarter).

Racial differences exist with regard to exposure to drugs. For example, more African American adolescents report cocaine and heroin as easy to come by, but this same group has the lowest rate of consumption. With regard to marijuana, ease of obtainment is more closely linked to use among White adolescents than for African American and Hispanic youth (Tarter, 2002).

"Women who use drugs and experience their negative consequences initiated use typically during adolescence.... Accordingly, efforts to prevent drug use and drug-related problems among women should begin with an accurate understanding of drug use among girls" (Wallace et al., 2003, p. 225). Across the board, studies show that the earlier the onset of drug use (or alcohol use, or processes of addiction for that matter), the greater the likelihood that addiction will manifest (Tarter, 2002). Conversely, and equally importantly, studies also show that adolescents who experiment with drug use actually have better psychosocial prognoses than those with no experience with alcohol or other drugs (Tarter, 2002). As contrary as these two statements may seem, what is known for certain is that there is no one distinct path for addiction for any one person. Instead, the complex interplay among biological, sociological, psychological, and environmental factors impacts each person differently. No two cases are alike, and each client should be treated with individualized care.

Overall, drug use among adolescents has been on the decline in recent years (Tarter, 2002), and for much of the past few decades, boys were assumed to be the primary users of illicit and licit drugs. However, in recent years, girls have begun to surpass boys in marijuana use and prescription drug use (and in alcohol use, as described previously) (Peebles-Wilkins, 2006). In 2004, there were 675,000 new female adolescent marijuana users to 577,000 new male adolescent users (Peebles-Wilkins). Additionally, adolescent girls now abuse prescription drugs more frequently than their male counterparts: 9.2% to 7.5% (DATA, July, 2007). This trend mirrors that of adult women, who also abuse and become addicted to prescription drugs at higher rates than men. One reason for this trend may be that less social stigma is assigned to marijuana and prescription drug use than to other substances of addiction. Another is that prescription drugs in particular are free and readily available from parental medicine cabinets.

While all these statistics are indeed disturbing, it is important to remember that many adolescents are left out of the surveying processes conducted by researchers. Specifically, adolescents who are homeless, incarcerated, in drug rehab, or truant from school tend to be ignored when it comes time to take polls. Adolescents who are substance abusing or dependent often have significant environmental factors that prevent active day-to-day participation in mainstream social expectations. Thus, their underrepresentation in contemporary surveying methods is likely. Among students who do take the surveys, underreporting is likely due to social stigma and fear of reprise by authority figures. Thus, we must consider these statistics inaccurate or deflated (Tarter, 2002).

GIRLS AND PROCESS ADDICTION

Food Addiction

Along with drug and alcohol addictions, girls also have their own set of process addictions. While some of these issues may be similar for adult women, particularly food addiction, the process is very different for girls. Eating disturbances can include anorexia, bulimia, and binge eating disorder (BED). While there are many self-help books and articles about body image and eating disorders, the experiences of girls who are unable to stop themselves from eating are vastly underresearched in the counseling literature. They are often seen as binge eaters, but the addiction may be slightly different, with a great amount of shame and guilt that comes from a lack of control. Girls with BED experience the same emotions as alcoholics after a drinking binge, including guilt and shame.

Adult-counseling clients with BED typically begin binge eating behaviors during adolescence in conjunction with other disordered eating behaviors, such as restrictive dieting. Girls who begin bingeing in earlier adolescence (ages 11–13) meet the criteria for BED earlier and exhibit greater psychiatric distress than those who have a later onset of binge-eating behaviors (Marcus & Kalarchian, 2003). A recent survey of girls ages 9 to 13 found that nearly 15% reported an eating disturbance in the month prior to taking the survey (Colton, Olmsted, & Rodin, 2007). These statistics are particularly disturbing in light of the fact that research on early adolescent substance abuse demonstrates that these girls have a greater likelihood of progression to addiction than girls who begin using substances in late adolescence. Similarly, it appears addictive behaviors become more entrenched in adulthood the earlier they emerge, an area of concern and attention for counselors.

Early onset of BED is also associated with childhood trauma (including sexual abuse), parental depression, and negative self-evaluation. "Dieting, the pressure to be thin, modeling of eating disturbances, appearance overvaluation, body dissatisfaction, depressive symptoms, emotional eating, body mass, and low self-esteem and social support predicted binge eating onset with 92% accuracy" (Marcus & Kalarchian, 2003, p. 51). With regard to childhood sexual abuse, African American women with BED are more likely to have been sexually abused (66%) than White women (24%) (Marcus & Kalarchian). Interestingly, adolescents and adults with addiction issues often have similar qualities. It appears links exist between those who use substances compulsively and those who abuse processes, such as eating. What is fascinating and alarming, however, is the gender difference with regard to binge eating patterns. Assessment studies reliably demonstrate that adolescent boys actually engage in binge eating behaviors far more often than adolescent girls, often at a rate of 4:1. This is generally attributed to the large number of calories boys need to intake to keep up with growth spurts during this age. The disturbing part lies in the fact that girls report feeling guilty and shameful for their binge eating behaviors at rates twice those of their male counterparts (Marcus & Kalarchian). Thus, while boys actually engage in eating binges much more frequently than girls, they do not carry the psychological and emotional stigma of their behavior. Boys appear to carry some immunity to social pressures about weight, while girls do not. And the girls pay a heavy price for this shame, in later diagnoses of mood disturbances and disordered eating.

Self-Mutilation or Cutting

Self-inflicted wounds, fortunately rarely seen in pediatric practice, can be particularly difficult to diagnose and frustrating to
treat. Although children with psychotic disorders such as schizo-
phrenia or mental retardation may deliberately injure themselves,
few who are not severely disturbed will do so. (Simpson & Hawke,
1970, p. 1008)

Most counselors who work with adolescent girls in today's cultural
climate would find the above quote quaint and perhaps even laugh-
able. Since the above article was published, the act of cutting or self-
mutilation has become relatively commonplace among adolescent
girls in particular. Self-mutilation involves the act of consciously
causing harm to one's own body. Common tools include razor blades,
knives, or other items with sharp edges, as well as burning or bruis-
ing the skin, pulling out hair, or breaking bones. Excessive piercing
or tattooing is also considered self-mutilation by some researchers,
but this area is debatable. Cutting on the arms and wrists is the most
commonly reported type of self-mutilation (Purington & Whitlock,
2004). Typically the act of self-mutilation is not suicidal in intent, but
rather an effort to either cope with negative emotions or, conversely,
stimulate emotion when the self-mutilating individual feels the need
for release. We quantify self-mutilation as an addictive behavior
because it meets the general criteria for addiction (pattern of compulsive behavior that is resistant to change and contains physiological and psychological components) and generates chemical releases
in the brain and body that mimic other drugs of addiction. Once
an individual begins self-mutilation, the endorphins released in the
brain following the act become quite addictive. Like any addiction,
more and more of the "drug" (in this case, self-mutilation) is needed
to reach the same high. Accidental suicide can be the result of "overdose" (Purington & Whitlock).

Exact rates of self-mutilation among adolescent girls are difficult to
determine, as self-mutilation is often a hidden behavior. Nonetheless, it
appears rates are consistently on the rise, and have even been cited as
the most significant problem facing adolescents today. Approximately
two-thirds of all adolescents who self-mutilate are female (Purington &
Whitlock, 2004).

Historically, the medical profession detailed three primary reasons one might choose to self-mutilate: suicide attempt, mutilation
with unconscious motive, and mutilation as a conscious attempt to

gain some benefit (Simpson & Hawke, 1970). When the act of self-mutilation or cutting first entered the broader consciousness of counselors and mental health professionals in the late 1980s, it was often quantified as a presuicidal or semisuicidal act. The clinical assumption often drawn was to treat the self-mutilating client the same as the suicidal client, often mandating inpatient care. We know now that self-mutilation is more complex than any of the above definitions imply. By 1998, the phenomenon of "cutting" was officially dubbed a "hot topic" by the editors of *Publisher's Weekly*, as new books on the subject flooded the marketplace in an effort to bring healing and relief to frustrated parents, counselors, and adolescents. In spite of this, our understanding of the etiology and progression of self-mutilation is in its infancy, as little research attention has been paid to this subject since its initial discovery in the 1970s (Purington & Whitlock, 2004).

Internet Gaming Addiction

Concern has been rising, particularly in Asian countries, about the growing problem of Internet gaming addiction for adolescents. Massively multiplayer online role-playing games (MMORPGs) are different from traditional video game consoles. Adolescents now have an alternate universe of online games played in real time with other players throughout the world. Gamers create *avatars*, or alternate identities, and thus are able to create elaborate fantasy worlds with other online players. Because these games are ongoing with no end goal, players can consume hours in front of their computers, playing to the detriment of other areas of life, including work, wellness, and relationships (a classic sign of addiction). The American Medical Association (AMA) is currently considering creating a psychiatric diagnosis for Internet gaming addiction to address these concerns. The 12-Step movement has joined in the concern, creating Online Gamers Anonymous to help alleviate the problem. While most online gamers are male (62%), this continues to be a significant concern for adolescent girls, as 70 to 90% of all youth play Internet games, 31% of all gamers are under age 18, and 38% of all gamers are female (Olson, 2007). Currently, the literature often refers to Internet gaming addiction as a male problem. Similarly, alcoholism and drug addiction have been traditionally viewed as diagnoses of men more often than women. Research studies thus focus on the male experience of a particular addiction. The danger here is that girls are engaging in Internet gaming, perhaps at lower rates, but at rates high enough to cause concern. And as the gap between male and female alcohol and drug behaviors has narrowed, so will the gap in Internet gaming addiction. Gender-specific research needs to be conducted now, so the needs of girls experiencing compulsive behaviors in this area are not ignored for the long term.

CONCLUSION

Our aim with this text is to identify ways in which addiction for women and girls is socially constructed. We do not deny the importance of understanding the individual and collective biological, psychological, and social precursors to addiction. But we feel the problem is larger than individual addicts. According to Angove and Fothergill (2003), "Society is responsible for pushing some women into chemical solutions" (p. 215). This is not meant to absolve any one person of her responsibility for her own well-being. Rather, it acknowledges the incredible bind in which women live each and every day. Women experience remarkable social pressures: scarcity of adequate childcare, lower pay than their male colleagues, homemaker responsibilities, and inadequate benefits and health care (Angove & Fothergill). Furthermore, as we discussed in this text already, women are expected to maintain the moral purity of the home, a role handed down by society through the ages and still very much in effect today. Finally, women are socially conditioned to relate: to our families, our friends, and ourselves. Most addiction and mental health treatment modalities conceptualize recovery as an individual process, relying on personal will for success. However, women don't become addicted in isolation, nor do they recover that way. So the very system of treatment is stacked against them from the outset, further enhancing an addicted woman's sense of isolation and loneliness (Crawford & Unger, 2004; McNeece & DiNitto, 2005).

Case Study

Sheila began using alcohol in early adolescence, a time quantified as most risky for young girls. Because her identity development was in its early stages at that time, it was developmentally more likely for her to become addicted than if she began drinking later in adolescence. Sheila began drinking with friends after the leader of her social group encouraged them to sneak vodka from her parents' liquor cabinet after school. Sheila liked how drinking made her feel grown-up and confident and seemed to take away all her insecurities. Her whole life, Sheila has combated dueling gender and cultural norms for an African American. On the one hand, it is considered unladylike for her to consume alcohol to excess. However, as an African American, her racial identity has been undervalued within the majority culture, and stereotypes exist about alcoholism and being Black. As an adolescent, Sheila was warned about her image by her mother, who was concerned that her smart, successful daughter might be pigeonholed due to her race. Sheila experiences these dueling messages as a double bind.

Counselors working with a client such as Sheila would be wise to ask about the developmental stage at which her addictive behaviors began. Because Sheila began drinking in early adolescence, her addiction may be quite far along. Understanding the social pressures that compelled her addiction also provides insight into her motivation for and barriers to treatment. While counselors should avoid stereotyping clients based on race or gender, having an understanding of the vast and complex social norms that impact behavior can be beneficial in creating therapeutic conditions for change. It would behoove Sheila's counselor to discuss her perceptions of her race and gender with regard to her addiction. Sheila can inform the counselor about her feelings about her culture.

DISCUSSION QUESTIONS

1. It is important for counselors to understand their perceptions, stereotypes, and biases about certain populations or behaviors. After reading this chapter, what particular perceptions, stereotypes, or biases were elicited for you? How do you plan to address them?
2. Think back to your own adolescence. What role did social pressures play in your development?
3. Do you think gender stereotypes about drinking, drug use, or other behaviors (gambling, etc.) still exist and impact women and men? Why or why not?

II

Biopsychosocial Issues

3

BIOLOGICAL FACTORS

The male and female organisms differ both in construction and in chemical makeup. Some feminist theorists have disputed claims that men and women are inherently different with regard to biology. Indeed, perceptions of women as the weaker sex contribute to sexist attitudes in the United States and in other cultures around the world. With regard to alcohol use, for example, it is commonly believed "women can't hold their liquor"; thus, women in the process of having a drink (or several) at a public bar are expected to exhibit side effects of alcohol more quickly than a man consuming the same amount. For men, drinking to excess is an expression of strength, masculinity, and prowess; for women, the same behavior denotes a tomboy, an alcoholic, or a slut. With regard to biology, current research is finding that indeed, women and men are different when it comes to addictive behaviors, the body, and the brain. In this chapter, the impact of addiction on the brain and the body will be explored. For the sake of clarity, *gender* will refer to a person's male or female social identity, while *sex* refers to one's anatomical and hormonal identity.

CHANGING PERCEPTIONS: ADDICTION AS A PUBLIC HEALTH CRISIS

As presented in Chapter 2, addiction has long been tied to morality in the United States. Perceptions of drug, alcohol, sex, or gambling addicts as morally deviant and corrupt are commonplace. Identifying addicts as weak, undisciplined deviants implies moral judgment. And moral judgment generally occurs in a trickle-down fashion: from the powerful majority (agent group) to the underclasses (target groups). In the case of addiction, judgment usually passes from the upper and middle class to the lower-class socioeconomic groups; from Caucasians to African Americans and Latinos; from men to women. This passing of judgment is sadly ironic as addiction cuts across socioeconomic status, racial identity, and gender. But by envisioning addiction as something that happens to "bad people out there," the agent group is effectively able to distance itself from the messiness of addiction, creating a buffer from reality.

The moral model of addiction led to Prohibition in the 1920s. One key player in the passing of this amendment was the Reverend Billy Sunday, an evangelical preacher who reached millions first through radio and later through television. After the passing of Prohibition, Sunday said, "The reign of tears is over. The slums will soon be a memory. We will turn our prisons into factories, and our jails into storehouses and corncribs. Men will walk upright now, women will smile and children will laugh. Hell will be forever rent" (Gray, 1998, p. 66). These powerful words are indicative of the moral mood at the time. Alcohol was seen as a tool of the devil, corrupting families and leading to the victimization and downfall of women. While these ideals and attitudes may seem antiquated today, the moral model is still active in spite of the passing of decades.

In part to combat the polarizing effects of the moral model, the medical community introduced the disease model in the 1950s to bring addiction into the sphere of public health. The disease model asserts that addiction is like any other disease in that it is chronic, progressive, and often fatal. The American Medical Association (AMA), the American Psychiatric Assocation (APA), and the World Health Organization (WHO) all support this model. Additionally, most addiction counseling programs emphasize the disease model within psychoeducational curriculum. In spite of this widespread support, the disease model has failed to take hold within the larger cultural mindset, where addiction continues to be perceived as a violation of the U.S. cultural moral code.

Evidence of this can be seen in our continued criminalization of addicts who find their way into the court system. In particular, if offenders belong to a target group (women, African Americans, and Latinos, for example) they can expect to be treated particularly harshly by the criminal justice system. In his excellent book, *Drug Crazy*, Gray (1998) noted that in the 1980s and 1990s, while the majority of cocaine users were actually Caucasian, 96% of defendants for cocaine-related charges identified as African American. This mirrors the current status of African American and Latino inmates in the U.S. prison system.

According to the U.S. Department of Justice (USDOJ, 2007), for every 100,000 White males in the United States there are 773 White male prisoners; for every 100,000 Latino males there are 1,747 sentenced prisoners; and for every 100,000 African American males there are 4,618 sentenced prisoners. Similarly disproportionate numbers exist for women of color, as African American women are four times more likely to be incarcerated for drug charges than Caucasian women, and Latina women are about 1.5 times more likely to be incarcerated for drug charges (Drug War Facts, 2005). Currently about 10% of all prisoners incarcerated received drug-related charges (USDOJ, 2007). In fact, the frequency of imprisonment due to drug-related charges has escalated dramatically since the 1980s. Between 1980 and 2004 the numbers of those incarcerated for violent crimes increased fourfold, and for property charges threefold. However, the numbers of those incarcerated for drug-related offenses increased from 19,000 in 1980 to a quarter of a million in 2004, a staggering 13-times increase (USDOJ, 2007).

This dramatic increase in drug-rated incarcerations is a direct result of the stringent drug laws enacted in the 1980s during the height of the War on Drugs commenced under the Reagan administration. Fed up with drugs perceived to be a blight on humanity, the War on Drugs discarded the notion of rehabilitation and moved toward punishment, believing this attitude would serve as a deterrent for potential drug users. The results include an exploding prison population, an overburdened court system, increased racial profiling for drug charges, and no decrease whatsoever in the rates of drug addiction or dealing (Gray, 1998; Drug War Facts, 2005). In short, the supposed War on Drugs that stemmed from the moral model of addiction has failed. In spite of the strong presence of the disease model in U.S. medical and counseling communities, the moral model continues to prevail in many legal and counseling decisions made in the United States. This perspective unfairly punishes those from outside the majority culture for their addiction problems, and prevents effective treatment from reaching those most in need.

What decades of failed policy has taught us is that a radical transformation in cultural perception of addiction must occur in order for any lasting change to occur. This idea is summarized by a law enforcement professional from northern Michigan:

> During his annual report to the Emmet County Board of Commissioners last month, Lt. Ken Mills of the Straits Area Narcotic Enforcement admitted the job of a drug enforcement police officer can be downright depressing. According to Mills,

70 percent of all crimes are related to drug abuse and many of the people he and his colleagues arrest for drug offenses are repeat offenders. "We tell them what they are doing is bad, that it hurts their families and even their bodies," Mills said. "But they continue to do it. I don't understand." (Fowle, 2008, ¶ 1 & 2)

This quote perfectly embodies the conflicted feelings of most Americans who consider addiction. The moral perspective has become so ingrained in the culture that in spite of general awareness to the contrary, most people who experience addiction in their communities will throw up their hands in despair and conclude, "Since addicts know what they're doing is *bad*, why don't they *stop*?"

Most addicts cannot stop easily because the behavior is a complex mixture of biological, psychological, and social influences. A more productive perspective considers addiction a public health concern rather than a moral issue. Since the beginning of the War on Drugs, dollars spent on punishment has outstripped dollars spent on prevention and treatment. Even though the disease model asserts otherwise, addiction is not treated the same as other chronic diseases: Imagine incarcerating patients with diabetes for adding sugar to their coffee, or heart disease patients for failing to take their medication. One drug counselor asserts, "'There's no parity with addictive disorders. Addiction is covered only 50 percent by insurance, if at all,' he said. 'But if a person has high blood pressure they are not discriminated against having their past behavior examined'" (Fowle, 2008, ¶ 11). Lack of parity in health insurance reimbursement, lack of quality treatment for the uninsured, and socially condoned punitive efforts have all perpetuated a culture of alienation for many addicts craving treatment.

Adopting a public health perspective eliminates stigma for addiction counseling. One contemporary example exists in the Netherlands. It's a common misconception that Holland is a safe haven for drug dealers and addicts and that drug laws are nonexistent. This is inaccurate. In fact, Holland approaches drug trafficking and addiction as two separate problems. Major drug dealing operations are actively prosecuted by law enforcement. Yet addicts are perceived not as criminals, but as a public health concern to be treated with compassionate, effective treatment. As a result, "about 70 percent of Holland's drug addicts are in treatment programs; only 10 to 15 percent of America's are" (Grose, 2007, ¶ 3). Because women addicts in particular are likely to experience intense shame and stigma, this supportive perspective may make counseling seem less threatening or punitive. Furthermore, addiction prevention and treatment save taxpayers money in the long run: It costs about seven times as much to prosecute and incarcerate an addict as it does to provide counseling to one (Grose, 2007). Thus, creating a culture of support and healing for addicts makes fiscal sense as well.

Cultural attitudes in the United States have largely shaped public policy and counseling accessibility for addicts. Our current system focuses on punitive measures for those caught breaking the law as a result of their addiction, including prosecution, incarceration, fines, community service, or mandated drug treatment. However, low-cost, effective addiction counseling is rarely available to those who might choose counseling for themselves. Even though addiction is largely perceived as a brain disease within the medical community, these attitudes have failed to reach the public at large. In other nations where addiction is perceived as a public health concern and treatment is seen as a pragmatic, cost-effective effort, rates of addiction and criminal behavior have declined. It's a stance worth exploring here in the United States.

BRAIN AND BODY

The brain is a miraculous organism indeed, and researchers still know very little about how it actually works in spite of decades of research. The complex interaction between brain and body is additionally confounding. In this section, we present a brief overview of brain functioning and the impact of addictive substances and processes on the brain. We also provide gender-specific considerations for women and adolescent girls with regard to hormonal and biological functions.

A Brief Overview of the Brain

To talk to an expert on brain functioning is to speak in a foreign language. Most practicing counselors will never have need of such terms as *membrane-bound subunit proteins* or *ligand-gated ion channel receptor family*. As counselors and educators, we are grateful for and indebted to the researchers who make the brain their subject. However, we also know from personal experience that clients suffering the effects of addiction care little for scientific terminology; they need their condition explained to them in ordinary terms, and with compassion. So that is what we relay to you in this section: how the brain works in ordinary language.

In the simplest language possible, drugs, alcohol, or processes of addiction are reinforcing because they simulate pleasurable experiences that make our brains feel happy. Take a moment and remember the first time you fell in love. Remember the giddy sense of well-being, the excitement and euphoria, the sudden appreciation for even mundane daily tasks. Remember the absolute joy in seeing the face of your beloved, perhaps in the hallways at school or at work. Most of us remember that first love vividly because it was the first time our brains were flooded with such a potent cocktail of pleasurable biochemicals. Love is truly intoxicating.

Drugs, alcohol, or processes of addiction work in much the same manner. "In fact, the reason why addiction is so powerful is that it mobilizes basic brain functions that are designed to guarantee the survival of the species" (Kuhn, Swartzwelder, & Wilson, 2008, p. 247). Addiction mimics first love, eating incredibly delicious food, or the euphoria after accomplishing a great task. And, like first love, most addicts are able to remember vividly their first encounter with their drug of choice: It was literally and figuratively intoxicating. Unfortunately, also like first love, the effects of the drug or process of addiction diminish over time. The brain becomes familiar with the biochemical flood and loses responsiveness to it. Most couples remember their first weeks and months of their relationship as a time of great connection and joy. Often they wonder, "Where did the love go?" when problems arise down the line. In fact, the love remains, but the intoxicating rush of pleasurable chemicals in the brain has stalled. The same is true for addicts. Over time, addicts strive to recreate the rush of those first encounters with the drug of choice, replicating the behavior and increasing the dose in order to generate a stronger high. It's a futile effort, as the brain has acclimated and the high of first rush can never be repeated.

As research on brain functioning becomes more sophisticated, it becomes clear that processes of addiction (e.g., gambling, sex, pornography) elicit similar pleasure responses in the brain as drugs. The metaphor of falling in love is one way to conceptualize this phenomenon. No drug is ever administered, yet new lovers will describe the experience as a high. Also, researchers have determined that for drug addicts, seeing images of the drug of choice or handling drug paraphernalia alone can elicit a pleasure response in the brain (Kuhn et al., 1998). Thus, certain behaviors and activities can enact the biochemical wash in the brain that activates pleasure and reduces pain. But these effects are ultimately short-lived.

After a pattern of addictive behavior is established, there is a price to pay for pleasure; addicts begin to experience withdrawal, or pain, when the drug or process of addiction is not available to them, "a yang for the yin" (Kuhn et al., 1998, p. 249). Potent biochemicals begin to leave the brain, and withdrawal begins, resulting in craving and a wide variety of other adverse symptoms, depending on the drug or process of addiction. For example, an individual addicted to an opiate such as heroin will experience flu-like symptoms including body aches and pains, fever, nausea, runny nose, and lethargy (Kuhn et al., 2008). The body becomes so acclimated to the pleasurable mix in the brain it has a difficult time coping without it. What is most frustrating to many addicts is that they are often unable to feel any pleasure at all for a while after beginning withdrawal from the addictive substance or process. Because the brain has been fed such high levels of pleasure-causing chemicals for so long, simple everyday pleasures no longer hold any interest. This sensitivity does return over time, but the first months of abstinence are a dangerous time for relapse for addicts. To better understand this phenomenon, it helps to have a general working knowledge of how the brain creates the conditions for reinforcement.

There are two major neurotransmitters working in concert to regulate the level of excitement and activity in the brain. The first is the gamma-amino butyric acid (GABA) system. The GABA system inhibits excitement in the brain. Thinking metaphorically, the GABA system is the brakes on a racy sports car. Balancing out the GABA system is the glutamate neurotransmitter system. Glutamate is the main excitatory neurotransmitter, or the gas pedal on our hypothetical sports car. There are many subtypes for each of these neurotransmitters, and drugs, alcohol, or processes of addiction "work" because they activate one type of transmission, sending the brain out of balance (Kuhn et al., 2008). What is potentially scary about substance addiction in particular is that the brain not only generates ideas, perceptions, thoughts, and our very personalities, but it also regulates basic life-sustaining behaviors such as breathing or the heartbeat. Thus, if the delicate balance of communication via neurotransmitters is knocked too far out of whack, basic survival functions cease to occur. For example, humans have a built-in reflex that activates when the back of the throat is touched. This gag reflex is purely automatic and is essential to survival as it keeps the airway clear for breathing. After heavy drug use, this reflex may be shut down, resulting in choking and suffocation (Kuhn et al., 2008). Celebrity deaths have occurred because of this diminished reaction, including those of Jimi Hendrix and Chris Farley.

In addition to stimulating pleasure and pain, and regulating the body, the brain is constantly changing, evolving, growing, and learning about itself and the world. Researchers used to believe the brain was essentially done growing by adulthood, and it remained static until death. We know now that the brain is constantly building new connections as it learns, and that much of this growth occurs without our awareness. This quality is called *plasticity,* and it can be deterred or altered in the presence of too many drugs or too much alcohol (Kuhn et al., 2008).

Many of the effects of alcohol occur in part because of the relationship between the GABA system and glutamate, including loss of coordination, social lubrication, and sedation (Devaud, Risinger, & Selvage, 2006). Also, alcohol appears to block certain receptors in the brain, which limits the ability to create new memories. This is what is responsible for blackouts or memory loss during heavy drinking episodes (Kuhn et al., 2008). Drugs also significantly impact memory by inhibiting memory creation, enhancing learning, or causing memory distortion (creating particularly dramatic memories that are labeled good or bad). Most commonly, drugs suppress the creation of memories through inhibition by increasing release of GABA neurotransmitters alone or in concert with suppression of glutamates. Neurons are unable to fire in a way that is necessary to learning and retention of events. What's so interesting about all this is that our brains differ in their level of excitement or inhibition in response to alcohol, drugs, or process of addiction: Because each person's biochemical cocktail is unique, and because brain functioning is still largely a mystery, there is simply no way to fully predict how alcohol or drugs will impact the brain.

One fascinating area of contemporary research lies in the work of Dr. Daniel Amen, a clinical neurologist and psychiatrist who specializes in brain functioning and activity. Dr. Amen uses single photon emission computer tomography (SPECT) scans to "see" mental illness and addiction by measuring blood flow and activity in the brain. Since 1990, Dr. Amen has conducted literally thousands of brain studies using nuclear imaging, and has established himself as the foremost expert in the field today. What follows is a brief summary of Dr. Amen's findings regarding various drugs of abuse on the brain. For a more exhaustive description, refer to his best-selling book *Change Your Brain, Change Your Life* (1998).

- Cocaine/methamphetamine: Even though these stimulant drugs may temporarily increase activity in the brain, over time they ultimately reduce blood flow and brain activity, creating what can be described as "mini-strokes" (p. 226) within the brain. Over time, use inhibits intellectual abilities, including attention deficits and inability to concentrate, memory, and verbal impairment.
- Opiates: These drugs, including heroin, methadone, codeine, and oxycodone, among others, are among the most destructive to brain functioning, causing what Amen describes as "brain melt" (p. 235). Opiates cause decreased brain functioning overall, and long-term chronic use can cause permanent brain damage.

- Marijuana: Use can cause decreased blood flow and activity in the temporal lobe that can decrease learning ability, memory, attention, and motivation. These complaints are common among long-term marijuana users.
- Inhalants: These "drugs," including paint thinner, gasoline, and lighter fluid, are fast acting and cause general decreased blood flow throughout the brain. The effects appear similar to those of cocaine or methamphetamine on SPECT scans.
- Alcohol: While small amounts (no more than one to two drinks per day) can be beneficial for the heart and perhaps the brain, long-term chronic use causes overall cerebral dysfunction, causing the brain to appear shriveled in SPECT scans.
- Caffeine and nicotine: Often ignored because harder drugs warrant more research attention, caffeine and nicotine can nonetheless cause negative effects on the brain. In fact, "Cigarette smoking makes everything worse" (Amen, 1998, p. 227). Both also cause lessened blood flow to the brain, particularly in the prefrontal and temporal lobes (areas of the brain that regulate attention, impulsivity, memory, and temper).

What is most compelling about Amen's work is the visual impact of SPECT scans on counselors and clients alike. Areas of inactivity in the brain appear as large holes or craters presented in three-dimensional space. It does not take a doctor or scientist to understand immediately the degree to which damage has taken place. Amen describes many patients expressing immediate and dramatic desire to change their behavior after seeing startling images of their own brains slowly deteriorating. For many patients, abstinence from drugs or alcohol can result in restored brain functioning; for some, deterioration may be permanent.

Understanding the workings of the human brain can be confusing! For an interactive and informative tour of this most important organ, we recommend Dr. John Medina's Web site, *Brain Rules*, at http://www.brainrules.net/.

Hormones

Over the past decade, scientists have become increasingly curious about the impact male and female hormones have on other bodily processes. Research studies about the effect of hormones on psychological and cognitive processes have exploded in number (Devaud et al., 2006). Most of these studies have been conducted on rodent populations, presenting both benefits and disadvantages. On the benefits side, rodents do not experience socialization of gender as humans do. So researchers are able to isolate one alcohol-dependence consequence at a time without the complication of stereotypes or labels. On the disadvantageous side, rats are not human and never will be. Obviously, our physical makeup differs from that of a rat or mouse. So there is truly no way to be completely certain of findings based solely on rodent research. That being said, these studies are the very best research available to us. Throughout the chapter, we'll attempt to designate when studies refer to rodent versus human participants.

The way men and women respond to stress is quite different hormonally. This is important to addictions counselors because most drugs of addiction, including alcohol, and processes of addiction create stress on the body. Women tend to secrete more cortisol when stressed than men, demonstrating a greater physiological response to stress than men (Devaud et al., 2006). Cortisol is the hormone that causes weight gain in the middle section of the body. This is why women who are chronically stressed find it difficult to lose weight in that area of the body. This holds true for both humans and rats administered alcohol in lab studies. What this means for human women is that chronic alcohol consumption excessively stresses the body over time, resulting in significant and dangerous health stressors such as heart disease (Devaud et al., 2006). On the flip side, studies with rodents also determine that withdrawal symptoms following chronic alcohol consumption are worse for male rodents, due to a greater increase of a particular hormone (called *plasma corticosterone*). Female rodents experienced an increase of this hormone as well during withdrawal, but not to the extent of the males. Thus, female hormones appear to exacerbate the negative effects of excessive alcohol consumption on the body, but lessen the effect of withdrawal. They recovered more quickly from withdrawal than the male rats, and suffered less severe symptoms, including fewer seizures. Female rats also gained certain sensitivities back more quickly than did male rats, including motor coordination (Devaud et al., 2006).

Estrogen appears to play a role in women's subjective experience of certain drugs. In studies, researchers have noted that reactions to amphetamine and smoked cocaine appear to be more enhanced when estrogen levels are high (before ovulation) than when they are low (after ovulation). Study participants note a more significant sense of "feeling high" during higher estrogen periods and decreased feelings of "wanting more." In contrast, nicotine and alcohol seem to have greater effects postovulation, when estrogen is lower and progesterone is high. Thus, elevated intake of nicotine and alcohol during this phase may equate to self-medication, as women often experience dysphoria, or mild depressive symptoms, during this phase (premenstrual; Lynch, Roth, & Carroll, 2002).

Just as the menstrual cycle impacts cravings for substances of addiction, so do substances impact the menstrual cycle. Chronic use of alcohol can also disrupt the menstrual cycle in women, leading to problems in reproduction (Devaud et al., 2006). So for adolescent girls and women, alcohol and drug use enters into a complex relationship with hormones and monthly cycles that can ultimately impact the course of addictions counseling. There are additional considerations specific to adolescent girls that can further complicate the addiction and recovery processes.

The Adolescent Brain and Body

Adolescence encompasses a broad, vague range of years that differs from individual to individual. For girls, adolescence is assumed to begin as the body develops womanly features such as breasts, and when hormones kick off the menstrual cycle. But again, these processes can begin for some at age 11 and for others at age 16 or 17. There is no predetermined marker for the beginning of womanhood as marked by biological changes. Thus, it is difficult to categorize typical adolescent development. Nonetheless, distinctive features do emerge when examining the correlation between adolescent brain and body development and the onset of substance and process abusive behaviors.

The adolescent brain is particularly volatile in its reaction to addictive substances or processes. The adolescent brain is growing and changing at a breakneck speed. If the sports car metaphor introduced earlier in this chapter is extended here, while for adults the sports car is tooling down a quiet country lane, for adolescents the sports car has been entered into the Indy 500. Research over the past 10 years has demonstrated that adolescents have both rapidly growing synapses and many areas of the brain that are unconnected, making adolescents "easily influenced by their environment and more prone to impulsive behavior, even without the impact of souped-up hormones and any genetic or family predispositions" (Ruder, 2008, ¶ 4). In fact, the human brain may not be fully functioning until age 25 or 30, when the frontal lobe (critical in reasoning, decision making, and judgment) finally becomes fully connected to the rest of the brain (Ruder, 2008). This means that adolescents are literally not "playing with a full deck." And differences exist between male and female adolescent brains: Girls' brains seem to peak in their ability to absorb information between ages 12 and 14; for boys this peak occurs about two years later (Ruder, 2008). What this indicates is girls and boys may be ready to learn more complicated material at different times in life (such as information about how the brain functions when exposed to alcohol or drugs).

At a time when adolescents lack the ability to make rational decisions about their substance use they are also most susceptible to brain damage as a result of intoxication. It's a dangerous combination indeed. Neural connections are made and dismantled daily for adolescents, and toxins introduced into the brain (including drugs and alcohol) that may simply impair adults can wreak havoc and cause permanent damage to the adolescent brain (Kuhn et al., 2008). The very plasticity of the adolescent brain that allows rapid learning and absorption of information also makes the brain vulnerable to outside stressors such as alcohol or drugs. Studies with rats have demonstrated that the younger brains of "adolescent" rats remained disabled after alcohol use, even as the adult brains recovered (Ruder, 2008). Thus, adolescents are among those at greatest risk of permanent impairment as a result of addictive behaviors.

Girls who reproductively mature at a younger age are more likely to develop a variety of adverse outcomes, including substance abuse. This may be due in part to sexual attention given early-maturing girls by older boys, who then prematurely introduce girls to "adult" behaviors, including substance abuse. Other factors include features of brain development and physiology that when paired with the lower emotional maturity of younger, reproductively mature girls, opens the door for earlier initiation to addictive behaviors (Tarter, 2002).

There are several biological factors that are particularly important to consider when examining risk factors for the development of addiction. First, adolescents appear to have lower sensitivity to the pharmacological effects of drugs of abuse. In other words, it takes more of a substance to get a high feeling when used by an adolescent. If an adolescent is using a substance at high amounts from the get-go, there is a greater likelihood for the development of abuse or dependence (Tarter, 2002).

It's no secret that adolescents can be moody, irritable, and changeable. This is due in large part to the chaotic wash of hormones enveloping the brain during this developmental period. Incidentally, negative mood, labile mood, and irritability are also key psychological factors related to the development of substance abuse and dependence. Poor self-control and low self-esteem, common features of both adolescence and affective disorders, correlate to substance abuse and dependence. So by virtue of their very nature, adolescents gain one more tally mark in the risk column (Tarter, 2002).

The seemingly benign act of sleeping may further impact adolescents' risk of developing problematic substance use behaviors. Adolescents tend to go to sleep and wake later than children or adults. An early school schedule, however, can interfere with these normal sleep patterns, resulting in chronic sleep deprivation. The result may include lower academic performance, discipline problems, and impaired concentration. All these factors are correlated to alcohol and drug abuse (Tarter, 2002).

Brain maturation during adolescence includes a spike in dopamine concentration, resulting in part in a greater propensity for risk-taking and stimulation-seeking behaviors. Not surprisingly, these behaviors also correlate with substance and process abuses (Tarter, 2002). Conversely, during this period of maturation the adolescent brain also has immature capabilities for cognitive reasoning. As a result, adolescents are less able to think objectively about the potential impact of substance or process abuse, resulting in higher risk of negative impact subsequent to this use (Tarter, 2002). The prefrontal cortex, or the part of the brain that conducts self-regulation, does not fully develop until adulthood. At the same time, neurotransmitters responsible for regulating inhibition and excitation are changing substantially. So adolescents are impacted by both the anatomical and biochemical processes (Tarter, 2002).

There is some fascinating new research indicating that early exposure to nicotine affects the reward circuitry of the brain. Specifically, adolescents who smoke and consume alcohol are more likely to develop alcohol use disorders than their peers who don't smoke but who drink similar amounts. Teens who smoke and drink alcohol experience up to 50% higher risk of developing alcohol abuse problems later in life in comparison to their nonsmoking peers (DATA, February, 2007). It appears then that the developing adolescent brain may be particularly susceptible to the chemical mix of these two substances.

It is important to remember that in spite of this potent mixture of hormones impacting the adolescent body and brain, most adolescents who experiment with drug or alcohol use do not go on to develop dependence. Environmental and psychological factors play an important mitigating role in how significantly adolescent developmental changes impact future addictive behaviors (Tarter, 2002). Nonetheless, both women and girls can experience significant health consequences from substance abuse that are worthy of consideration.

HEALTH CONSEQUENCES OF ADDICTION
FOR WOMEN AND GIRLS

Alcohol Use

Because of unique features in brain and body function, women and adolescent girls both are at risk for specific health problems as a result of their problematic drinking or drug use behaviors. Ancillary health problems are often overlooked in the presence of substance dependence, but are worthy of attention if counselors wish to treat clients holistically. In this section, we discuss the impact of alcohol and drug use disorders on the body.

Regardless of gender, heavy alcohol consumption appears to contribute to a number of health issues leading to death, including various cancers, hypertension, liver disease, brain disease, accidental injuries, and violence (U.S. Department of Health and Human Services [USDHHS], 2005; White, Altmann, & Nanchahal, 2002). Women in particular experience greater sensitivity to drug and alcohol abuse than men, demonstrating heightened physiological responses to the presence of the substance in the system (Lynch et al., 2002). Birth control pills can also slow the body's ability to process alcohol-enhancing intoxication effects (Kuhn et al., 2008). While overall, women have a lower frequency of alcohol abuse and dependence than men, they tend to exhibit greater health problems more rapidly, including liver disease, brain damage, and heart damage (Devaud et al., 2006) as well as problems with the pancreas and high blood pressure (Kuhn et al., 2008). For adolescent girls, health risks from excessive alcohol consumption include death due to drunk driving, greater vulnerability to sexual assault, and great susceptibility to developing alcoholism later in life if drinking begins before age 15 (USDHHS, 2005). Also, because the adolescent brain is so undeveloped, greater risk for permanent brain damage from excessive substance use is a major concern.

There is one significant area where women tend to fare better than men in treatment for alcohol problems. Once in treatment for alcohol dependence, women tend to exhibit less severe alcohol withdrawal symptoms than men do. Most significantly, women are less likely to go into withdrawal-induced seizures, one of the most distressing consequences of withdrawal (Devaud et al., 2006). One of the true benefits for women is that often relapse to drinking during treatment occurs because clients are simply overwhelmed by frustrating, unnerving, and often painful withdrawal symptoms. Thus, treatment providers may find women less likely to relapse due to unmanageable withdrawal symptoms (Devaud et al., 2006).

Drug Use

There are particular health concerns for women using both licit and illicit drugs. As described previously in this text, women are more likely than men to be prescribed medication, and are more likely than men to become addicted to prescription medication. Among the most frequently prescribed medications are benzodiazepines that have high potential for abuse and dependence (Schnoll & Weaver, 1998). Unfortunately, much of the research done on the effects of prescription medication on the body has been conducted on laboratory animals or on male volunteers as participants. There are liability issues in using women participants, especially when they are of childbearing age. These concerns give researchers and drug companies pause in their research endeavors; thus, counselors have little information to go on when identifying health risks of prescription medications for women (Schnoll & Weaver, 1998). Benzodiazepines have potential for abuse and dependence, can cause seizures during withdrawal, and should not be used with other central nervous system drugs, including alcohol, opioids, or some over-the-counter cold and allergy medications (National Institute on Drug Abuse [NIDA], 2005). Other highly addictive prescription medications may also be responsible for significant health damage. Prescribed opiates carry risk of dependence, can cause respiratory depression or death if too large a dose is taken, and can cause drowsiness and constipation in the short run. Stimulants prescribed for attention-deficit hyperactivity disorder (ADHD), some forms of depression, or narcolepsy might cause high body temperature or irregular heartbeat, cardiovascular failure, or feelings of hostility or paranoia (NIDA, 2005). Clearly, counselors must be aware of the negative impact these prescribed medications may have on clients' physical well-being.

Illicit drugs also carry significant health risks for regular users. With regard to drug use women tend to become addicted more quickly than their male counterparts (Nelson-Zlupko, Kauffman, & Dore, 1995). Women are also at greater risk for developing malnourishment, hypertension, and sexually transmitted diseases (Gordon, 2002). Age also plays a role in health risks as a result of drug use. For example, younger women are most at risk of accidental death or injury, suicide, and overdose related to their drug use; middle-aged women who abuse drugs are more likely to develop breast cancer or osteoporosis; and older women who abuse substances are prone to fractures, such as in the hip, due to accidents or falls (Gordon, 2002). Additionally, the death rate for female addicts is higher than that for male addicts (Cook, Epperson, & Gariti, 2005). There are obviously many additional health risks for all clients who abuse or become addicted to illicit drugs. For a more comprehensive breakdown of risks by individual drug, please refer to the NIDA InfoFacts publications, available for download from http://www.drugabuse.gov/Infofacts/InfofaxIndex.html.

OTHER AREAS OF HEALTH CONCERN FOR WOMEN AND GIRLS

Telescoping

One of the most important concepts counselors need to know about with regard to alcohol and drug abuse by women is *telescoping*. Typically, women and girls begin engaging in substance abusive and addictive behaviors later in life than men and boys do. Why this is so is unclear. Perhaps younger women and girls are more reluctant than boys to engage in high-risk or rule-breaking behaviors in adolescence. Perhaps boys are more stimulus-oriented than girls, and seek out excitement and danger at an earlier age. Regardless, once girls and women begin to use substances, their behavior progresses to abuse and addiction on a much faster trajectory than that experience by men. Women and girls who progress through the addictive cycle often do so at a breakneck pace. And once they enter treatment (generally earlier than men), they demonstrate greater severity of use (Rahman & Clarke, 2005).

The health consequences of this behavior are equally rapid. Some examples: Women who engage in abusive or addictive alcohol behaviors more rapidly develop cirrhosis of the liver than men. Women who smoke heavily develop myocardial infarction and lung cancer more rapidly than men. Women who abuse crack cocaine are more likely to wind up in the emergency room than men. And women who use drugs intravenously are more likely to contract HIV than men who shoot up (Lynch et al., 2002).

Why does telescoping happen? First, as discussed previously, there appears to be significant biological differences in male and female functioning. There is also a sociological component to the development of addictive behaviors. Historically, it has been generally less appropriate for women and girls to engage in alcohol and drug use than for men and boys. Thus, boys tend to have an earlier age of initiation to substance use. However, there is some evidence that girls are as likely to use alcohol and other drugs as boys once they are exposed to it. Due to social stigma, girls are exposed to alcohol and other drugs later in their development. But once it is available to them, they are just as likely as boys to imbibe. All these components contribute to telescoping.

HIV and AIDS

Of the entire world's population, just under half of those infected with the human immunodeficiency virus (HIV) are women and girls. An additional 7,000 women and girls become infected each day. While the majority of those infected with HIV live in the Caribbean and sub-Saharan Africa, infection rates are on the rise in Eastern Europe, Latin America, and Asia (Joint United Nations Programme on HIV/AIDS, Global Coalition on Women and AIDS [GCWA], n.d.). Within the United States, HIV infection is also on the rise, particularly in rural areas. Between 1994 and 1999, reported AIDS cases rose 82% in rural areas, compared with 59% in urban ones (Wright et al., 2007). Substance abuse behaviors have been linked to the increased spread of HIV and acquired immunodeficiency syndrome (AIDS) (Wright et al.). These behaviors include unprotected sex, sex with multiple partners, sharing of needles, and sex with intravenous drug users (Wright et al.). Stimulant use, in particular, has been linked with increased risk for HIV, particularly methamphetamine and crack cocaine use (Wright et al.).

While abstinence and condom use education programs have impacted the global spread of HIV, often women and girls find they are unable to consistently use condoms or abstain from sex due to conscripted gender roles. In the most extreme cases, sexual slavery or prostitution prevent women and girls from abstinence or condom use. Young girls forced into the sex market are entirely unempowered in choosing their fate when it comes to partners or safe sex practices. With regard to condom use, under 5% of women and girls globally use condoms regularly, largely due to social stigma or lack of access to condoms. This is discouraging, as condom use has been shown to significantly lower the risk of HIV infection (GCWA, n.d.).

Within the United States, studies have shown that female drug users are less likely to engage in consistent condom use, and thus are at greater risk of exposure to HIV/AIDS. Drug abusing women who trade sex for drugs also place themselves at greater risk (Wright et al., 2007). Incarcerated addicted women demonstrated more high-risk behaviors with regard to both their sexual and drug use behaviors (sharing needles, for example) (Guyon, Brochu, Parent, & Desjardins, 1999).

With regard to treatment and prevention programs for substance abusing women and girls, gender-specific interventions are important. These might include skill development in negotiating condom use and risk reduction strategies, particularly with regard to trading sex for drugs (Wright et al., 2007).

Pregnancy and Childbirth

There is one area where women can experience health problems while men cannot: pregnancy. One possible consequence of alcohol use during pregnancy is fetal alcohol syndrome (FAS), one of the more common types of mental retardation occurring in newborns (Lynch et al., 2002). FAS is noted by low birth weight, facial abnormalities, and brain damage that can impact learning, memory, attention, and problem-solving (USDHHS, 2005). FAS is the most preventable cause of developmental disabilities, and women are encouraged to abstain from alcohol use if they are pregnant or planning to become pregnant.

While pregnancy is generally glorified in U.S. society, there is an underlying, pervasive attitude emerging where women are identified more as the carrier of a child than as an individuated human with personal rights. In other words, there are legal and ethical situations emerging where the rights of the unborn outweigh the rights of the mother. For example, in some states, laws already exist that treat alcohol or drug use during pregnancy as child abuse. What this does for currently substance abusing mothers is drive them underground rather than enticing them to treatment. The laws are deeply flawed: These women aren't intentionally abusing their unborn child; they are struggling with a complex and baffling addiction that has biological, psychological, and sociological foundations. Treatment is needed, not prison time.

For pregnant adolescent girls who abuse substances, the stigma is even greater. These girls are struggling with a host of identity development issues, from being an individual to parents and to identity as a sexual being. For pregnant women and adolescent girls, school- and community-based prevention and treatment programs are needed to effectively deal with the health consequences of substance abuse and pregnancy.

CONCLUSION

Many counselors lack knowledge about the physical impact of alcohol, drugs, and processes of addiction on the female brain and body. Possessing basic information about the complicated interactions among addiction, brain functioning, hormones, and other physiological processes can help counselors educate clients about the holistic impact of addiction. Furthermore, this knowledge assists counselors and clients alike in reconceptualizing addiction as a public health concern rather than an issue of moral depravity. Removing stigma from addiction and recovery can only benefit women addicts, who may hesitate to seek counseling due to shame and stigma.

Case Study

Sheila has only been using pain medication for a short period of time, but is already experiencing symptoms of addiction, including tolerance with withdrawal. She feels deeply ashamed about her behavior because she sees herself as a negligent or deviant mother as a result of her abuse. She feels she is failing as a wife and mother and cannot understand how weak she has become in fighting her cravings for the drug. Sheila normally takes good care of her body, eating well and engaging in exercise. However, she finds she just feels bad so much of the time, she has begun sacrificing her normal routine in order to sleep or watch TV due to lethargy. Because her symptoms of depression and anxiety are on the rise, she is also consuming more alcohol than is typical.

Sheila is clearly exhibiting signs of telescoping as evidenced by her short-term but heavy drug usage, resulting in signs of dependence. And like many women, Sheila may have been prescribed incorrect levels of medication by her physician, and may not be receiving regular check-ups to monitor her medication use. Complicating the situation, Sheila experiences the impact of the moral model of addiction that dictates she overcome her weakness and control her drug use. Her value as a mother and wife appears diminished in her own eyes, and possibly in the eyes of her family as well. As Sheila seeks counseling for her problem, she must be educated about biological components of addiction so she can begin to reduce her anxiety about her drug dependence. By alleviating anxiety, worry, and fear, Sheila becomes able to problem-solve and examine her situation rationally. She then engages in effective searching for solutions to her problem.

DISCUSSION QUESTIONS

1. How does the moral model impact your perception of addiction? The disease model? Are you in agreement or disagreement with the perspective of drug treatment in the Netherlands? Why or why not?
2. "Falling in love" is one metaphor to understand the development of addiction. Using metaphors can be an effective counseling technique when educating clients about addiction. What other metaphors may be helpful in explaining complex brain processes?

3. When counseling addicted women, health concerns are likely to be an issue. Often counselors are undereducated about health and wellness and may feel uncomfortable delving into this area. Assess your own level of confidence with this area, and how you might enhance your awareness and knowledge.

4

PSYCHOLOGICAL FACTORS

Women are particularly susceptible to psychological problems in conjunction with addiction. In fact, every diagnosis in the *Diagnostic and Statistical Manual* (DSM) is more likely to be found in an addicted woman than in a nonaddicted woman (Gordon, 2002). What is remarkable is the complex interconnection of many related factors: gender socialization, addiction, sexuality, and poor mental health, all of which appear to become inextricably linked. This chapter presents an overview of the range of psychological dysfunction experienced by addicted women and adolescents. Precursors to addiction, including sexual and physical abuse, are reviewed. Risks of suicide and self-harm related to addiction are included.

The simple fact of addiction counseling is that "poor psychological functioning reduces drug treatment success" (Risser, Timpson, McCurdy, Ross, & Williams, 2006, p. 646). It is a troubling reality that many, if not most, mental health and community counselors never receive training in treating addictions, and many addiction counselors have little to no educational background about other psychological issues. Furthermore, it has been a long-held truism within the addiction counseling community that before any underlying issues can be addressed, the addiction must be in full remission and the client must be well into abstinence. This attitude is absurd at best and maleficent at worst. Since most clients who have reached the point of full-blown addiction also carry a DSM psychological diagnosis, ignoring these issues equates to tapping the first nail in the coffin of treatment failure.

As is true with women, adolescent girls who face addiction are much more likely to be struggling with a mental health diagnosis; in fact, it is likely that the mental health issue drove the addiction. Some addictions that initiate due to social appeal, such as alcohol or drugs, may have been exacerbated by friends or romantic partners. Others, such as food addiction or self-harm, are much more likely to be a symptom of an underlying mental health issue. Regardless, mental health problems and addiction appear correlated for women and girls across the life span.

It is important to examine just how prevalent mental health issues are for addicted women and girls and the difficulties that exist in diagnosis. Currently, the DSM-IV-TR has a clear set of criteria for diagnosing substance-related disorders. While the diagnostic criteria can assist counselors working with adult women, a lack of clear guidelines exists when defining problematic substance use or dependence for adolescents (Winters, Latimer, & Stinchfield, 2001, as cited in Wilmshurst, 2005). Without clear guidelines, it becomes up to the individual counselor to determine if substance use is problematic. Prior to entering treatment, an adolescent girl may be subject to a nonprofessional's opinion about the appropriateness of her substance use. For example, a concerned parent or friend might determine she is "addicted" and coerce her into counseling. Thus, treatment is off to a shaky start.

In terms of prevalence of substance use, a recent national survey found that 45% of all 8th graders, two-thirds of all 10th graders, and three-quarters of all 12th graders reported alcohol use within the last year. When asked about illicit drug use, 22% of 8th graders, 41% of 10th graders, and 51% of 12th graders reported using within the last year, with marijuana being the most reported drug used (Wilmshurst, 2005). For adolescents, this often represents experimentation: While most will not become addicted, some will struggle with lifelong substance use problems. There are many issues that contribute to why experimentation may lead to an addiction; having a mental health issue, diagnosed or not, is at the top of that list.

WOMEN'S EMOTIONS, COGNITIONS, AND ADDICTIVE BEHAVIORS

Women and men are geared to experience emotions differently. Whether this difference is a result of biological or social influence is an ongoing issue of hot debate. Regardless, what is apparent from anecdotal and research evidence is that gender differences do exist. Men tend to have an outward emotional experience. For example, anger and aggression are more socially acceptable emotional states for men than for women.

Anger is generally expressed outward toward other people or events. Women, on the other hand, tend to focus emotions inward. Anger is a socially taboo emotion for women to express, while sadness is acceptable. Thus, women might experience depression, often defined as anger turned inward, rather than anger toward an external object, person, or event (Verona, Reed, Curtin, & Pole, 2007). These differing emotional experiences impact the way addiction forms and manifests in women and men.

Gender differences exist in how women and men engage in addictive behaviors with regard to emotional states. Women tend to engage in substance or process abusive behaviors to cope with or suppress difficult emotions and relieve stress, while men engage in these behaviors to get high or enhance emotions, including anger or aggression (Haseltine, 2000). "It has been proposed that women use substances more often as a means of coping with … traumas and stressors, as opposed to men who may be more likely to use substances for hedonistic reasons" (Back, Sonne, Killeen, Dansky, & Brady, 2003, p. 171). This pattern reflects the inward versus outward emotional experiences of women and men. If counselors fail to understand the unique emotional experiences women endure in conjunction with their addiction, treatment may miss the mark.

Reflect again on the philosophy of the 12 Steps incorporated into most addiction treatment programs: Addicts are expected to acknowledge how their substance use has resulted, in part, from their own ego-centeredness, and thus amends must be made to those injured by their substance abusing behavior. For women, the person most often hurt by the addictive behavior is the user herself. Rather than exhibiting egotistical self-absorption via substance abusing behaviors, women are more likely to have lost the sense of ego entirely. Addiction evolves in an effort to detach from psychic wounds, serving as a balm against the pain. Addicted women become detached from their emotions, from community, and ultimately, from their sense of self. Healing may come from the recognition of this sense of separateness, and through careful attention to these deep, emotional wounds.

Specifically, intense guilt and shame can impede addiction counseling for women. Women are apt to internalize all responsibility for negative life events, including addiction. Women also often suffer harsh judgment from family, friends, and society when they engage in addictive behaviors; thus, the guilt and shame can cut even deeper (Haseltine, 2000). Overall, women experience more feelings of guilt, shame, and sadness, or anxiety about their addictive behaviors than men (Nelson-Zlupko, Kauffman, & Dore, 1995). As women tend to engage in addictive behaviors in order to cope with negative moods, this cycle of guilt and shame can become particularly impactful. Women may also experience feelings of hostility about addiction treatment, perhaps in part due to limited gender-specific treatment options. This hostility has been shown to be a greater precursor for counseling termination for women than for men (Haseltine, 2000). Counselors must address the emotional experiences of women clients in order to be successful.

Women also experience unique cognitions regarding self-identity that can impact the progression of addiction and treatment. One very disturbing factor is that addicted women tend to have lower expectations for their lives than addicted men do. Addicted women are more likely to be focused on mere survival rather than on improving life and truly making positive change. This is disturbing in light of the fact that women often face greater economic challenges (such as unemployment) than men, and are more often the primary caregiver for children (Nelson-Zlupko et al., 1995). Thus, what counselors are potentially faced with are difficult barriers to recovery coupled with a mindset of survival. This is not to quantify counselors' experiences with all women addicts, but to acknowledge the significant exacerbating factors that may occur alongside the addiction itself.

DUAL DIAGNOSIS

The traditional separation of mental health and addiction treatment services does a significant disservice to counseling clients. From the addictions counseling angle, most clients come to treatment with a concurrent mental health disorder that needs attention before the mitigating factors contributing to the addiction can be resolved. Mental health counselors who are not trained or prepared to ask about substance abuse practices are missing a huge piece of the overall treatment puzzle, as many clients will use drugs or alcohol to self-medicate their mental illness.

Dual diagnosis, or concurrent addiction and mental health issues, presents a "chicken and egg" type dilemma: Which comes first? The relationship between the two appears complex and reciprocal. Often, individuals with a mental illness will use a substance to cope with the symptoms of their disorder. For example, women with depression might consume alcohol to deaden the pain, or use stimulants to raise energy levels in order to function in their daily lives. Women with anxiety disorders who also compulsively gamble may drink alcohol to calm their nerves prior to going to the casino. On the flip side, once the pattern of problematic use has been established, mental health or emotional disorders may worsen as a result of chronic use. For example, women who abuse an illicit substance may feel intense guilt and shame for neglecting parenting responsibilities, developing depression as a result. Or, women who gamble in excess may experience intense anxiety in part due to financial losses and stressors. While the relationship between mental health issues and addiction has not been clearly defined to date, there does appear to be a reciprocal link between the two, where one may reinforce or exacerbate the other.

Both Axis I and Axis II disorders have been found to be highly prevalent among adults suffering from addiction. Approximately 78% of men and 86% of women with alcohol dependence also meet the criteria for at least one other psychiatric disorder (Sonne, Back, Zuniga, Randall, & Brady, 2003). One Canadian study showed that while 4.4% of the nonalcoholic population suffered a major depressive episode in the 12 months prior to the study, about 15% of the alcoholic respondents reported having one. About 21% of respondents who were dependent on illicit drugs reported a major depressive episode in the previous 12 months (Koehn & Hardy, 2006). Furthermore, drug users (typically polysubstance users) experience greater prevalence of both Axis I and Axis II disorders than those who are addicted to alcohol alone. Additionally, both Axis I and Axis II disorders tend to be more prevalent in women than in men. These findings appear consistent both in the United States and among international populations (Landheim, Bakken, & Vaglum, 2003). Studies also consistently confirm that women who abuse drugs are more likely to suffer from a concurrent mental illness (Webster et al., 2007).

The most prevalent Axis I disorder for women with alcoholism is major depression. Addicted women are also more likely to have a diagnosis of posttraumatic stress disorder (PTSD), anxiety disorders, simple phobias, social phobia, and eating disorders than men (Landheim et al., 2003). This information reinforces the concept that women tend to drink or use drugs as a means for coping with difficult or painful emotions. Evaluating from the mental health provider's perspective, one study determined that of 867 women seeking treatment for depression, over 30% reported problematic substance abuse (Roeloffs, Fink, Unutzer, Tang, & Wells, 2001). With regard to depression and alcoholism, it appears that in general, alcoholism precedes depression for men while depression precedes alcoholism for women (Nolen-Hoeksema & Hilt, 2006). In addition, some DSM diagnoses can inhibit the success of drug treatment interventions if not taken into account. For example, depressive and depressive-like symptoms have been shown to lower the likelihood of abstinence from drug use and to raise the chances of relapse (Lynch, Roth, & Carroll, 2002). Mental health counselors untrained in addiction intervention, or vice versa, are at risk of doing more harm than good if they avoid one area or the other.

Like Axis I disorders, Axis II disorders can also play a significant role in the recovery process. For example, polysubstance addicts are more likely to be diagnosed with a personality disorder (Axis II) than those who are addicted to alcohol alone. With regard to gender, most studies find women are more likely to be diagnosed with a personality disorder than men. There is one exception: Antisocial personality disorder tends to be more prevalent among male addicts, though studies have been mixed (Landheim et al., 2003). Women who were diagnosed with antisocial personality disorder were more likely to have alcohol problems than nonantisocial women (Nolen-Hoeksema & Hilt, 2006). Thus, personality disorders, which are particularly resistant to treatment, seem especially prevalent among addicted women. Since personality disorders include a high degree of emotional reactivity and weak ego functioning, these clients are in particular need of effective dual diagnosis attention in the counseling setting.

In addition to emotional problems and treatment complexity, dual diagnosis can also worsen functioning in other areas of life. For example, women who have concurrent mental illness along with addiction (and this accounts for most addicted women) also perceive greater employment barriers due to both their gender and mental health status (Webster et al., 2007). Employment is important to mental health as it provides income, daily structure, community, and a sense of purpose. Thus, women who struggle with addiction and mental health problems will experience even more severe symptoms if unemployment is added to the mix. Un- or underemployment can lead to poverty, homelessness, and problems with transportation and childcare. The downward spiral can be rapid and treacherous.

Dual diagnosis also significantly impacts counseling considerations for adolescents. Many adolescents who use substances do not become addicted. The old idea of alcohol and marijuana being "gateway drugs" to other substances has not been found to be true for the majority of adolescents. However, for the adolescents who are at risk for progressing to other substances or adopting a compulsive substance use pattern, dual diagnosis may exist (Wilmshurst, 2005). Some of the more common comorbid disorders for adolescent girls are depression, anxiety, and PTSD.

As the increasing awareness of concurrent conditions among adolescent girls increases, counselors need to be looking for mental health conditions along with addictions issues as the rule, rather than the exception (Chi, Sterling, & Weisner, 2006). Treating both mental health and addictions issues is often difficult and requires more comprehensive treatment than what is usually available at most addictions facilities. As we have discussed, the traditional 12-Step model is often ineffective with girls suffering from substance abuse problems alone. For those girls whose concurrent diagnosis is depression or anxiety, simply relying on the 12 Steps is entirely inadequate.

Substance Dependence and Depression

Overall, women are more likely to suffer from depression than men. One contributing factor is that women are more likely to be exposed to negative life events and stressors than men, including genetic or biological predisposition to depression, sexual and emotional violence, domestic violence, negative gender role socialization, poverty, and lower socioeconomic status (Koehn & Hardy, 2006). While men are also susceptible to depression concurrent with addiction, women are more likely to be so: One Canadian-based study revealed that among alcoholics, 21% of the women also suffered depression compared to 13% of the men. Similarly, among those addicted to illicit drugs, 32% of women suffered depression compared to only 24% of men (Koehn & Hardy, 2006).

Women who are depressed may also self-medicate using substances that actually exacerbate depressive symptoms rather than alleviate them. For example, while women may be less likely than men to engage in problematic alcohol or marijuana use while depressed, they seem to be significantly more likely to be abusing sedatives or tranquilizers (Roeloffs et al., 2001). This is a dangerous situation in that tranquilizer abuse along with depression will exacerbate both problems or lead to accidental or intentional suicide. This is a frightening example of why both addictions and mental health counselors must possess the capabilities to explore both dimensions of client functioning within the counseling relationship.

While much of the research on dual diagnosis has been conducted on adult women, there are specific considerations for working with adolescent girls who also suffer high rates of depression concurrently with substance abusing or addictive behaviors. According to the American Academy of Child and Adolescent Psychiatry (AACAP), about 5% of children and adolescents suffer from depression during any particular point in time (AACAP, 2008). During adolescence, the risk of developing depression ranges from 15% to 20% (AACAP as cited in Drysdale & Rye, 2006), and it is twice as likely to be found in girls than in boys (Wilmshurst, 2005). There are many causes of depression, including abuse or neglect, stress, loss of a parent or significant relationship, having a chronic illness, other trauma, a high prevalence rate of alcoholism in first-degree relatives, family poverty, and conflict between parents (Wilmshurst, 2005). Just as there are numerous causes of depression, there are numerous signs of depression.

Recognizing that adolescent girls may be suffering from depression can be very difficult. Part of the difficulty is that it may be complicated to detect or separate depression from what is considered "typical adolescent stuff," and so adolescent depression often goes undiagnosed. Some of those signs may be low energy, boredom, social isolation, difficulty with relationships, poor performance in school, and extreme sensitivity (AACAP). Many of these symptoms may be associated with puberty and thus dismissed as just another bad day or typical teenage behavior. Other, more extreme signs, such as major changes in eating or sleeping patterns, frequent illnesses, talking about or making efforts to run away, feeling hopeless, and thoughts or expression of suicide (AACAP), may also be ignored. When left untreated, depression is a major risk factor for school failure, impaired relationships, suicide attempts or completions, and substance use and abuse (Drysdale & Rye, 2007). Comprehensive treatment is needed, and the question of whether to include psychotropic medications is still highly debated in the literature. Like adult women, adolescent girls who suffer from depression and who are not treated or who are treated poorly are at high risk for turning to substances in order to treat themselves. Self-medication occurs so often for adolescent substance addictions that depressive disorders are among the most common comorbid diagnosis category along with substance use (Cornelius & Clark, 2008).

ANXIETY

Just as depression is more likely to precede addiction for women (where the reverse tends to be true for men), it appears that anxiety disorders are also more likely to precede addiction diagnoses for women, and that childhood trauma can contribute to the development of both disorders (Marquenie et al., 2007). Thus, for anxiety disorders such as generalized anxiety disorders, simple phobias, or panic disorder, women may drink or use drugs as a means of self-medication to mitigate unpleasant symptoms. However, social phobias and pressures may also give way to problematic substance use. Women may use drugs or alcohol to relieve social pressures, to conform to peer groups, and to alleviate anxiety about negative evaluation from others (Stewart, Morris, Mellings, & Komar, 2006). Therefore, both state and trait anxiety features are linked to addictive behaviors in women.

Anxiety disorders are also common among adolescent girls; they are often undiagnosed, and often lead to substance use. Using substances to self-medicate and manage anxiety is an appealing option for adolescents with several of the more common anxiety disorders. The onset of social phobias is most consistently observed in adolescence, which makes sense given adolescence is a time of great concern with regard to peer relationships and social pressure to conform (Pither, 1994; Wilmshurt, 2005). From a feminist perspective, social phobia may stem from adolescent girls' attempts to define their social identities to navigate a new social system of peers, friends, and parental relationships. The phobia can evolve as girls are overwhelmed and unable to face these social changes. Higher social expectations at parties or large social gatherings can lead to alcohol consumption to cope with social anxiety. Drinking may be socially acceptable or socially required by peer groups. The alcohol helps to calm anxiety and "treats" the anxiety disorder without the shame of having to reveal to anyone what emotions are being experienced. The same is true for adolescents who have test anxiety or difficulty with panic disorder in stressful situations like school. Turning to substances helps to calm the anxiety, which serves two purposes: It is socially acceptable in their peer group and may help them to fit in or raise their social status, and it eliminates the anxious feelings.

There is also enormous sexual pressure on girls during adolescence. A girl may be simultaneously required to perform sexually in a romantic relationship while remaining virginal to others in her life, particularly family and other adults. If there is anxiety about being sexually active or distress about sexual development, substances may help to medicate uncomfortable feelings in order to fit in sexually and to perform in socially mandated ways. Simultaneously, substance use will likely help her to fit in and elevate her social status among peers, a difficult balance to maintain. What this all adds up to is a dramatic mix of self-medication and confusion about symptoms. Thus, comorbid anxiety and substance use can be one of the most difficult of the dual diagnoses to treat. They essentially blend into one issue, and separating the anxiety and substance use is very difficult and time-consuming— another example of the importance of including both a mental health and substance use component in counseling.

WOMEN, PTSD, AND ADDICTION

Posttraumatic stress disorder (PTSD) is defined as a clinical disorder triggered by a trauma where the symptoms last for more than one month, impede functioning, and severely affect one's ability to regulate affect (DSM-IV-TR). Some of these symptoms include "flashbacks, numbing, avoidance, heightened physical arousal, and a sense of foreshortened future" (Wilmshurst, 2005, p. 224). PTSD is a prevalent psychiatric disorder in conjunction with addiction: About 26% of women and 10% of men who are diagnosed with alcohol dependence also experience PTSD. Other studies estimate the prevalence of PTSD to be even higher, perhaps as high as 38% to 59% for women who are chemically dependent (Najavits, Sullivan, Schmitz, Weiss, & Lee, 2004; Sonne et al., 2003).

As with other aspects of addiction, much of the preliminary research about PTSD examined only male clients, particularly addicted men who were returning from combat situations. The results of these studies were generalized to women. However, contemporary research is more gender balanced. Modern studies demonstrate significant differences between men and women with PTSD and simultaneous substance use disorders. Specifically, female substance abusers are more likely than male substance abusers to be diagnosed with PTSD, females are more than twice as likely to have lifetime PTSD, and females are more likely to be revictimized or to suffer multiple traumas than males (Back et al., 2003). Once again, gender-specific research shows that generalizing results found with one gender cannot be translated to the other gender.

In one study of participants seeking treatment for both PTSD and alcohol dependence, 97% of women reported a history of sexual assault (including rape and molestation), and some history of physical assault during their lifetime (Sonne et al., 2003). Other studies demonstrate percentage rates of 89% for sexual abuse and 73% for physical abuse (Najavits et al., 2004), particularly at the hands of an intimate partner. In fact, some evidence demonstrates those who suffer violence by an intimate partner are more likely to eventually develop symptoms of PTSD than those who suffer violence by a stranger (Dansky, Byrne, & Brady, 1999). Women may also experience trauma related to both natural and manmade disasters and victimization due to crime (Najavits et al., 2004), or to have witnessed the death or homicide of someone close to them (Back et al., 2003). Because women are more likely than men to have suffered sexual abuse, rape, or domestic violence, treatment can be particularly complicated, as these events result in the greatest trauma (Hapke, Schumann, Rumpf, John, & Meyer, 2006). As a result, for women, PTSD is more likely to precede alcoholism than men (59% to 28%); addicted women are likely to experience social impairment and cognitive and emotional avoidance due to their PTSD (Sonne et al., 2003).

PTSD is also more likely to occur in conjunction with harder drug use than with alcohol use. For example, women cocaine addicts are 10 times more likely than nonaddicted women to have a diagnosis of PTSD, while users of "softer" drugs are only about four times more likely than nonaddicted women to be concurrently diagnosed with PTSD (Dansky et al., 1999). A recent study of women diagnosed with PTSD and either cocaine or alcohol dependence showed additional differences: Women in the cocaine/PTSD group were more likely to be African American (than Caucasian, the dominant ethnicity in the alcohol/PTSD group), isolated from community and unmarried, to have legal problems related to prostitution, and to suffer employment problems, including un- and underemployment (Back et al., 2003). Thus, in addition to considering gender differences in clientele, cultural factors and drug of abuse must also be taken into consideration. Women with PTSD and substance use disorders are not a homogenous group.

With regard to treatment, addicted women with PTSD are often perceived as difficult, due to the interpersonal difficulties that often arise from severe trauma. Additionally, limited effective treatment modalities exist to meet the needs of this specific population (Najavits, Weiss, Shaw, & Muenz, 1998). As a result, counselors are often stymied or frustrated in their attempts to be helpful. Traditional models of addiction treatment may be ineffective for women with PTSD and substance use disorders. Many of these clients may find the 12-Step philosophies particularly difficult to navigate (Najavits et al., 1998), or traditional models may dictate that the substance use disorder must be treated before the mental health issues. However, many women wanted both to be treated simultaneously; one study demonstrates that 80% of women participants indicate this preference (Najavits et al., 2004). Simultaneous treatment of PTSD with substance use disorders is particularly relevant for addictions counselors as the presence of PTSD can lead to more dysfunctional clinical profile, poorer prognosis (Back et al., 2003), poorer treatment outcomes, greater likelihood of relapse (Sonne et al., 2003), and lower compliance with aftercare (Najavits et al., 2004). In addition to the fact that women with concurrent PTSD and substance use disorders express a preference for simultaneous treatment, there is promising evidence that contemporary models of treatment that treat both are effective (Back et al., 2003). Many women with comorbid PTSD and substance use disorders also suffer from affective disorders, including depression and anxiety (Back et al., 2003). As we've demonstrated throughout this text, when counseling interventions are designed to meet the specific needs of this population, both counselors and clients alike report greater therapeutic alliance and indicate higher levels of treatment succes (Najavits et al., 1998).

PTSD is also a companion diagnostic area to anxiety for adolescent girls. Girls experience PTSD at higher rates than boys due to the types of traumas that often trigger this level of reaction, such as assault and rape. While any individual can experience PTSD after traumatic incidents such as car accidents or witnessing a crime, the more common triggers are often crimes that affect adult women. In a relatively small study (total of 297 participants), Deykin and Buka (1997) looked at the link between PTSD and chemically addicted adolescents. The findings were compelling: 58% of the girls began to use substances after the traumatic event. Substance dependence emerged after the PTSD. One must ask, did these girls begin to use substances as a result of the PTSD in order to self-medicate? According to Deykin and Buka, "In females, chemical dependence may be secondary, resulting from repeated substance use to deaden the psychic discomfort of PTSD" (p. 756). They did state that because adolescent girls had a higher probability of being raped than adolescent boys, they had higher rates of PTSD, and there were gender differences in the response to the PTSD, but for girls, the substance use clearly followed the PTSD symptoms. This study, while somewhat small and limited, points to the importance of understanding the connection between a mental health issue and an addictions issue. Counselors can no longer continue to try to treat the addiction without looking for the underlying cause.

What all of these concurrent diagnostic areas have in common is that they increase the likelihood that women or adolescent girls may develop addiction, to either substances or other harmful behaviors, and that they decrease the likelihood that counseling will be successful. The complexity of these diagnoses also speaks to the importance of viewing each woman or girl as an individual and screening for social history, substance abuse patterns, mental health, and emotional needs, and tailoring treatment to both the addiction and the mental health issues.

PHYSICAL VIOLENCE

Physical violence against women and girls can create psychological trauma that may be self-medicated with drugs, alcohol, or other compulsive behaviors, even in the absence of a PTSD diagnosis. In this section, the psychological impact of violence on the development of addictive behaviors will be discussed.

A strong link appears to exist between excessive alcohol use and intimate partner violence (IPV; DATA, 2006). While a correlational relationship between heavy alcohol consumption and IPV has long been acknowledged, some experts in the field are ready to assert a causal relationship between the two. Though excessive alcohol use is not implied to be the only cause of IPV, it is thought to be one contributing factor, as multiple studies have demonstrated a decrease in IPV once abstinence or reduction in drinking is achieved (Leonard, 2005). There also appears to be a similar relationship between excessive illicit drug use and IPV. Interestingly, it is not just the substance use of the perpetrator that seems to correlate to IPV, but all the substance abusive behavior of the victim. One hypothesis for this correlation is that victims (typically women) who use illicit drugs also suffer from lower social status and lower self-esteem, which may make them more vulnerable to abusive partners (DATA, 2005). Following abuse, women are also more likely to use drugs or alcohol to cope with the emotional aftereffects. For the perpetuators of violence, many theories attempt to explain increased violent behavior after drug or alcohol use. Theories focus on social learning within families and communities regarding the role of violence in relationships. Feminist theories tend to focus on the gender disparity between men and women that perpetuates the mindset of women as subordinate to male dominance. Two additional theories in particular help frame violent behavior in relationships: The first, *deviance disavowal* theory, implies that substance abuse is used as an excuse to commit premeditated violent behaviors. The second, a theory of *alcohol expectancies*, indicates that if a person believes drinking will make him or her violent, then he or she will act violently as a result (Galvani, 2004). This theory extends to sexual behavior as well.

For adolescent girls, the experience of physical violence typically takes place in two places, either at home or with an intimate partner. In 1997, Harrison, Fulkerson, and Beebe discussed the connection between the rates of physical abuse and the use of substances. Their research was not surprising, but helped to demonstrate in a sparsely researched field the strong connection between being abused and using substances earlier and more frequently. They found that girls had higher rates of abuse at all grade levels. Addictions counselors who work with adolescents acknowledge that girls who come in for treatment frequently have a history of abuse, but there is little research to support what is known anecdotally.

The other issue of concern is where this abuse is occurring. Counselors who work with abused girls know that abuse occurs both at home within families of origin and with romantic partners, but there is little research to confirm this. Silverman, Raj, Mucci, and Hathaway (2001) found that approximately 25% of adolescents have experienced dating violence, either physical or sexual. This is equivalent to the adult population. For girls, the risk is "three to six times that of IPV (intimate partner violence) against males" (Silverman et al., 2001, p. 572).

There is a wide range of mental health concerns for both women and girls who experience IPV. IPV is associated with heavy substance use, unhealthy weight control (e.g., diet pill use or laxative use), sexual risk behaviors, and higher levels of suicidality (Silverman et al.). Support for the link between physical abuse and alcohol abuse comes from a study by Clark, De Bellis, Lynch, Cornelius, and Martin (2003). This study does not separate out physical and sexual abuse, but it does show a strong link between an abuse history and addiction. What is interesting about this study is they also include the link between the abuse history and major depression: Girls who had a history of sexual and physical abuse also had higher rates of major depression and higher rates of addiction. Part of the reason for the connection may be that girls who are abused are more likely to have difficulty with regulating their emotions, which may contribute to their depression, which in turn contributes to addictive behaviors (Clark et al.). Again, we see the complex interplay between mental and chemical health in action.

Another area where physical abuse may have a negative effect in spite of the dearth of research is domestic violence that children witness. In the authors' work with children, and in my (Pepperell) several years working in a domestic violence shelter, we have seen many children and young girls shattered by witnessing violence in the home (while not experiencing violence directly). In our opinion, this vicarious trauma is still abuse. Yet, there are no studies to indicate the rate of addiction related to witnessing violence directly. The trauma of witnessing physical violence as a young child or adolescent may be a link to addiction, similar to what we've observed in the literature between direct sexual or physical violence and substance use disorders.

SEXUAL VIOLENCE

Women who have suffered repeated sexual violence episodes, especially in childhood, appear to be at higher risk for abusing drugs and alcohol than their peers (Cook, Epperson, & Gariti, 2005; Gordon, 2002). In addition, these women are also more likely to develop mental health problems and contract HIV/AIDS than women who have not experienced chronic sexual violence. In this section, the correlations among childhood sexual violence, mental health, and addiction are explored.

Just as with physical abuse, there are many ways in which one may experience sexual violence, and each of those experiences will have a different clinical impact. Studies show a correlation between sexual abuse and substance use or addictive behavior (Chen, Tyler, Whitbeck, & Hoyt, 2004; Clark et al., 2003; Howard & Wang, 2005; Silverman et al., 2001). There is uncertainty about how many women and girls are sexually abused before the age of 18, but most estimate around one in four (Howard & Wang, 2005; Walker, Scott, & Koppersmith, 1998). Part of the variation is due to the underreporting of this experience. Many episodes are not reported due to "embarrassment, denial, self-blame, or fear of breach in confidentiality and/or the possibility of retaliation if the perpetrator is known to the victim" (Howard & Wang, 2005, pp. 372–373). As a result of this violation, many individuals turn to drugs, alcohol, or other addictive behaviors as a way to cope with the abuse. Drugs can be used to alter neuron functioning, to aid with affect and mood (Walker et al., 1998), which may feel helpful for individuals struggling with symptoms resulting from sexual violence.

In a more recent and explorative study, Howard and Wang (2005) found that girls who had been sexually abused were also more likely to have suicidal thoughts, use substances, engage in more risky sexual behaviors, and have generalized feelings of sadness or hopelessness. This study was one of the only ones to split the findings by gender, demonstrating that the impact of sexual abuse on boys and girls is, in fact, qualitatively different.

Finally, while there is limited research to support this next point, anecdotal evidence points to the negative impact of sexual harassment on girls and women. Working or attending school in a sexist environment can lead to increased rates of depression, anxiety, and anger (Ross & Toner, 2003). As previously discussed, these emotional states are often associated with drug use, alcohol use, or other compulsive behaviors. Women and girls are sexually harassed in school hallways and in the workplace across the country on a daily basis, subjected to sexist jokes and comments, as well as institutional sexism such as the "glass ceiling" that often keeps women locked into middle management positions. Often sexual harassment is done with no specific threat and no physical touch. Administrative personnel then either choose not to handle it, or are not sure how to handle it. This constant harassment leads to fear, confusion, and anxiety and may produce some of the same symptoms that a sexual assault does. Thus, women and girls may turn to substances or process addictions to cope with their experiences. In particular, Ross and Toner (2003) state, "It will be important to examine the impact of sexist experiences on key life transitions, such as puberty ..." (p. 34). This is an area worthy of further consideration and research.

Psychological Effects of Prostitution

In U.S. culture, a woman who uses substances, particularly to excess, may be perceived as promiscuous and sexually available (Koehn & Hardy, 2006). This misperception negatively impacts addicted women and their relationships with potential partners and with their own sexual selves. The resulting behaviors may include sexual victimization or prostitution. There appears to be a significant correlation between prostitution and drug use. Unlike glamorous portrayals of prostitution in the media, where women are portrayed as sensual and empowered, prostitution exacts an intense mental and emotional toll on women in the sex trade. Women do not become prostitutes for sexual pleasure. Generally, selling or trading sex stems from necessity, either because of lack of options for financial resources or stability, or for a desperate need to procure drugs. Unlike higher-paid prostitutes or escorts, street-level prostitutes often turn to the sex trade to finance an already-existing drug addiction. This street-level prostitution is often the most dangerous for women, more so than working in a brothel or as a call girl, or as a stripper or exotic dancer.

The decision to trade sex for drugs or to engage in prostitution is intensified by preexisting situations and worsens current psychological problems. With regard to preexisting trauma, addicted women who engage in prostitution or trading sex for drugs are significantly more likely to have been victimized by childhood physical or sexual abuse than women who have never traded sex for drugs (Edwards, Halpern, & Wechsberg, 2006). Some studies of prostitutes have demonstrated that as many as two-thirds meet the criteria for PTSD, though for many, the trauma occurred during childhood or from other sexually violent events, rather than from the prostitution itself (Young, Boyd, & Hubbell, 2000). Women engaging in prostitution often lack the educational background or work skills to earn money in legal or less harmful ways: They tend to be younger, unmarried, un- or underemployed, and are more likely to be homeless (Edwards et al., 2006).

Street-level prostitutes often have little control over their working conditions. They are often subjected to particularly demeaning, violent, and degrading sex acts. Because of the psychologically harmful effects of the sex trade, women frequently turn to drug use (particularly crack cocaine and heroin) to dull the emotional trauma of violence and to lessen inhibition for sex. This correlation creates a downward spiral of drug use, leading to helplessness and hopelessness (Young et al., 2000). In fact, in some crack houses, one woman acts as a "house girl," providing sexual acts and services in exchange for drugs, even doses as small as a hit on a crack pipe. This role further debases drug-addicted women, creating more trauma and psychological distress (Young et al., 2000).

Emotional disturbance as a result of prostitution can include psychological distress, loneliness, isolation, and fear (Ling, Wong, Holroyd, & Gray, 2007). With regard to specific diagnoses, prostitutes show heightened levels of depression, anxiety, and paranoid ideation; these are even more likely to occur in drug-abusing prostitutes. PTSD in particular is likely to be diagnosed in drug-abusing prostitutes. Participating in the sex trade can result in physical health problems as well, including exhaustion, cervical cancer, STDs, HIV, traumatic brain injuries, and respiratory problems (Edwards et al., 2006; Ling et al., 2007). Prostitutes are also likely to experience violence, physical assault, and sexual assault, often contributing to lifelong patterns of abuse and assault.

Even among addicts, women who have not traded sex for drugs seem to be more psychologically healthy. A recent study of African American women who smoke crack cocaine demonstrated that women who had never traded sex for money "had better scores on self-esteem, decision making, confidence, anxiety, and depression … current traders [of sex for money] reported the most childhood problems …" (Risser et al., 2006, p. 651). Thus, counseling interventions for addicted women who have currently or previously traded sex for money or drugs must move beyond addictions treatment alone to include self-esteem enhancement, job skills development, and decision-making skills (Risser et al., 2006). These are essential for success.

ADDICTED AND INCARCERATED

There is evidence that alcohol and drug use can aggravate violent criminal behavior. Aggression and violence have long been perceived as a behavioral consequence of male substance abusing behaviors, particularly with regard to alcohol. In fact, aggression in men as one outcome of alcohol intoxication is a phenomenon well supported by the research literature. Researchers have even asserted that aggression following alcohol intoxication is exclusively a male problem; thus, research in this area for women is unnecessary (Hoaken & Pihl, 2000). As feminist scholars, we resist the notion that any area of potential research is inconsequential for either gender. And when an assertion is made that one social problem or another is exclusively the domain of either gender, we believe both women and men suffer from such stereotyping. Perhaps women's aggression is not as widely recognized a phenomenon as men's, but it is certainly worthy of attention. One such study demonstrated that under provocation, women were as likely as men to demonstrate aggressive behavior, regardless of intoxication status. Other studies have had mixed results regarding women's aggressive responses when intoxicated (Hoaken & Pihl, 2000). However, there is one group of women that is often viewed as aggressive, even though that is not the norm.

Female inmates are one of the fastest-growing populations in the U.S. penal system—particularly women of color. Up to two-thirds of incarcerated women meet criteria for mental illness and require medication management at rates of two to three times those of non-incarcerated women. Additionally, dual diagnoses of mental illness and substance use disorders are prevalent. Alcohol and drug use have been shown to increase the likelihood of criminal behavior in women, and thus many women entering prison have a substance use disorder (SUD). One study demonstrated that 83% of incarcerated women met criteria for an SUD (Singer, Bussey, Song, & Lunghofer, 1995). In fact, women are often engaging in criminal behavior not because they are bad or evil (as is often assumed by our society) but because of crushingly difficult life circumstances that lead to nonviolent acts as a means of survival.

Because many of the criminal acts committed by women are non-violent, this population often goes unnoticed. Thus, few studies have attempted to address the specific needs of this population. Similar to preexisting conditions found in prostitutes, female inmates often have a history of childhood physical or sexual abuse (Singer et al., 1995). Thus, the psychological factors impacting mental health and substance use behaviors are often deeply entrenched and more difficult to treat. Additionally, substance abusing incarcerated women struggle with feelings of loneliness and isolation, and have experienced physical or sexual violence during adulthood, including rape, physical assault (stabbings, shootings, beatings, attempted murder), and similar assaults as a result of being victimized while engaging in prostitution (Singer et al.).

Postincarceration, addicted women are clearly in need of multiple services in order to reacclimate to society and to find some level of safety and satisfaction in life. Services including housing assistance, addiction counseling, mental health counseling, financial assistance, education and training, medical care, and family support were listed as most important by incarcerated women (Singer et al., 1995). It is interesting to note that these women perceived jail as a positive place to achieve temporary abstinence from drugs or alcohol because effective addiction counseling services were not available to them out in the community (Singer et al., 1995). This is a powerful insight for counselors working with recently released women.

SELF-HARM AND SUICIDALITY

Among adult women, alcoholism, addiction, and depression all increase the likelihood of successfully completing a suicide attempt. As many as 90% of people who die by suicide have a diagnosable substance use disorder or mental illness, or both (Suicide Prevention Council, n.d.). Among the nonaddicted population, women are more likely to attempt suicide than men, though men are more likely to successfully commit suicide than women. However, women who are alcoholic or addicted are more likely than nonaddicted women to successfully commit suicide (Lisansky-Gomberg, 1989). Surprisingly, even cigarette smoking is a predictor for suicide (Tanskanen, Tuomilehto, Viinamaki, Vartiainen, & Lehtonen, 2000). According to Wilke (2004), "Suicide thoughts, attempts, and completions are highly related to substance abuse, particularly with co-morbid depression. Substance abuse has been related to a greater frequency of suicide attempts, repeat suicide attempts, and more serious ideation" (p. 232). Thus, the possibility of suicide must be of serious concern for addiction counselors.

Concern about self-harm and suicidal behavior is also warranted when working with women and girls with comorbid PTSD and addiction. One study demonstrates that among women with both diagnoses, about 32% attempted self-harm or suicidal gestures, mainly in the form of cutting, scratching, or overdosing (Harned, Najavits, & Weiss, 2006). The use of drugs and alcohol prior to self-harm or suicide attempts is prevalent (Harned et al.).

The same is true when thinking about adolescent suicide and self-harm behaviors. When partnered with addiction, rates of self-harming behaviors and suicidality go up. In the literature, self-harm and suicidality are often discussed together, yet they are clearly two very different issues. With regard to self-harm behaviors, it is important for addictions counselors to understand not only why this occurs with other addictions, such as substance use, but also to begin to think of this behavior as an addiction itself. Self-harm has also been termed *cutting, self-mutilation,* or *self-injury,* but broadly, it is any behavior that an individual engages in where there is an intent to alter or destroy body tissue for nonaesthetic purpose (tattoos and piercings are considered aesthetic, though excessive body alterations such as these might constitute self-injurious behavior) (Purington & Whitlock, 2004). Typically self-injury occurs on the arms or wrists, but can occur on any part of the body. Self-injury is usually a way to express emotions; clients often say that it helps them to "feel something" and to connect with a part of themselves when they often feel disconnected with the world. Because it is used as a coping mechanism, it can become addictive. Clients often have stated that they cannot get through the day or any tough times without harming themselves once they begin to use this method of self-soothing. Purington and Whitlock stated:

> Once the behavior is started, the endorphins released by self-injurious behavior can become quite addictive. The process can be likened to that of a growing drug addiction, where at first, small amounts (of the drug or self-injury) provide a sense of calm and well-being that provide a temporary escape from the pain of life. As tolerance builds, the user needs increased amounts (of drug or self-injury) to achieve the same effect. (p. 2)

Understanding self-harm as an addiction in and of itself has critical implications for counselors who work with adolescent girls. For example, one of the common mistakes is to assume self-harm behavior is related to suicidality. The two are not automatically linked. In fact, the self-harm behavior is a way of coping and may prevent a suicide attempt. Clearly, concern about suicide should be addressed via assessment and follow-up, but counselors would be wrong to assume all self-harm is suicidality. This behavior is like any other addiction in that it stems from an inability to manage other mental health issues, such as depression, anxiety, or PTSD. It is critical to treat the underlying issue, not just the behavior or resulting addiction.

Self-harm behavior and substance abuse are often connected. Girls who are engaging in self-harm behaviors are more likely to take other risks with their bodies, such as using drugs or alcohol to "try on" new coping skills, to fit in socially, or to manage another underlying mental health diagnosis. Also, if counselors are not explicit in providing new coping strategies while encouraging girls to stop self-harm, they are at higher risk to take on new maladaptive strategies, like drug and alcohol use (Purington & Whitlock, 2004). This is similar to when drug or alcohol addicts "switch addictions," from alcohol to caffeine or cigarettes to sunflower seeds. It is a common phenomenon in this line of work, and needs to be considered with regard to self-harming behaviors.

While girls' suicidality may not be related to self-harming behavior, in some ways they are related. Silverman et al. (2001) found connections among higher suicidality, substance use, and IPV. Suicidal ideation was "six to nine times as common among adolescent girls who had been sexually and physically hurt by dating partners" (p. 578). While they do not report what percentage of those girls have a substance abuse problem, given their other finding, it is safe to infer that it would be higher than the general population. Most girls turn to suicide because they no longer are able to cope with either an internal or external stressor—the same reason most turn to an addictive behavior. We know that girls are three times as likely to attempt suicide as boys (Wilmshurst, 2005), though they are less likely than boys to be successful in their attempts because the methods used by girls are often less lethal than those used by boys. What is also clear is that girls who are addicted are also more likely to be suffering from a mental health issue, such as depression or anxiety, which increases the risk that they will be suicidal. Treatment must address all three areas, not just one.

CONCLUSION

For women and girls, addiction to substances or processes involves a complex interplay of psychological factors. Counselors must begin the therapeutic relationship by assessing mental health functioning, past trauma, suicidality, and the potential for self-harm before treatment can begin. Then, throughout the treatment spectrum, counselors must bear in mind that in order for recovery from addiction to take place, underlying causes and correlates of addiction need attention as well. Dual diagnosis treatment must not be the exception in addictions counseling; rather, necessity compels it to become the rule.

Case Study

During the early stages of counseling, Sheila reveals she was sexually assaulted by two boys while in high school. The assault included coerced sexual activity with two boys she considered friends. The three were drinking at the home of one of the boys while his parents were out of town. Believing she was partially at fault for what happened, Sheila stuffed the memories of the assault and never revealed what happened to anyone, including her husband. Since the assault, Sheila has struggled with symptoms of depression, including difficulty sleeping, depressed mood, and irritability. She also has symptoms of anxiety and social phobia. When these symptoms emerge, Sheila typically deals with them by withdrawing and increasing her alcohol intake. Sheila feels she has been effective in hiding her symptoms, as well as her alcohol use, from her family. But lately, she finds it more and more difficult to hide her pain, and has begun withdrawing, experiencing greater psychic pain as a result of her many psychological issues.

By this time in the counseling relationship, you have begun to realize that Sheila's alcoholism is far bigger than a simple DSM diagnosis. Her drinking began as a social behavior during high school to fit in with her peers and to feel socially accepted. Her alcohol intake increased after the sexual assault. Sheila always blamed herself for the assault: Because she was drunk that night, Sheila harbored a secret fear that she somehow asked for the assault to happen. Sheila also worries that she somehow led her male friends on sexually, and perhaps communicated romantic interest that was misinterpreted. Sheila self-medicated her internalized guilt and shame by drinking more and more heavily.

Additionally, Sheila experienced symptoms of depression and anxiety since the assault. A comprehensive assessment of her psychological profile can assist you, her counselor, in determining what steps need to be taken to address these potential diagnoses. Because alcohol is a depressant, if Sheila is suffering from clinical depression, her drinking behaviors are intensifying her symptomology. In addition to determining an accurate diagnosis, it would benefit Sheila to receive education about how her alcohol use is contributing to her psychological distress. It would also be prudent to assess for PTSD, as the symptoms following her assault are persistent and enduring.

DISCUSSION QUESTIONS

1. What are your own opinions about women's culpability in sexual assault? Are there biases or prejudices that might inhibit your work with her? How would you assist her in releasing her self-blame for the assault?
2. Discuss how to intertwine addiction counseling and mental health counseling in working with women like Sheila. Develop three goals that would benefit Sheila if they were a part of her treatment plan.
3. Traditional (i.e., the 12-Step model) addiction counseling discourages addicts and alcoholics from taking any medication during recovery. What are your perspectives on medication management for mental health issues for addicted clients?

5

SOCIAL FACTORS

In addition to biological and psychological issues, women face a multitude of sociological pressures that contribute to addiction. Women are shaped by society and gender norms in many ways beginning in childhood. This chapter will review the influences of socialization, peer pressure, sexualization, and family of origin on the growing rates of both substance and process addictions. Because socialization is distinctive during different life stages, this chapter will review concerns for adolescent girls separately from those experienced by adult women.

SOCIOLOGICAL ISSUES FOR ADOLESCENTS

For adolescents, one of the primary social concerns is simply the normal developmental process itself. For girls, transitioning through puberty into adolescence can be extremely difficult. Pipher (1994) described three components that contribute to the struggle for adolescent girls, all related to developmental changes. The first component relates to the physical changes girls experience during the transition into adolescence, including hormonal changes. The second component is specific to the way society reacts to girls changing and developing. Pipher stated, "American culture has always smacked girls on the head in early adolescence. This is when they move into a broader culture that is rife with girl-hurting 'isms,' such as sexism, capitalism, and lookism" (p. 23). And finally, girls are expected to distance themselves from their parents during this time. We know from feminist theory about the importance of connections and relationships in adolescent girls' development of a sense of self; thus, this can be a treacherous time for girls to disconnect from their families, especially if they are not able to find other connections.

One complication during this transition is that it seems to come suddenly. Girls tend to be accepted for who they are in elementary school, but once they hit middle school and high school there is much more pressure to achieve popularity and to conform to social and gender norms for girls in their school. This conformity often includes pressure to use substances or to become sexually active. For women, relationships are primary in all areas of life, while for adolescent girls maintaining a connection with peers is the most critical and often the most difficult (Stern, 1991). Girls attempting to find social connection feel compelled to conform to the behaviors of their peers. These behaviors may be contrary to their self-identities, but to be accepted they do what their peers are doing. Stern presented this struggle to build relationships as important when considering the effects of peer pressure, media images, and academic pressure upon girls' identities. For example, if there is pressure in a peer group to dress a certain way, adolescent girls may feel pulled to comply even if it does not feel congruent with who they are. This conflict also exists when there is pressure to behave in a specific way, such as drinking alcohol, drug use, or self-mutilation behaviors. To decrease the ensuing dissonance, Stern stated, adolescent girls may begin to feel disconnected from their peers, which can cause stress (which may contribute to mental health concerns, process addictions, or substance use to cope with the stress).

The development of self in connection with others is a challenging dilemma that is central to the lives of adolescent girls. Unfortunately, the model of perfection presented to girls is typically teens in movies, on television, or in pop music bands. Usually these girls are posed in magazines that have been digitally retouched in ways that make the girls themselves unrecognizable. While adults may be cognizant of this, most young girls are not. Ultimately adolescent girls end up striving for a level of perfection that does not exist (Kilbourne, 2004). There are multiple systems at work here, and we will examine all of them.

Social Norms and Stereotypes

One of the primary developmental tasks during childhood is to establish a gender identity. Children are socialized early in life to perceive themselves as either a boy or a girl. They learn to label those around them as boy or girl, and that gender is permanent from birth. Wehren and De Lisi (1983) attempted to address the important developmental issue of gender understanding. Their aim was to show the age at which children understand gender as consistent and the influence of gender norms. They found that at age 3 children could identify gender but not gender consistency. By age 7, children understood gender as consistent, and by age 9 they were able to distinguish gender norms and societal influence. This study was important, as it established that children understand gender early and that societal norms and pressures are influential. This understanding of gender norms and roles contributes to pressures that girls feel to find relationships that are secure. Young children also learn very early that boys have specific preferences, like trucks, dark colors, and not crying. They also learn that girls are sensitive, play house, and will wait for a man to kiss them and make them happy (yes, that is a Disney reference). Socialization begins in early childhood, and while children become more aware and relearn more fluid concepts about gender, the social norms and roles assigned based on gender continue into adolescence and adulthood.

For adolescent girls, contending with gender roles and norms that have been established for them can be very difficult. For girls who in some way do not fit the social norm, whether that is because they identify as transgendered or they enjoy more traditionally male activities or characteristics, adolescence can be very difficult. Alice Miller (1981) described children splitting into a true self and false self during this time. Children, according to Miller, had to make a choice between being their authentic or true self or being loved: They had to determine which behaviors would bring love or abandonment. For example, if a girl believed her parents did not value expression of feelings, she would stop expressing her feelings. The more she stopped expressing feelings, the more she felt loved, but this created a false self. The true self, the one with feelings, would be pushed aside so often that it would be lost. Miller focused on children needing and wanting parental approval. Other theorists expand on these ideas to girls, and to include peer groups.

Pipher (2005) found that adolescent girls had the difficult task of balancing the true self, being who they believe they really are, with the false self, being who they think they need to be. The more girls have to push aside their true self, the more they get lost. Social roles are very complicated for adolescent girls; for example, they should get good grades to please their parents, but not get such high grades they alienate their friends. They should be active in whatever sport is popular, regardless if that is what they really want to do, but they should not be better at sports than boys. They should be interested in boys, even if they identify as lesbian. They should be virginal in appearance, but be sexually active. Clear as can be? And finally, girls should look perfect all the time, be thin, and know exactly what kind of clothes are most fashionable in order to look just like the girls in magazines.

All of these social norms only support the false self. There are very few, if any, that support the true self. Losing the true self contributes to depression, anxiety, and stress. All of these can lead to addictive behaviors such as alcohol use, eating disorders, and self-harming behaviors as a way to try to self-medicate, or as a way for the adolescent girl to try to reconnect with her true self.

Media Images

As two well-educated adult feminist women we (the authors) have frequent conversations about how women are portrayed in magazines, movies, and television (and how we don't live up to those standards for appearance). We are also both very active and physically fit women, and yet we will never look like the women we see in the media who are falsely presented to us as normal. What most adult women are cognizant of is that most of the women we see in print media don't look like that either; their images have been retouched to model perfection. However, women are bombarded with these images of physical ideals. It is difficult not to be influenced in spite of the fact that we (the authors) and you (the readers) are highly educated individuals.

If understanding the influence of media on self-image is difficult for grown women, imagine how difficult it is for 13-year-old girls. They don't realize that their favorite pop idol is not really 5 feet 10 inches and a size 2, with no fat anywhere on her body (yet with large breasts). The amount of retouching and airbrushing to assist in creating "perfect" bodies for girls to emulate is often not understood by girls. Adolescent girls perceive these images as normal, attainable bodies. Girls may begin to attempt to look like these models through dieting, restrictive eating, or exercising to extremes. These behaviors may lead to disordered eating patterns. Adolescent girls may also begin to use substances such as cigarettes, caffeine, or stimulants to help them lose weight. Girls may also become depressed or anxious about conforming to media images and social pressure from peers to lose weight. These behaviors sustain the false self. The emotional and physical consequences are significant, and can impact self-esteem, social development, and the development of future problems.

Researchers such as Moore and MacKinnon (2001), Kilbourne (2004), and Tiggemann, Gardiner, and Slater (2000) are just a few whose work has focused on the social influences of girls' identity. Moore and MacKinnon (2001) stated that a girl's sense of self is shaped and forged primarily through social interaction with peers and in school. Peer pressure stems in part from the media. While the media has influence on both boys and girls, the research shows that its influence is more harmful for girls. Moore and MacKinnon found that girls understand the impact of media. They found girls "clearly illustrate how social interaction and personal identity are potently influenced by the pervasive and compelling nature of their messages" (p. 310). Tiggemann et al. (2000) also found that girls understood the influence of the media. They found that girls "very clearly and articulately described how the constant barrage by the media of thin, attractive, glamorous women leads to the belief that thinness and attractiveness are the cultural norm" (p. 655). The girls in this study could discuss these influences, but they expressed powerlessness to stop the pressure from the media and society. What is interesting about these studies is that the girls talked about being surrounded by images, yet feeling unable to stop them, much in the way one talks about addiction, being unable to stop, and feeling out of control. Yet, it is these images that contribute to low self-esteem, poor body image, high rates of eating disorders, substance use, and a loss of self.

The influence of the media was also examined in Kilbourne's (2004) work. She reported that girls are taught by the media to be quiet, not talk too much or too loudly, and not to have needs. Young women often perceive media images as the norm, and look for peer confirmation of what is expected. The influence of the media is powerful, and this power becomes stronger as girls enter middle school and high school (Kilbourne, 2004). Stern (1991) described these years as the time when girls feel drawn to maintain relationships with their peers. If relationships stem from gender socialization of what young women "should be," media will have ongoing power over girls and young women.

Another concern is not just how media images may affect girls' self-image but the way the media targets girls in order to sell products to them. The tobacco industry has often been accused of marketing to younger and younger individuals, individuals who may not have the maturity to realize that cigarettes are dangerous and toxic. The results of this advertising focus are clear: About 90% of smokers began smoking before the age of 21 (American Lung Assocation, 2008). "Corporate America encourages girls to consume products such as Coke and designer jeans, and chemicals such as alcohol and nicotine, to sedate their natural and understandable pain. As the cigarette companies have discovered, adolescent girls are perfect targets for anyone peddling sophistication" (Pipher, 2005, p. 202). Marketing and advertising will continue to target adolescent girls because it works.

One powerful presence in the media that has been foisted upon girls is a Disney character known as "Hannah Montana," played by Miley Cyrus. What is so fascinating about her is that her show is a startling visual depiction of a girl having to give up her real self in order to gain fame and popularity (her false self). On her show, Cyrus's character has two names. During the day she attends school as Miley, but at night she becomes rock star Hannah Montana. This one girl now represents two people, a split persona who changes her image and sense of self via costume changes; girls are told that because of her splashy outfits and blond hair, Hannah is a much cooler rock star. Who is Cyrus when she is on tour and which of her selves is the real girl? In the end, neither. While this show is rated for teens, girls as young as 4 are watching and being influenced by these messages. Parents pay outrageous amounts of money for CDs, merchandise, and concert tickets. And while clearly no one is saying out loud that Hannah is "better" than Miley, the message is clear: Hannah Montana is the one to be, a false identity created from a real 15-year-old girl. The result is that girls who don't feel adequate or connected may have difficulty forming their identity and self-concept. This may lead to feelings of anxiety, depression, and isolation. These girls are at a much higher risk for substance use and other addictive behaviors. They are also at a higher risk because they may try risky behaviors to fit in, to belong. Friends are critical to girls, and when girls don't know themselves, they have a very difficult time establishing connections to others.

Influence of Friends

There is little in an adolescent girl's life that has as much influence on her development as her peer relationships. Those relationships are what help girls develop their own sense of self; in many ways friends work like a mirror reflecting back to a girl who she is or who she could be. Because they are the most influencing relationship in an adolescent girl's life, they also have an influence on whether substances are used, and how often. While it is important for parents and guardians to teach young children to abstain from drugs, alcohol, and tobacco use, and to make their own choices, we must be aware that approximately 45% of 8th graders, two-thirds of 10th graders, and three-quarters of 12th graders reported using alcohol within the past year when asked (Wilmshurst, 2005). So, by the time they get to high school, most adolescents are already drinking.

For girls, the data are even more troubling. For the first time in U.S. history, adolescent girls are poised to pass boys in levels and frequency of substance use. "Among 8th and 10th graders, girls drink more ... girls are more likely to use inhalants and stimulants ... once girls use harmful substances, they are more apt than boys to become dependent" (Schinke, Fang, & Cole, 2008). Much of this increase may be related to the higher needs for girls to seek peer approval by using substances. If girls' peers use alcohol or marijuana, the likelihood of substance use increases (Hussong, 2000; Wilson & Donnermeyer, 2006). For example, girls may drink to fit in at a party, to avoid standing out as abstainers, or simply to be part of a group. Many, if not most, adolescents go through experimentation with drugs or alcohol, which allows them to connect with friends and fit in with peer groups. Experimental use generally does not cause any long-term damage or raise the risk for substance use disorders later in life. It is important for counselors to determine what behaviors are problematic and what behaviors are typical. Peer groups are not the only influence on girls' substance use behaviors. The degree to which peers are able to influence adolescent girls' substance using behaviors relates back to the girls' family of origin (Hussong, 2000; Schinke et al., 2008; Wilson & Donnermeyer, 2006).

Influence of Family

While peer groups may have a greater direct effect on an adolescent girl's choice to use substances during middle school or high school, it is the influence of the family that underlies those choices. There is significant documentation that children with substance abusing parents are at a greater risk of developing a substance-related issue themselves (Su, Hoffmann, Gerstein, & Johnson, 1997; Thompson & Henderson, 2007; Wilson & Donnermeyer, 2006). There are several risk factors that impact whether a child uses substances or not. The first is related to the connection between generations of substance use. There are many different theories about why this may occur. The first is the notion that there may be a genetic predisposition to addiction. Another theory is that adolescents may be learning the substance using behaviors from their family member per a social learning theory model (Su et al., 1997). Su et al. also test a stress-coping model, one that proposes the substance use of the parent increases the adolescent's risk of experiencing other negative life events. These negative life events further lower family cohesion, which contributes to the adolescent's use of substances to cope with those life events. In their research, this model appeared to have the most impact, particularly on adolescent girls' depressive symptoms, which is significant due to the frequency of comorbity with depression and substance use.

The second risk factor is what messages and type of supervision the family is able to provide their children. If parents are battling with an addiction, they are less likely to provide supervision after school. When adults are not present to monitor substance use, the use goes up (Hussong, 2000; Schinke et al., 2008). In addition to monitoring substance use, being present has an impact on attachment. How girls attach to their parents may have an effect on how they then attach to their peers. With solid family attachments, while they will still need to bond and shift their focus to their peers, they will take the messages with them that they received at home. Without those attachments, they will only have their peer messages to utilize.

Family interaction theory describes the intersection of both of these influences and what happens when the family attachment is not strong. One criticism of this theory is that it looks primarily to the mother as the primary caretaker (Schinke et al., 2008), and the one that is responsible for what occurs at home. While that may be the case, this is where many counselors incorrectly blame the mother for what happens in the family, and from a feminist perspective, that can be damaging to the family and the girl you are counseling.

So, in considering the impact of parents' addictive behaviors on the familial bond, use caution in assigning blame if addiction problems also arise for the children. The problem is not that simple. However, "low parental attachment correlates more highly with smoking, drinking, and drug use among girls than among boys" (Schinke et al., p. 70). This also fits with Su et al.'s (1997) finding that girls in their study were more affected by a lack of family cohesion than boys.

The final effect the family has on adolescent girls' addiction issues is that children who grow up in homes that are unstable or abusive are at greater risk for depression and substance use (Schinke et al., 2008; Su et al., 1997). Girls who do not feel safe or secure look for other ways to cope with those emotions. This coping may come in the form of alcohol, drug, or tobacco use with friends. It may also come in the form of self-mutilation or disordered eating.

Sexualized Culture

The last contributing factor is the way our culture has oversexualized adolescent girls. The American Psychological Association's (APA) task force on the sexualization of girls (2007) described sexualization as occurring when:

- A person's value comes only from his or her sexual appeal or behavior, to the exclusion of other characteristics;
- A person is held to a standard that equates physical attractiveness (narrowly defined) with being sexy;
- A person is sexually objectified—that is, made into a thing for others' sexual use, rather than seen as a person

with the capacity for independent action and decision making; and/or
- Sexuality is inappropriately imposed upon a person. (p. 1)

We see sexualization everywhere—in the media, the clothes that girls wear, and the songs that are on the radio. But nothing demonstrates the sexualization of girls better than the *Girls Gone Wild* phenomena. *Girls Gone Wild* (GGW) is a multimillion-dollar direct-to-video series of (assumed) college-aged girls exposing their bodies in public (Pitcher, 2006).

Not only are the girls on the tapes performing sexual acts, or conducting a striptease for men, but they all meet a homogenous criterion of beauty: almost all white, between 100 and 110 pounds, blond, blue eyes, thin and firm body types, clearly falling into a constructed routine of self-care and makeup. They dress in a specific way and appear to be "good girls" (Pitcher, 2006). GGW sets up a carnival-like atmosphere that helps draw these girls into the moment, which makes them more likely to consent. The consents of the young women, along with their age (all of them knowing to say they are 18), are all captured on tape; however, "many women featured on GGW appear to be under the influence of alcohol or drugs. On the videos, slurred speech and wobbly posture sometimes allude to inebriation. Some are actually holding beer cans or sipping cocktails" (Pitcher, p. 206). This party atmosphere not only encourages the substance use, but it is that substance use that creates the atmosphere where the girls feel free enough to strip or engage in sexual acts on camera for a T-shirt.

For some, it may feel empowering, but if it were truly to empower women, all women would be a part of it, and the goal would not be a multimillion-dollar enterprise. These videos provide yet another perspective of beauty and sexuality that is not real and likely unattainable for most girls, and the message to both genders is that this behavior is indeed normal when in fact it communicates misogyny. It sends that party atmosphere message, the girls look fun and inviting, and along with other aspects of our media, it damages girls.

This is just one extreme example of the sexualization of girls and young women; there are many more. What is critical is that there are consequences for oversexualization of girls. "These consequences include harm to the sexualized individuals themselves, to their interpersonal relationships, and to society … can contribute to body dissatisfaction, eating disorders, low self-esteem, depressive affect" (APA, 2007, p. 2). The task force on the sexualization of girls found the three most common mental health consequences to sexualization are eating disorders, low self-esteem, and depression or depressed mood.

Finally, this sexualization affects society in general. These images perpetuate sexism, sex bias, and sexist attitudes (APA, 2007). With exposure to sexualized images, men, women, and adolescents may begin to take on the roles in the images, with men and boys perhaps becoming more aggressive and women perhaps being more passive and more sexualized. This contributes to the rape myth (the belief that girls or women invite rape by their behavior or dress) and to the minimization of women. It also contributes to the ways in which adolescent girls engage in substance use; it is often to connect with either friends or boys they like. They are often invited in, and may feel as if this is the only way to connect with a guy that they like. This is a big part of the reason for the disparity between the reasons adolescent girls come into substance use.

Sexualization begins at a very young age, with the word *princess* written on the bottom of toddler girl shorts. And in college, drunk women on spring break are asked to strip for a video that will make one man very rich so they can get another item of clothing with the words "Girls Gone Wild" written across the breast. Both of these examples influence how girls define themselves as sexual beings: simply made of parts to be looked over by men. They tear apart girls' self-concept and self-esteem and contribute to high levels of depression, anxiety, eating disorders, and addiction. High levels of depression, low self-esteem, and anxiety all contribute to adolescent girls' addiction, whether the addiction is to food, self-harm, or substances. The link between unhealthy sexualization and addiction is significant.

SOCIOLOGICAL ISSUES FOR WOMEN

As described in the historical overview that began this book, women are affected by socially constructed gender norms about alcohol, drugs, and addiction. Social factors may influence how women seek treatment for addiction and also affect women's likelihood of becoming addicted in the first place. According to Angove and Fothergill, "Society is responsible for pushing some women into chemical solutions" (2003, p. 215). In other words, gender norms and stereotypes can have an oppressive influence on women, resulting in emotional distress and substance use as a coping mechanism.

Familial Systems and Relationships

Similar in some ways to adolescents' development, women's development of problem substance use appears inextricably linked to relationships. Within their families of origin, a history of alcoholism or drug dependence puts women at greater risk of becoming dependent themselves (Gordon, 2002; Kaskutas, Zhang, French, & Witbrodt, 2005; Nelson-Zlupko, Kauffman, & Dore, 1995). This link appears to be related to both genetic and family cultural factors. Women may use substances to fit into their family culture, or as a defense against the emotional distress caused by living with an alcoholic or drug-dependent family member.

After leaving the childhood home and creating families of their own, addicted women experience overresponsibility within their families, high levels of familial tension, and are often discouraged from seeking counseling by their family members (Nelson-Zlupko et al., 1995). Women internalize a high level of shame and guilt because of their addiction, feeling they are failures as wives and mothers. Additionally, families of addicted women are often unsupportive of their seeking treatment; there is no clear understanding of this phenomenon, but perhaps families are ashamed to admit the primary female figure has become addicted, and perhaps it parallels traditional gender roles to keep addicted women disempowered and dependent on a caregiving spouse. The relationship between spouses who are addicted is a strong influential factor.

Women seem more susceptible than men to social pressure to drink or use drugs, and are more likely to have a substance abusing partner (Gordon, 2002). For example, women heroin addicts are more likely to be introduced to the drug by a male friend or romantic partner, while men are more likely to be introduced to heroin by other men. Also, these women are more likely to buy heroin from or for their male partners, to support their drug habits with their partners, and to share needles with their partners than men do with their female partners (Cook, Epperson, & Gariti, 2005; Gordon, 2002). Again, this phenomenon parallels traditional gender roles of influential, powerful men and disempowered, dependent women. Women are dependent on their male partners for drugs, and rely on them to assist in maintaining addiction.

On a broader cultural level, society tends to judge women's problem drinking and drug use more harshly than men's (Angove & Fothergill, 2003; Haseltine, 2000; Lynch, Roth, & Carroll, 2002; Kaskutas et al., 2005; Matthews & Lorah, 2005). Thus, women often feel compelled to hide their drinking from family and social supports out of a sense of guilt and shame (Angove & Fothergill, 2003), and may hesitate to seek counseling (Roeloffs, Fink, Unutzer, Tang, & Wells, 2001). Women entering counseling for addiction are less likely than men to have family support, and are more likely to have a lower socioeconomic status, lower education, and to be unemployed (Gordon, 2002; Haseltine, 2000; McCance-Katz, Carroll, & Rounsaville, 1999). Therefore, they often need more support from counselors and treatment centers to continue counseling and to be successful.

SOCIAL CONSIDERATIONS FOR WOMEN WHO PARENT

Addicted women often have serious concerns with regard to their children, both during and after pregnancy. These concerns stem from legitimate biological risks of addiction on unborn fetuses, as well as social stigma related to mothers who are addicted. In U.S. culture, women are socialized to domestic responsibilities, so special judgment is reserved for addicted mothers, who are perceived as failing in their responsibility to hearth and home.

As mentioned, true health risks exist for women who abuse drugs or alcohol while pregnant. Abusing alcohol during pregnancy puts babies at risk of developing fetal alcohol syndrome (FAS), the most preventable form of intellectual or developmental delays. About one-third of women who consume six alcoholic drinks a day or more give birth to a child with FAS, resulting in developmental delays, behavioral problems, and facial and neurological abnormalities (Gordon, 2002). Other birth defects that can occur as a result of alcohol or drug abuse during pregnancy include heart problems, growth delays, and mental and behavioral abnormalities (March of Dimes, n.d.). Addicted pregnant women might also deliver prematurely, experience vaginal infections, or suffer miscarriages (Nelson-Zlupko et al., 1995).

Indeed, alcohol or drug use during pregnancy can result in significant and grave consequences for babies, parents, and families. Most would agree that delivering healthy babies is a worthy and important goal. However, social and media perceptions of substance abusing or addicted pregnant women may create oppressive conditions for these women, who are perhaps the most in need of compassionate and effective treatment. For example, in the late 1980s, the U.S. media and legislative powers leapt upon crack cocaine as the next big drug crisis to impact society. Crack (a highly potent form of cocaine that is inexpensive and can be cooked up on an ordinary kitchen stove with water and baking soda) is a drug that evolved from poor urban neighborhoods and became the subject of national crisis once it began to hit more mainstream suburban markets. Like previous drug scares reported in this text, subordinate groups were particularly marginalized for using crack cocaine—in this case, poor, urban African Americans, particularly pregnant women. The reality was that only a tiny percentage of the population was using crack, and an even smaller number actually became addicted to it. But this next scourge of our society resulted in massive government financial investments, and elicited legislation to particularly punish those engaging in the crack trade (Reinarman & Levine, 1995). This had both gender and racial implications that are still being felt today.

By the early 1990s government and media attention shifted to babies born addicted to crack, and these crack babies were touted as a great American tragedy—that an entire generation was being lost to this drug, and these babies were not expected to thrive, meet developmental goals, or grow into fully functioning adults. The social impact on the United States was inflated to serve government interest, rather than to address a public health problem (Reinarman & Levine, 1995). In the end, no such catastrophic decimation occurred; while babies born addicted to crack were likely to experience some health problems before and after birth, in the long run they were as likely as nonaddicted babies to have normal, healthy lives, and research studies asserting otherwise were often flawed or biased (Litt & McNeil, 1994). In spite of the fact that the public frenzy around crack and crack-addicted babies did not bear out in reality, the mothers of these babies bore the scars of stigma related to their abuse of and addiction to crack. Seen as failures in their primary cultural roles as mothers, these women were submitted to the contempt of our society and to legal action due to their addicion (Litt & McNeil). Thus, the impact of addiction on pregnancy causes harm beyond just the biological.

Addicted women who are currently parenting also experience stigma and barriers related to their status as mothers. They may be hesitant to enter treatment for fear of retribution or investigation by social services (Gordon, 2002). Since the crack baby scare in the early 1990s, states have increasingly enacted legislation creating punitive measures for women who abuse illicit drugs during pregnancy. This unnecessary duality between mothers and their unborn fetuses created by legislation ignores obvious public health concerns that are of far greater gravity than legal concerns. While most states do not seek prosecution against pregnant women who abuse illicit drugs during pregnancy, South Carolina and Texas have both arrested and prosecuted dozens of women over the past decade. These laws are generally regarded as misguided and based on frenzied public concern. Interestingly, few if any laws seek to punish women who smoke cigarettes or drink alcohol during pregnancy. These more socially sanctioned substances, though as dangerous as illicit drugs, if not more so, are generally ignored within the legal community (Drug Policy Alliance Network, 2001). Thus, addicted mothers often internalize shame, perceiving themselves as "bad mothers" (Hegamin, Anglin, & Farabee, 2001). For example, women who are single parents and who are referred to treatment through the court system may internalize complex feelings of inadequacy if they are parenting young children. Additionally, they may fear losing their children if they seek counseling for substance dependence (Greenfield, 2002). As drug-related charges are the most significant factor in women's prosecution and incarceration, addicted women may perceive the court system and treatment community as punitive rather than restorative. Eighty percent of incarcerated women have children, and three-quarters of these have children under age 18; thus, separation from young children can be particularly traumatic (Drug Policy Alliance, 2001). As women define themselves within community and in connection to others, this separation can cause significant harm to self-concept. In fact, children have been found to be a significant social support for women in recovery; maintaining strong relationships between mothers and children can only be a benefit (Tracy & Martin, 2007). After separation during incarceration, lack of trust of the legal system results, and women are not afforded opportunities to experience the potentially restorative nature of the justice system.

Finally, women who are the sole or primary parent often find a lack of childcare to be a barrier to counseling. Data suggest women are more likely to be successful in addictions counseling if services are provided to support and maintain strong mother–child bonds. Women seeking addiction counseling often suffer additional social deficits, including poverty and unemployment. Thus, lack of affordable and accessible childcare can all but prohibit substance abuse counseling. Unfortunately, most service providers lack services for women with infants and young children (Fendrich, Hubbell, & Lurigio, 2006). In fact, only 41% of U.S. treatment facilities that accept women clients offer special programs or groups for women; of these, only 18% offer childcare (Drug and Alcohol Services Information System [DASIS], 2006). Addicted women thus perceive counseling as unsupportive of their needs, and may fail to benefit from counseling treatment (Fendrich et al., 2006).

WOMEN, ADDICTION, AND VIOLENCE

Women are at risk of experiencing a range of violence-related consequences as a result of drinking and drug use behaviors (both their own use and the use of others). Increasingly, counselors and researchers alike are aware of the dangerous relationship between addiction and violence against women. This relationship appears bidirectional: Women who experience violence are more likely to become addicted, and addicted women are more likely to experience violence (Gordon, 2002; Matthews

& Lorah, 2005). The number of women addicted to alcohol or drugs who are also victims of violence is astonishing: As many as 90% of women with drug abuse and dependence problems report being sexually abused at least once in their lifetime, and 40% to 74% of alcoholic women have been victimized by sexual assault, incest, or rape (Gordon, 2002). These numbers far exceed those among the general population, where approximately one in six women has been the victim of rape or attempted rape (Rape, Abuse and Incest National Network [RAINN], n.d.).

Intimate Partner Violence

Intimate partner violence (IPV) is a significant social problem in the United States and one that plays an important role in the development and perpetuation of addictive behaviors for both women and men. "Close relationships are, in some respects, the most dangerous ones for women" (Lips, 2006, p. 447). In the United States, approximately 30% of women homicide victims are killed by their intimate partners, four out of five spousal murders in the United States involve the male spouse killing the female spouse, and IPV makes up 20% of violent crimes against women (Lips, 2006). Because IPV occurs within relationships that should be a safe haven for women, and because IPV is so often hidden due to shame or fear, it exacts a particularly extreme toll on the psyches of women victims. As mentioned in the previous chapter, women will often use alcohol or drugs to cope with the negative psychological effects of IPV.

For the perpetuators of violence, many theories attempt to explain increased violent behavior after drug or alcohol use. Theories focus on social learning within families and communities regarding the role of violence in relationships. Feminist theories tend to focus on the gender disparity between men and women that perpetuates the mindset of women as subordinate to male dominance. Two additional theories in particular help frame violent behavior in relationships: The first, *deviance disavowal* theory, implies that substance abuse is used as an excuse to commit premeditated violent behaviors. The second, a theory of *alcohol expectancies*, indicates that if a person believes drinking will make him or her violent, then he or she will act violently as a result (Galvani, 2004). This theory extends to sexual behavior as well.

Sexual Violence

Sexual violence against women is a multilayered and complicated issue. One layer is the perception that men often expect a positive correlation between alcohol use and possible sexual encounters, while women may feel the opposite: that drinking with a man will lead to unwanted sexual advances (Galvani, 2004). Paradoxically, there exists a misperception between alcohol use and sexual prowess. For example, women may believe that drinking improves sexual performance. In fact, the opposite is true: Sexual appetites are generally decreased by alcohol use. The cultural stereotype that women who drink are more likely to have sex may be part of the reason that women are often the victims of sexual assault while under the influence. Men who are sexually aggressive toward women impaired by substances may justify their attacks by implying that the victim "wanted" to have sex (Gordon, 2002). Here lies the complicated intersection in gender roles and substance use.

Specifically with regard to alcohol use, gender socialization dictates that it is "unladylike" for women to drink to excess. At the same time, women who drink to excess are assumed to be sexually available. Male perpetrators also drink to excess in part to disinhibit behavior. Add to these social behaviors the chemical fact that alcohol is an extremely effective social lubricant. The result of this intersection can be unwanted sexual advances, abuse, assault, or rape. In the author's (Briggs) experience of working as a sexual assault advocate on a college campus, many sexual assaults follow this very pattern. What is most alarming and destructive about this trend is that often the male perpetrators were unaware of their role in the assault until campus charges had been filed. And the women victims felt intense shame and guilt because of their own drinking behaviors.

As a result of sexual violence, women who have suffered repeated attempts appear to be at higher risk for abusing drugs or alcohol than their peers (Cook et al., 2005; Gordon, 2002). In addition, these women are also more likely to develop mental health problems and to have contracted HIV/AIDS than women who have not experienced chronic sexual violence.

CODEPENDENCE

The topic of codependence for women in treatment for addiction is rife with gender implications. Because feminine attributes (emotionality, for example) are admonished in our culture, male attributes are assumed to be normal, while women's ways of being are considered abnormal (Cook et al., 2005). Thus, women's caretaking of family members (especially male partners or spouses) may be labeled as codependent or pathological. Women are encouraged to pull away, disengage, and separate from significant others who are in treatment for addiction. When women themselves are in treatment for addiction, their significant others are encouraged to pull away from them. If partners are encouraging or compassionate, they are labeled as codependent and accused of assisting in the addiction. This leaves women again feeling inadequate and alone in their addiction. This is another way traditional models of addiction counseling fail to support women's natural and instinctual method of self- and other-care. Instead of labeling women as codependent for desiring to support partners in recovery, or for expecting the same when women themselves are in counseling, counselors might facilitate their normal, nurturing, supportive instincts in healthy ways.

CONCLUSION

While addiction rates for women of all ages continue to rise, it is clear that much of the increase is due to the trauma and difficult social systems that women must navigate beginning in early adolescence. Adolescent girls face issues of family violence, sexualization, peer pressure, and navigating complex social relationships. As adults, women face similar social pressures of parenting, IPV, and sexual violence. Gender socialization supports male dominance and, at its worst, allows for continued victimization of women and, at best, fails to support women's development. These issues all contribute to substance abuse and process addictions as ways of coping, or in some cases to develop or maintain relationships.

Case Study

After revealing her sexual abuse history to her partner, Sheila reports that her partner is having a difficult time relating to her. While he now understands why she has been hesitant to talk about her high school years, he still finds himself pulling away. Sheila shares with her counselor that her partner often drinks on the weekends and that she often feels afraid when he drinks to excess. While she says she is not afraid of her husband, his drinking contributes to her anxiety. She also shares that when he drinks, he wants her to drink with him, and that she does not like to be out of control in that way. She also mentioned that she is down to only two pain pills left and she is not sure what to do to get more. She does not feel like she can stop taking them, but she is afraid to ask the doctor for more because of what he might think of her.

As your work progresses with Sheila it is important to consider the sociological factors related to addiction. At this stage, understanding the gender-based relationship dynamics of her partnership is critical. Her husband now knows that she has been sexually abused, and their relationship has changed. It will be important to counsel her to understand her feelings toward her husband and to improve her communication with him. The sexualization and victimization of women take a great toll on relationships. It will also be important to keep an eye on her partner's drinking and his interest in including her in another addictive behavior. As we mentioned, many women are introduced to addictive behaviors by their partners, and this is an example of how that may happen. Sheila is likely experiencing old fears about her sexual assault and may be feeling unsafe sexually. This contributes to her anxiety, which leaves her more vulnerable to addiction. Finally, it is important to remember that her concern about her physician's opinion of her is multifaceted. She may be concerned about being seen as addicted, and about what that would say about her as a person and most importantly as a mother. And if her physician is Caucasian, she may be wondering about how he will perceive her as an African American woman with a possible addiction.

DISCUSSION QUESTIONS

1. In what way might Sheila's sexual abuse history affect the way in which she communicates with her children?
2. Talk about the relationship between her depression and anxiety and her partner's weekend drinking. How might they be connected? Does the way in which he pressures her have any impact on her own substance use?
3. As a substance abuse counselor, what do you believe your role is in relation to the sociological issues that Sheila is currently facing?

III

Prevention, Treatment, and Relapse Prevention Across the Life Span

6

COUNSELING CONSIDERATIONS FOR WOMEN
An Overview

Addiction counseling in the United States has historically proven inadequate to meet the full spectrum of needs of addicted women. Research over the past 30 years demonstrates that women are underserved by the addiction counseling community, with regard to both treatment availability and services necessary to assist women to successfully complete treatment (Marsh, D'Aunno, & Smith, 2000). Women seeking counseling for addiction deserve specific considerations, including treatment modalities, access to social services, and childcare. In this chapter treatment considerations for young and middle adult women are considered, including specific considerations for college-aged women, women who parent, and women across the socioeconomic and cultural spectrum.

My introduction to the profession of addiction counseling went something like this: My first counseling job after completing my master's degree in community counseling (no training in addictions counseling) included conducting the intensive outpatient treatment (IOP) program at a small hospital-based counseling facility. At about 5 p.m. on my first day of work, my supervisor prepared to clear out for the night. She had given me some resources and worksheets for planning the evening's group counseling experience, and as she was showing me around the group counseling room, she noted the 12 Steps listed on the wall. "Just stick to the first three steps and you'll be fine," she said, and then she departed into the darkening night. In addition to the 12 Steps, I also knew the agency expectations: Clients could not be late or absent without some sort of remediation or retribution; any excuse for missing treatment was considered resistance and should result in a confrontation with the client; and I was to do much of the talking during the session. These expectations were the equivalent of swallowing glass for me: I could feel the sharp corners in my throat and stomach as I considered approaching my clients in this confrontational, rigid, nonempathic manner. I was trained to express unconditional positive regard, empathy, and compassion toward my clients. On that first night of work, I felt as though I'd been asked to disregard two years of clinical training in order to counsel these addicted clients.

As a new addictions counselor, it felt entirely incongruent, counterintuitive, and just plain wrong to greet my new clients with a set of rigid rules and a confrontational attitude. My socialization as a woman and my training as a counselor urged a different set of norms and behaviors: My instinct was to work collaboratively with clients, to encourage their sense of self-efficacy, to accept them where they were at, and to understand that in spite of their best intentions, occasionally life got in the way of their treatment. It was as though all my natural and professional instincts needed to be suppressed in order to be an addictions counselor. Furthermore, rigid adhesion to the 12 Steps required me to disregard the individual hopes and expectations of my clients.

It is important to note that this recollection is not meant to disparage the 12-Step movement. Alcoholics Anonymous (AA) and others have helped countless people achieve and maintain sobriety, and are free and available to all. Clients struggling with addiction should be encouraged to use any venues available to them to promote their recovery. However, the 12-Step movement was never intended to be a counseling paradigm. Furthermore, the 12 Steps possess a philosophical base that may prove oppressive to women clients.

First, the 12-Step philosophy focuses on the notion of powerlessness. As noted in Chapter 2, AA was founded by two white men who enjoyed a degree of affluence. In their lives, an overinflated sense of self-power led them to believe they could control their compulsion to consume alcohol (Matthews & Lorah, 2005). For women seeking treatment for addiction, an inflated sense of personal power is generally not a problem. Rather, many women come to counseling with feelings of shame, guilt, failure, and other concerns, including histories of sexual and physical violence, unsupportive family structures, socioeconomic problems, and legal issues. Women with addiction struggle to feel any level of power in their lives, which worsens addictive behaviors. Thus, encouraging a woman who has no sense of personal power to accept her powerlessness is like encouraging a fish to admit its need for water. It is unnecessary, detrimental, and potentially cruel. In fact, many clients placed in this situation will exert their personal power by leaving treatment—hardly the effect counselors want to have on their clients (Matthews & Lorah, 2005).

Issues of oppression become even more significant for women of color, lesbian women, women who are differently abled, and elderly women (the last to be covered more thoroughly in Chapter 8). Women who experience multiple oppressions come to treatment with a sense of powerlessness, and often the alcohol, drug, or process abused is a coping mechanism for dealing with the effects of oppression. Again, to encourage these women to accept their powerlessness is unnecessary and can promote further victimization.

Traditional models of addictions counseling also focus heavily on overcoming resistance through confrontation. This is problematic for women clients for two reasons. First, behaviors labeled "resistant" often result from simply being female. For example, the vast majority of addiction counseling programs in the United States do not provide childcare for clients. However, clients are expected to attend treatment for long blocks of time over weeks (many intensive outpatient programs last three hours per night, four nights per week). If a woman is struggling financially, is single parenting, or lacks significant social contacts (for example, all her friends are addicts), it may be impossible for her to find or afford childcare so she can attend treatment on a regular basis. Is she being resistant? Or has the counseling agency set up impossible standards, condemning some mothers to treatment failure? The latter seems more accurately the case.

Overcoming resistance through confrontation is also problematic because most women in U.S. society are not socialized to be openly confrontational: Women are characterized as nurturers and tenders of others, not confronters. Recent studies have determined that the old adage of "flight or fight" does not necessarily apply to women. In fact, women who experience stress, anxiety, or fear may in fact "tend and befriend." Instead of running away from a problem or slugging it out (confrontation), women seek relationships for comfort. Women might care for children, reach out to loved ones, or seek physical comfort from a spouse. So, when stressed due to addiction problems, women seek support, not confrontation. Harsh confrontation may cause anxiety, shame, and fear to spike for women clients, perhaps forcing them out of counseling altogether.

Thus, assessment, diagnosis, and treatment planning for women clients must emerge from a revised paradigm. Traditional addictions counseling interventions require modification to meet the unique needs of women clients. In this chapter, treatment considerations for young and middle adult women will be considered, from assessment to discharge. Specific and concrete suggestions for counseling agencies will be offered to make addictions counseling more supportive of women's recovery.

ASSESSMENT AND DIAGNOSIS: GENDER CONSIDERATIONS FOR ADULT WOMEN
Politics of Diagnosis

The process of assessment and diagnosis is fraught with political undertones. The *Diagnostic and Statistical Manual* (DSM) published by the American Psychiatric Association (APA) is the benchmark publication for mental health professionals. With each subsequent revision, writers of the DSM have attempted to eliminate potential biases inherent in certain diagnostic criteria. For example, after much controversy in 1973, homosexuality was removed from the DSM-II as a mental disorder. It was replaced in the DSM-III by the category of sexual orientation disturbance, which allowed for a diagnostic category for those (implied homosexuals) who struggled with their sexual orientation identity (Spitzer, 1981). This shift is a classic example of the embedded nature of gender and sexuality issues. Via the DSM, counselors are able to observe shifting attitudes about what is "normal" and "healthy" and what is not. In this case, heterosexist attitudes continued to impact our clinical impressions of homosexual clientele: While homosexuality itself was no longer a category of mental illness, it was assumed that only homosexuals struggled with identity issues around their sexual orientation. Today, our awareness has expanded to include bisexual, transgender, transsexual, and asexual as possible sexual or gender orientations. Also, we are beginning to be aware that heterosexual individuals may also struggle with sexual orientation issues. Ideas and attitudes are constantly evolving. Therefore, it is important to consider gender biases and stereotypes when applying information from the DSM.

In the current incarnation of the DSM (DSM-IV-TR), women and men benefit from increased awareness and sensitivity to gender issues in creating diagnoses and conducting assessments. However, caveats remain. First, assigning a diagnosis alters a woman's perception of herself. For example, general symptoms such as nervousness or listlessness may be translated into an anxiety or depressive disorder. Assignment of a diagnosis may pathologize or victimize a woman already experiencing powerlessness in her life (Lips, 2006). In the case of substance abuse treatment, assigning a diagnosis too early may frighten, intimidate, anger, or threaten a client who is not yet ready to identify as a substance abuser or as substance dependent. Thus, using caution when assigning a diagnosis is warranted.

Assigning a diagnosis can also change others' perception of clients. Receiving a mental health diagnosis can result in the assumption that other symptoms are simply related to the diagnosis, rather than a result of other health problems. For example, for a woman who is assigned a diagnosis of depression, fatigue might be assumed to be related to the diagnosis, and other medical explanations may not be explored (Lips, 2006). With regard to addiction, because U.S. society continues to place such a stigma on treatment recipients, others may make value judgments about addicts' reliability, honesty, integrity, or worth to society. Overcoming addiction is difficult enough without additional societal stigma. This stigma is particularly potent for women, as cultural norms assume addiction to be more of a male problem. Women may have their worth as a wife and mother questioned by friends and family members once the label of "addict" has been assigned.

Finally, diagnoses both impact and can be impacted by stereotypes of whole groups. As an example, I once posed to an addictions counseling group this question: "What does an addict look like?" The group members thought for a moment, looked around the room, and began to describe themselves: predominantly African American, male, middle-aged, low socioeconomic status. These stereotypes burden all of us. They burden the addict who fits the stereotype and thus contends with the exacerbated stigma of his race, class, or gender. They burden the addict who does not fit the stereotype, because her addiction is often overlooked or minimized by others. Stereotypes and assumptions offer detrimental shortcuts in assessment and diagnosis of clientele. Another example: According to the National Institute on Drug Abuse, most crack users are white, while 96% of crack defendants in federal court are black or Hispanic (Gray, 1998). Stereotypes and perceptions of what is normal can dramatically influence a counselor's objectivity when assigning diagnoses, regardless of the counselor's gender identity (Lips, 2006).

Conducting a Holistic Assessment

The diagnosis of a client is only one small piece of the assessment process. Sadly, over the years mental health and addiction counseling branches have rarely converged in assessment efforts. Typically, agencies and practitioners identify as either addiction-oriented or mental health–oriented, and never the twain shall meet! However, many women clients struggle simultaneously with addiction and mental health issues (Covington, 2008). Thus, conducting an assessment based only on addiction-related behaviors is to the detriment of clients' recovery processes. Similarly, counselors working in mental health settings should heighten awareness of lurking substance abuse issues, and should build addiction inquiry into the assessment process. For example, clients who struggle with symptoms of depression (e.g., sleep disturbance, loss of interest in normal activities, loss of energy) may use alcohol as a coping mechanism: to dull painful feelings, or to help with insomnia or sleep disturbance. As alcohol is a depressant, use can exacerbate these symptoms and can negate any positive impact antidepressants may provide. Therefore, it is clearly in counselors' best interests to inquire about possible addiction or substance abuse issues.

The initial assessment interview for adult women should be holistic and integrative in nature, including inquiry about all major areas of clients' lives. Gathering information about all the possible liabilities and strengths present greatly increases the possibility of effective treatment planning and subsequent treatment success. Some examples of major areas to cover in an assessment interview are listed below.

Addiction and Mental Health History　　In addition to the areas listed below, determine prior treatment history and understanding of clients' impressions of that treatment (i.e., helpful or harmful).

1. Substance use history: Including substances used and amount and frequency for each substance. Counselors should be aware that phrases such as "a couple" or "a few" mean different things to different people. For example, "couple of beers" can mean two 12-ounce cans, two 40-ounce bottles, or two 6-packs, depending on who is doing the reporting. Thorough and sensitive questioning on the part of the counselor will clear up any confusion. Also, clients may use alcohol- or drug-related terms that may be confusing to counselors. For example, terms such as *eight-ball, speed-ball, double-deuce,* or *ket* may confound counselors who have limited exposure to drug culture or terminology.

2. Mental health history: Inquire about clients' histories with mental illness: diagnoses in particular, and symptomology in general. Clients seeking treatment for addiction issues may have never sought or received treatment for mental illness issues, and in fact may have been self-medicating to cope with symptoms. Inquiring about general symptoms of depression or anxiety, as well as determining orientation to place, person, time, and situation, will assist counselors in gathering important information

for designing treatment plans or for auxiliary treatment needs. Women in particular are more likely to have a concurrent mental health issue than men (Covington, 2008).

3. Process addiction issues: Asking clients about compulsive behaviors outside of substance use will provide information needed for comprehensive treatment. Inquire about gambling, Internet, spending, or sexual behaviors that may be of concern to the client. Keep in mind that women clients in particular may be experiencing intense shame about engaging in these behaviors, and may be reluctant to disclose during the initial assessment interview. Patience and ongoing assessment may be necessary to fully flesh out all the issues.

Major Life Areas   Identify both strengths and liabilities.

1. Employment or education: Understanding employment status provides important information about clients' abilities, interests, and financial resources. Understanding a client's educational status will help determine readiness for counseling participation, particularly if reading and writing skills are needed for treatment.
2. Family relationships: Women are less likely than men to have family support for seeking addiction treatment (Nelson-Zlupko, Kauffman, & Dore, 1995), and may be the victim of threats or intimidation if determined to quit using (Covington, 2008). Determine level of family support (both family of origin and family in household). Assess family history of addiction or mental health issues, as well as issues of abuse. Genetics may play a part in current addictions issues for clients. Determining current family status will also help identify problems meeting basic needs, particularly if a woman is underemployed or single parenting.
3. Social relationships: Are her relationships based primarily on substance abuse or other addictive behaviors? Are there relationships that involve healthy communication and behaviors that she can rely on? Is she isolated and alone?
4. Legal problems: Having legal problems may impact clients emotionally and financially. Parents in addictions counseling may be at risk of losing their children to social services or foster care. If a legal problem resulted in referral to treatment, clients may be reluctant to fully disclose all behaviors due to fear of retribution from the court system.

5. Financial problems: Having enough money to live and sustain a family is a major concern. Clients having financial problems may have difficulties with transportation, childcare, nourishment, or employment flexibility to attend treatment. Some women clients may feel financially dependent on a partner who is unsupportive of treatment and recovery. These issues, in addition to the general emotional distress financial problems can cause, may significantly impact the course of counseling.
6. Medical problems: Issues such as chronic pain, recent surgery, or ongoing medical issues may contribute to or exacerbate addiction issues. Furthermore, addictive behaviors may make certain conditions worse. For example, clients suffering from liver disease may be required to achieve sobriety from alcohol use in order to qualify for a transplant.
7. Issues of abuse or sexual exploitation: Counselors need to be aware that women who were sexually abused as children are more likely to develop an addiction and enter the sex trade in adulthood. "Childhood victimization leads to a cascade of negative consequences for women that complicate addiction treatment" (Covington, 2008, p. 8).

TREATMENT PLANNING

Very few studies have been conducted to determine effective addiction counseling techniques for women. For example, between 1984 and 2005 only one randomized trial was published comparing the effectiveness of mixed-gender programs to women-only programs (Kaskutas, Zhang, French, & Witbrodt, 2005). Counselors must examine their theoretical approach and interpersonal dynamics to ensure they fit women's ways of being. For example, research has shown that women in addiction treatment respond more favorably to empathy, collaboration, respect, optimism, and process-oriented counseling (as opposed to problem solving; Stevens & Smith, 2009). This manner of counseling is contrary to traditional, confrontational approaches that include techniques that may alienate or drive women clients out of counseling. Also, traditional models of addiction counseling, including the Minnesota model, emphasize individual pathology over sociopolitical realities (e.g., sexism) experienced by women in U.S. society. The disease model reduces the moral stigma of addiction but ignores the impact of societal influences on personal development, focusing exclusively on individual issues (Matthews & Lorah, 2005). There are several counseling theories that appear effective with addicted clients overall, but seem especially congruent for women entering addiction treatment. Brief descriptions of each follow.

Motivational Interviewing

Motivational interviewing (MI) is both client centered and directive, and focuses on enhancing clients' motivation and confidence to make changes in their lives. Developed by William Miller in the 1980s, MI is a dramatic departure from the traditional model of addiction counseling in that it does not involve hard confrontation or "breaking" through resistance. Rather, resistance to and ambivalence about addiction treatment are perceived to be natural and expected parts of the change process. MI is based on the stages of change model of addiction recovery (DiClemente, 2003; Miller & Rollnick, 2002), where clients pass through five stages in their change processes. In brief, the five stages areas as follows:

- Precontemplation: In this stage, clients are essentially unaware of their potential problem with addiction. They may be aware of life problems, but generally attribute them to other sources outside of the addiction. Clients in this stage do not see change as necessary, nor do they exhibit much motivation for change.
- Contemplation: In this stage, clients are beginning to consider that problems experienced may be related to addictive behaviors, and change may be a possible solution. Clients become more willing to discuss possible strategies for change, weighing pros and cons of possible alternatives.
- Preparation: In this stage, clients have reached the point where they are getting ready to take action. They have come to understand the problems their addictive behaviors are causing in their lives, and are testing the waters around different possible solutions, determining which course of action is the right one for them.
- Action: In this stage, clients are making changes and are engaged fully in the process of recovery, either by reducing harmful use of substances or processes or by abstaining altogether. Their partnership with the counselor is solid, active, and highly functional.
- Maintenance: At this stage, clients may be ready to terminate counseling, as they have established new patterns of behavior and are no longer at high risk of relapse (DiClemente, 2003).

MI is not a counseling theory: Rather, it is a transtheoretical skill set that can be applied in a variety of settings and with clients in any stage of the change process. The spirit of MI is more important than specific techniques. Approaching each client as an individual with specific needs, strengths, and motivations who deserves to be treated with respect and trust constitutes the heart of MI. To accomplish this, counselors are encouraged to keep four basic principles in mind (Miller & Rollnick, 2002):

1. Express empathy: By relating to clients from a perspective of understanding and respect, counselors express engagement in clients' personal process of recovery.
2. Develop discrepancy: By listening and reflecting client-initiated change talk, counselors help create cognitive dissonance in clients. By querying whether current addictive behaviors facilitate individual clients' personal goals, uncomfortable "gaps" of dissonance can be created, producing motivation for change.
3. Rolling with resistance or avoiding argumentation: This is a dramatic departure from traditional models of addiction counseling that emphasize the importance of direct confrontation and breaking through denial. By rolling with client resistance to treatment and acknowledging ambivalence, counselors "come alongside" clients rather than working against them.
4. Support self-efficacy: In addition to motivation for change, clients must possess belief and confidence that they can change. By supporting clients' self-efficacy, counselors assist in building client confidence in abilities.

Efficacy of MI has been demonstrated via a multitude of research studies. Furthermore, it fits well with feminist perspectives in counseling as it emphasizes collaboration and mutuality over confrontation and authoritarianism.

Relational–Cultural Theory

Traditional models of human development describe healthy development as growth from dependence on others to independence from others. As with most traditional models in psychology and counseling, this theory was developed by and researched with majority-culture individuals, specifically Caucasian, heterosexual men. Relational-cultural theory (RCT) indicates that as women develop, their sense of connectedness is enhanced through the processes of growth and maturity. RCT evolved from research conducted at the Stone Center at Wellesley College and asserts that "true connections are mutual, empathic, creative, energy releasing and empowering for all participants" (Covington, 2008, p. 21). In fact, a woman's mental health and addiction problems can be traced to disconnectedness or a violation in her relationships

(Covington, 2008). Concepts such as *mutuality* and *empathy* are essential to RCT. Mutuality means that individuals in relationship are able to express their thoughts, feelings, and opinions, and are able to experience the thoughts, feelings, and opinions of others. Empathy is the experience of cognitively and affectively joining with another person while maintaining a sense of separate self. When mutuality and empathy are present in the counseling relationship, women benefit from (1) increased vitality, (2) empowerment, (3) self and other knowledge, (4) self-worth, and (5) a desire for greater connection to self and others (Covington, 2008).

Women may use drugs, alcohol, or processes of addiction in order to create or maintain connection to others. In particular, male partners influence women's addictions by introducing women to drugs and later becoming their steady supplier. Also, women may engage in addictive behaviors to deal with the emotional pain of abuse or domestic violence; women may come from families where addiction is the norm, and women appear to receive less support from male partners for entering treatment (Covington, 2008). Within female-to-female relationships, women may engage in addictive behaviors to bond with friends or to feel a part of a group; for example, college-aged women may engage in eating disordered or self-mutilation behaviors if they see peers doing the same. This type of compulsive behavior becomes a ritual of belonging for these young women. Finally, women may develop a relationship with the substance or process, which ultimately replaces interpersonal relationships. Women often speak of having a "love affair" or finding a "best friend" in addictive behaviors and substances (Covington, 2008). Understanding the nature of women's relationships and assisting in empowerment and healing is the ultimate goal of RCT.

Harm Reduction

Depending on their point of view, counselors and recovering substance-dependent individuals may perceive harm reduction as a destructive delusional denial, or a radical departure and compassionate alternative from the disease/12-Step models that dominate the current addictions counseling profession. Harm reduction is included in this text because it represents a possible alternative for some clients struggling with substance abuse and dependence, and because the spirit and philosophy of harm reduction align with feminist principles.

Harm reduction emerged because its developers felt the core assumptions of traditional models of addiction counseling were flawed. Assumptions of the disease model and 12-Step recovery programs were called into question, including the following (Denning, Little, & Glickman, 2004):

- *Clients must accept the title of "addict" or "alcoholic" and must admit their powerlessness over alcohol.* Many people are able to overcome addiction without ever calling themselves addicts, and research demonstrates that pushing clients to admit powerlessness actually makes them feel worse about themselves, not better.
- *Addiction is a primary disease: It must be "cured" before any other counseling can occur.* Often, addiction is not the first concern of clients. It is coupled with other issues, including mental heath or basic need deficiencies. Also, the addiction may have occurred because of something else, such as a severe trauma or chronic pain.
- *Lifelong abstinence from all psychoactive substances is required.* Clients entering treatment for the first time may be unwilling or unable to commit to such a hefty solution all at once. For example, future medical problems may require treatment with pain medication. Harm reduction allows clients to thoroughly explore the problem before determining their preferred course of action.
- *Clients must enter treatment ready and motivated, having hit rock bottom in their addictive cycle.* As providers of health care, it is entirely counterintuitive for us to require clients to suffer significantly before treatment is possible. Imagine telling a woman with Stage 1 breast cancer that she must wait until her cancer gets to Stage 4 and she is *really* motivated before treatment can begin.

Harm reduction offers an alternative for the 80% of addicts who fail to achieve abstinence via traditional addiction counseling (Denning et al., 2004). In summary, harm reduction philosophy asserts (Denning et al.):

1. Not all substance abuse results in addiction, but all substance use needs to be done safely and in an informed manner.
2. Though abstinence may be necessary or preferable for some, not all clients need to totally abstain from substances.
3. "Just say know"—clients should become aware of how much and how often they are using.
4. Self-care is essential, regardless of the status of use.
5. Addiction counseling should be nondiscriminatory, regardless of current status of substance use.

6. Mental health is treated concurrently with chemical health issues.
7. Prenatal care should be given to substance users without fear of sanction.
8. Clients should not be submitted to punitive measures for choosing to continue to use substances.
9. Fear, stigma, and shame should not be a part of the counseling process.

Harm reduction essentially approaches addiction from a humane public health perspective rather than from a moralistic or punitive one. Clients become experts on substances in general, and on their own use patterns in particular (Denning et al., 2004). The relationship between the counselor and client is humane, client centered, nonpunitive, and nonhierarchical. Thus, it fits well with a woman's way of being and with feminist perspectives.

SELF-HELP GROUPS: WOMEN FOR SOBRIETY

Women for Sobriety (WFS) serves as an alternative to traditional 12-Step programs. WFS stemmed from a common belief that methods that worked for men (AA or Narcotics Anonymous [NA]) would not necessarily work for women. Created especially for women alcoholics, WFS entails both self-help groups and free literature distributed to women participants around the United States. Rather than 12 steps, the WFS program entails 13 statements or positive affirmations that are supportive of a woman's way of being, of assisting her in overcoming self-destructive relationships (including her relationship to alcohol), and in achieving greater intimacy with herself and others while overcoming an addiction to alcohol. They are (WFS, 1993) as follows:

1. I have a life-threatening problem that once had me.
2. Negative thoughts destroy only myself.
3. Happiness is a habit I will develop.
4. Problems bother me only to the degree I permit them to.
5. I am what I think.
6. Life can be ordinary or it can be great.
7. Love can change the course of my world.
8. The fundamental object of life is emotional and spiritual growth.
9. The past is gone forever.
10. All love given returns.
11. Enthusiam is my daily exercise.
12. I am a competent woman and have much to give life.
13. I am responsible for myself and my actions.

Clearly, the 13 statements are meant to assist women in defeating negative thought patterns that can lead to self-destructive behaviors, including alcohol use. They appear based on a cognitive-behavioral model of counseling, which has been demonstrated to be effective with women overcoming addiction (Cook, Epperson, & Gariti, 2005). In addition, meditation, exercise, positive nutrition, and healthy group dynamics are all a part of WFS group meetings. For more information, visit the WFS Web site at http://www.womenforsobriety.org.

WOMEN-SPECIFIC ADDICTION COUNSELING

Components of the Treatment Program

It is not enough to simply offer women-only treatment programs in an effort to meet women's needs. While creating women-only treatment programs and treatment groups may be an effective tool for increasing women's likelihood to enter addiction treatment, it is simply not enough. In the words of one treatment provider,

> For a male client I may have two issues to address ... in treatment. For a woman client, I may have five. She may have DCFS involvement ... She may have medical needs that need to be addressed ... She may need to be referred to outpatient therapy for ... abuse issues. There are employment issues, she may need a GED.... You have to ... address what you can, and you really have limited time and resources. (Fendrich, Hubbell, & Lurigio, 2006, p. 675)

This powerful observation indicates two areas where addictions counseling agencies may encounter barriers to providing effective treatment to women clients. First, most agencies are set up along traditional lines. Many are set up to provide addiction counseling only from a traditional 12-Step or Minnesota model, and do not offer ancillary services or accommodations for women clients. Second, agencies that do wish to expand service options for women may find resources and support limited for such endeavors, making accommodations impossible. To demonstrate how these two realities collide, consider the following scenario. Lack of childcare is consistently cited as a barrier to women entering addiction treatment (examples: Fendrich et al., 2006; Marsh et al., 2000; Stevens & Smith, 2009). Thus, providing childcare would liberate some addicted women to attend treatment, particularly residential or inpatient treatment. However, because of funding cuts in the last decade, treatment facilities have a difficult time providing childcare, and inpatient facilities are hesitant to take on the additional liability providing childcare would bring (Fendrich et al., 2006).

For women entering addiction treatment, many of their coping mechanisms may have been focused on socially condoned emotive responses. In other words, women may have spent more time managing difficult and confusing emotions, within themselves and within their families or other relationships, rather than developing cognitive coping mechanisms. One important component of women-specific treatment is to teach cognitive skills as evidenced in cognitive-behavioral therapy (CBT) or reality therapy (RT; Cook et al., 2005).

In addition to interpersonal concerns, counseling agencies must also consider accommodations for women clients. For example, from a traditional perspective absence or lateness is perceived as resistance. For many women, however, barriers to treatment are very real and need to be addressed rather than negatively labeled. The following have been recommended as components of addiction counseling programs, either directly or through referral (Stevens & Smith, 2009):

- Medical resources for clients and their families
- Financial resources and education
- Stress management and assertiveness training
- Educational and vocational guidance
- Childcare
- Transportation
- Legal assistance and guidance
- Housing assistance or housing on site
- Case management services
- Family and couples counseling
- Parenting skill development

Traditionally, addiction counselors have projected the attitude of "sobriety first"; in other words, clients are led to believe that no other life areas can be addressed until sobriety has been achieved. In contrast, the above list indicates that women experience more successful treatment outcomes if multiple areas are addressed as they strive toward sobriety or abstinence, or both.

Counseling Group Composition

As with most areas of addictions counseling, the majority of counseling treatment interventions were originally designed for majority-culture men. Only in the past 20 years have funding dollars and clinical attention begun to shift to the specific needs of women (Cook et al., 2005). One important consideration for counselors is whether to offer women-specific addiction counseling. This might include women-only treatment groups and treatment programming, rather than the more typical mixed-gender model. One argument for such a system is that women come to addiction counseling with unique issues, including lower levels of self-esteem and higher rates of depression than men. Also, due to oppressive factors in U.S. society, women struggle with issues of guilt, shame, and stigma around their addictive behaviors, and thus may feel particularly isolated and lacking in support (Kaskutas et al., 2005). Women are also more likely to lack family support for treatment, to be entering treatment with lower educational and socioeconomic levels than their male counterparts, and to be entering treatment with a history of physical, sexual, or emotional abuse (Cook et al., 2005; NeSmith, Wilcoxon, & Satcher, 2000). Taking all these differences into account, there are some clear advantages to women-only addiction treatment groups.

Gender roles and dynamics exist within the group just as they do outside the group. Communication styles, for example, can play an important role in the functioning of the group. In Western cultures, it is more likely that men will use conversation as a means for establishing status, dominance, and control, while women use conversation to build connection and communication. Thus, in a mixed-gender group setting, men may dominate the rhythm and topic of conversation, while female members support and affirm the male perspective. Interestingly, this pattern seems most prevalent in European American gender relations, and less so in African American interactions, where greater gender equity in communication style seems to exist (Lips, 2006).

Similarly, as women often find themselves in the nurturer role in a heterosexual partnership, in mixed-gender counseling groups women may invest more energy into supporting male group members than in their own recovery (Kaskutas et al., 2005). Interestingly, some research shows that while women benefit more from women-only groups, men benefit more from mixed-gender groups than from men-only groups. The benefit for either seems to come from the social dynamics of the group: In male-only groups, men tend to avoid discussion of feelings or relationships (per socially constructed gender norms). In mixed groups, men talk more about these issues. The impact of the gender makeup of the group is exactly opposite for women: In mixed-gender groups, women tend to shut down, where in women-only groups they more freely express emotions and thoughts (Covington, 2008). Studies demonstrated that in mixed-gender groups men tend to dominate the discussion, interpersonal issues are minimized, and women tend to allow the men to select group topics for discussion (NeSmith et al., 2000).

Women may enter counseling expressing a preference for mixed-gender groups because they feel more comfortable with men or because they do not like women. This attitude is revealing and provides counselors with important information about client socialization. Often, women who are more comfortable with men also ascribe to traditional gender stereotypes, and prefer being with men because they rely on those stereotypes for information about how to behave. Women who profess not to like other women are essentially admitting their distaste for their own gender identity. In either case, these women could benefit from socialization with other women (Covington, 2008).

On the other hand, mixed-gender groups can also provide a healthy outlet for women and men to practice cross-gender relationship skills, and provide a more realistic social environment for people in recovery (NeSmith et al., 2000). Also, counseling groups that are women only but which retain traditional, confrontational models of counseling are not any more effective than mixed-gender groups operating from traditional models (Bride, 2001). Mixed-gender groups that employ feminist principles (e.g., mutuality and collaboration) are more likely to be effective. Thus, there are benefits and drawbacks to mixed-gender addiction counseling groups.

While outcomes research about the effectiveness of women-only counseling groups versus mixed-gender groups has been inconclusive (Cook et al., 2005), research does indicate that by offering women-only groups, counseling centers may attract women who otherwise would be reluctant to enter treatment (Weisner, 2005). By offering women-only groups, counseling centers remove a barrier and make counseling less threatening and more accessible to some women.

Counselor Gender

Women clients may prefer same-gender counselors. It has been theorized that counselor–client pairs based on shared gender traits (or ethnicity or both) may result in greater trust, understanding, and empathy due to shared cultural experiences (Fiorentine & Hillhouse, 1999). However, studies have failed to consistently support this hypothesis. In fact, male counselors may be preferred based on preexisting gender stereotypes (e.g., men are more competent in a professional setting), the nature of the presenting problem, and individual counselor characteristics (Hanna, Hanna, Giordano, & Tollerud, 1998). There are benefits and drawbacks to both same-gender and mixed-gender counselor–client pairings.

One perspective asserts only women counselors can fully understand the systemic oppression experienced by women clients. Studies demonstrate that most training opportunities focusing on women-specific counseling needs are attended primarily by women (Hanna et al., 1998). Both authors of this text have had similar experiences: We often present at conferences on women's issues in counseling and counselor education, and generally our audiences are 90% female (and the men who do attend are rarely from the majority culture). Research results and our own anecdotal experiences indicate women may be best prepared personally and professionally to counsel other women. There are also caveats to pairing a woman client with a male counselor. For women who have experienced victimization through physical or sexual abuse, a male counselor may serve as an uncomfortable reminder of past trauma. Also, women may have a more difficult time self-disclosing to a male counselor, especially about highly sensitive issues. Finally, negative transference may occur between a female client and a male counselor, thus impeding the therapeutic process (NeSmith et al., 2000).

There are alternatives to this perspective, however. As indicated throughout this text, a long-standing bias in addiction counseling is that "only an addict can counsel an addict." This norm emerged from the 12-Step movement, where newly recovering addicts and alcoholics are assigned a more experienced sponsor to support them through their recovery. These attitudes leapt from the self-help movement into the counseling milieu, where counselors who have gone through the 12-Step process and who are in recovery themselves may assert to clients that someone who has never experienced addiction will be at a complete loss as to how to treat them. This conclusion is absurd, in the same way assuming a cardiologist who has never had a heart attack cannot possibly effectively treat someone with heart disease. A similar criticism may apply to women counseling women: There certainly are men who are capable and adept at counseling women, and who long for a deeper understanding of women's experiences. Similarly, there are women counselors who may harbor oppressive tendencies themselves, ultimately harming women clients. Perhaps the competency and training of the counselor is more important than the gender.

Another consideration is that by working across genders, women clients may have a unique opportunity to experience a relationship with a man that is both healthy and helpful (NeSmith et al., 2000). For women who have been abused or denigrated by a man or men, this might be a particularly healing and transformative experience. Ultimately, it appears that regardless of counselor gender, the most effective counselors are those who are empathic, warm, genuine, and both self- and society-aware so as to understand the subtle effects of oppression on women clients (Hanna et al., 1998).

TREATMENT OUTCOMES

Retaining clients for the duration of an addiction counseling program is one of the most important outcome measures. Clients who complete treatment are more likely to abstain from substances, are less likely to be arrested, and are more likely to find or maintain employment (Bride, 2001).

Historically, research has demonstrated women to be less likely to initiate addiction treatment, and therefore less likely to complete it. More recent data suggest women are at least as likely as men to begin and complete addiction counseling. Women who do complete addiction treatment are nine times more likely to remain abstinent than women who do not complete treatment, though men who complete treatment are only three times more likely to remain abstinent than men who do not complete treatment (Green, 2006). Overall, women who have gone through addiction counseling have better long-term recovery outcomes than men (Green). Due to this encouraging information, designing addictions counseling interventions that are attractive, available, and accessible to women bodes well for addressing addiction problems in this population.

RELAPSE PREVENTION

In traditional addictions counseling settings, relapse is perceived as temporary or permanent treatment failure, rather than a normal part of recovery progression. Relapse triggers are different for women than for men. For example, men are more likely to relapse during happy occasions, such as parties or other social events. Women, conversely, are more likely to relapse in response to difficult or stressful life situations, such as a divorce or death. Women are also more likely to relapse as a result of past abuse or trauma (Covington, 2008). Women who undergo addiction counseling are less likely to relapse than men who seek treatment, and their reasons for relapsing tend to be different. Women seem at greater risk of relapse when their romantic partners are substance abusers, but women are less likely than men to relapse overall (Green, 2006).

LIFE SPAN DEVELOPMENT CONSIDERATIONS:
YOUNG ADULT WOMEN

Just as most addiction treatment research has been conducted on men, the research that has been generated from a woman's perspective tends to focus on middle adult women entering treatment for addiction issues, rather than abuse or misuse problems. Since most women who meet the criteria for full-blown addiction are well into adulthood, the needs of young adult women (aged 18 to 24) are often neglected in the research literature and in treatment program planning. This section will present a brief overview of treatment concerns specific to young adult women.

Developmentally speaking, young adulthood is a time of experimentation and self-exploration, when the attitudes and behaviors of peers become more important than familial, biological, or cultural influences (Huchting, Lac, & LaBrie, 2007). Thus, young adult women are likely to be influenced by peer norms with regard to addictive behaviors, including alcohol consumption, drug use, eating disorders, or other processes of addiction. Due to this vulnerability, counselors should not assume treatment that works for adults in middle age will work equally well with young adults, as value systems, attitudes, and beliefs are often dramatically different from one age group to the next.

The sheer numbers of young adults encountering problems with substance abuse and dependence mandates our attention to their screening and counseling needs. The 2002 College Alcohol Study (CAS) revealed that about 81% of college students had used alcohol in the previous school year. Forty-four percent of survey participants reported binge drinking episodes (four drinks in a row for women; five drinks in a row for men; Baldwin, Johnson, Gotz, Wayment, & Elwell, 2006). With regard to drug use, the core survey revealed that in 2002, about 43% of students used tobacco in the previous year, 20% used marijuana, 5% used amphetamines, about 2% reported cocaine, sedative, or other "designer" drug use; 1% used hallucinagens, and about 1% used opiates or inhalants (Baldwin et al., 2006). Among all young adults (college students or not), 25% of young adult males and 14% of young adult females met or have met the diagnostic criteria for alcohol dependence as defined by the DSM-IV-TR (Monti, Tevyaw, & Borsari, 2004/2005). There is some evidence that health care providers may be unaware of the range of substances used and abused by young adults: For example, health providers on college campuses named two primary substances abused by students, alcohol and marijuana. Students, on the other hand, listed more than 25 substances currently being used within the student body (Baldwin et al., 2006). Providers, regardless of location, should heighten awareness of all substances of abuse, and should not make assumptions about patterns of use.

Consequences for young adult women that use or abuse substances can be severe and distinct from those experienced by middle adult women. For example, young adult women may suffer sexual consequences for their drinking behaviors. Often women experience a power disadvantage in sexual relationships with men and feel unable or unwilling to disappoint potential male sexual partners (Lips, 2006). Adding alcohol to the mix often raises the risk of unwanted or pressured sexual encounters for women. Thus, unplanned or unprotected sex may be a consequence of excessive alcohol use for young adult women. In addition, the risk of sexually transmitted diseases, accidental death or injury, driving under the influence, psychiatric distress, and decreased academic performance are all potential consequences young adult women may face as a result of excessive alcohol use behaviors (Foote, Wilkens, & Vavagiakis, 2004).

Young adults have typically experienced fewer alcohol- or drug-related consequences than middle- or older-aged adults. Consequently, they are less likely to seek out addictions counseling or to perceive themselves as having a substance problem. Furthermore, many of the mainstream screening procedures and treatment modalities (outpatient treatment or AA meetings, for example) may only offer traditional addiction treatment geared toward full-blown addicts. With regard to screening, the CAGE questionnaire is often used to determine if alcohol dependence is possible. The CAGE is a series of four questions used by treatment providers as an initial screening to determine if more comprehensive assessment is necessary (Stevens & Smith, 2009):

1. Have you ever tried to *cut down* on your drinking?
2. Have you ever felt *annoyed* by others criticizing your alcohol use?
3. Have you ever felt *guilt* about your drinking behaviors?
4. Have you ever had an *eye-opener* in the morning?

While the CAGE questionnaire is typically about 90% effective in discriminating nonalcoholics from alcoholics (Stevens & Smith, 2009), in college populations, the CAGE fails to identify 43% to 69% of problem drinkers, and is even less sensitive when used with female students. Data suggest this common screening measure may fail to detect problem drinking among young adult women.

With regard to treatment, few young adults will follow through with referrals if they feel the treatment modality is irrelevant to their situation. For example, results of one study demonstrated that when referred to AA, less than 20% of college students attended even one meeting, and no students attended more than once (Foote et al., 2004). Screening opportunities must be made available once problems do arise. Examples include emergency departments, college campuses, military counseling centers, and at the workplace, often via Employee Assistance Program (EAP) counseling centers (Monti et al., 2004/2005).

At venues such as college campuses, alcohol and drug education programs typically include substantial educational components about the impact of substances on the body, brain, and lifestyle. These programs may be implemented via individual or group sessions, or lectures (Monti et al., 2004/2005). However, these programs have not been shown to effectively reduce substance abuse. Brief motivational interviewing (BMI) has been shown to be as effective or more effective than assessments alone or treatment as usual for young adults with lower-level substance abuse problems. Longer-term or more intensive treatment may be necessary if young adults meet the criteria for substance dependence (Monti et al.).

BMIs typically consist of one to four sessions conducted by a trained mental health professional for about 30 to 60 minutes per session (in fact, some research suggests a five-minute intervention can be as effective as a 20-minute counseling session [Baldwin et al., 2006]). In spite of its very brief duration, BMI has been demonstrated to be effective across settings. For example, on college campuses, participants in one BMI reduced their alcohol use by 56% and effects were maintained for up to four years after treatment ended. In emergency departments, one session of BMI reduced alcohol-related injuries more effectively than traditional interventions for up to six months following treatment (Monti et al., 2004/2005). In general, BMIs involving feedback and MI skills have been demonstrated to reduce alcohol-related problems and heavy drinking episodes.

In summary, the needs of young adult women are distinctly different from those of middle-aged women due to developmental needs and the range of severity of consequences that result from addictive behaviors. Generalization of addiction ideas and concepts from middle-aged women to this younger population limits the effectiveness of interventions. Sensitivity and care should be used when applying assessment and treatment techniques.

DIVERSITY ISSUES

Lesbian, Bisexual, and Transgendered (LBT) Women

Prior to counseling LBT women, counselors must examine their own biases and perspectives about lesbianism. Myths that exist in the United States about lesbian women include the following: Lesbians hate men, lesbians are all "butch" or masculine, or lesbians became lesbian after a negative sexual experience with a man. Stereotypes such as these can damage or prohibit an effective counseling relationship (Finnegan, 2001).

With regard to bisexuality, counselors may assume clients are confused or in denial about their sexual orientation or that they are sexually promiscuous (McVinney, 2001). Transgendered women (i.e., transsexuals, drag kings, bigender or androgynous individuals) are often defined by society as sick or disordered because of their orientation (Leslie, Perina, & Maqueda, 2001). Living in such a hostile environment can create incredible stress and emotional trauma (Finnegan, 2001).

Though enormous diversity exists among LBT women, certain risk factors may impact many. First, many of these women rely on lesbian- and gay-friendly bars for social outlets and peer support. Second, LBT women experience oppression heterosexual women do not. In addition to sexism, LBT women in the United States cope with ongoing social, political, and legal hostility. LBT women of color, with disabilities, or living in poverty cope with multiple oppressions. Third, the dissonance related to "staying in the closet" and the stress of "coming out" can both create conditions for substance abuse and dependence. Finally, the trauma related to discrimination and hostility related to sexual orientation can exacerbate the likelihood of substance abuse behaviors (Finnegan, 2001; Leslie et al., 2001; McVinney, 2001).

Recommendations for counselors working with addicted LBT women encourage an open, nonjudgmental stance that discourages labeling or stereotyping. Counselors should take time to explore the meaning of sexual or gender identity for each client who identifies as such, as there is no one way to be LBT. Counselors should approach client interactions from a collaborative, supportive stance, rather than engaging in heavy confrontation. Also, like many women, LBT women may find 12-Step meetings threatening or noninclusive. LBT women should be encouraged to attend only if it feels congruent or helpful to them as individuals (Finnegan, 2001; Leslie et al., 2001; McVinney, 2001). Counselors should also validate and support whatever sexual or gender identity is preferred by LBT clients, as counselors may be the only consistent source of support or encouragement these women have. Finally, counselors should assist LBT clients in finding and accessing LBT supportive agencies outside of the counseling center, including community employers or care providers (Oggins & Eichenbaum, 2002).

Issues of Race

It is outside the scope of this text to identify specific treatment needs for every racial group found in the United States. Indeed, the cultural landscape is expanding at such a rate that it is nearly impossible to identify all possible racial variations and ethnic backgrounds to be found within our borders, not to mention the needs of women who immigrate to the United States from other countries across the globe. Rather than examining race from an *emic* perspective (where individual racial groups are classified via specific descriptors), we chose to examine race and culture from an *etic*, or holistic, perspective, where universal truths are examined. "Ethnically diverse populations are heterogeneous. Any knowledge gained about members of a particular group must be balanced with the view that each person is also a unique individual, different from any other individual" (Wade, 1994).

Addiction counselors must be aware that women of color are impacted by multiple layers of oppression and one size most definitely does not fit all. Many counseling theories and theories of feminism were created from a middle-class Caucasian perspective, and thus may perpetuate covert or overt oppression upon clients who do not adhere to that value system (Alleyne & Rheineck, 2008). For example, the idea of a "good family" from a middle-class Caucasian perspective may include images of living in a single-family home, annual summer vacations, and weekly church attendance. These images may not resonate or be relevant to members from other cultural backgrounds. Women entering addiction treatment whose families do not match this image may be judged as inadequate, different, or strange. Similarly, an individual's relationship to drugs, alcohol, or processes of addiction may be strongly influenced by her cultural and racial background. Counselors should inquire with sensitivity about each client's perspective of her own addiction.

Interestingly, counseling centers are often similarly divided along racial lines. Frequently, the center directors, counselors, and other highly trained professionals are Caucasian, while paraprofessionals, administrative staff, and assistants tend to be people of color. Researchers in the counseling field (including the two authors of this text) belong to the majority culture. So with regard to policy making, theory, and counseling techniques, many decisions are made from a majority-culture perspective with limited direct impact from employees and clients of color (Alleyne & Rheineck, 2008). Consequently, the oppression that exists in society at large may also be present in the counseling center itself.

As a result of this disparity, researchers and practitioners have called for systemic change. On the one hand, culturally sensitive counseling practices are necessary to meet the needs of individual populations. Thus, understanding individual racial or cultural groups' historic and contemporary relationships to addictive substances and processes may be necessary to meet client needs. However, little empirical research has been done to quantify this claim (McNeece & DiNitto, 2005), and the sheer number of cultural and racial groups in the United States makes it all but impossible for practitioners to be intimately aware of all cultural variances. On the other hand, creating counseling programs sensitive to individual cultures may dilute services across communities, creating competition for funding and clientele at a time when addiction as a public health problem is epidemic. Rather, creating a holistic, outcomes-based community system to address addiction problems may be an effective alternative, where treatment communities come together to share a common goal (reducing the occurrence and impact of addiction; Holder, 2006).

Since both research and stereotypes about addiction come from a majority-culture perspective, counselors should be aware of any hidden assumptions or biases they may hold about clients because of their race. For example, African Americans are often perceived as having more severe levels of addiction, and are more likely to suffer legal consequences because of their substance abuse. Women of color are more likely to be reported for abusing substances while pregnant than white women. Often these punitive measures result from biases held against women because of their racial identity. African American women in the criminal justice system, for example, found greater barriers to programs related to finances, family reunification, and reduced criminal involvement than Caucasian women; Caucasian women are more likely to receive substance abuse and mental health services upon release from incarceration than African American women (U.S. Department of Justice [USDOJ], 2007).

When women of color also struggle with poverty, educational deficits, or unemployment, issues of race become even more significant. Due to societal perceptions, women of color may feel isolated from support and powerless to make changes in their lives. Women of color are more likely to experience social and legal consequences for their drinking and drug use behaviors, and are more likely to be charged with and prosecuted for drug crimes (Covington, 2008). In 1999, African American women were almost eight times as likely to be incarcerated than their Caucasian counterparts (USDOJ, 2007).

Issues of Ability

Addiction in the disabled community is a very real concern. According to the 2000 U.S. Census, just under 50 million people in the United States identify as having one or more mental or physical disabilities. Among these, it is estimated that between 6 and 13 million also suffer from chemical dependency, among other addictions. Among some subpopulations of disabled individuals, the estimates of addiction are as high as 80% (Stevens & Smith, 2009).

While feminist and counseling research on ethnic/racial minorities and women has increased in recent years, there are still populations of women that are ignored or rendered invisible by counseling research and practice communities. Disabled women fall into this category, as their specific needs are generally ignored outside of the vocational counseling arena. To clarify, *disability* refers to the specific physical or mental condition that can be defined by a medical practitioner. *Handicap* refers to the specific societal condition that limits a disabled person from fully participating in society (Stevens & Smith, 2009). For example, a woman unable to walk due to a traumatic brain injury is disabled because of her injury; she is handicapped when a building does not have an elevator to accommodate her wheelchair. Her physical condition is not the handicap; the building owner's disregard *is*.

In addition to the handicapping attitudes of others, some disabled women feel invisible because they may be unable to participate in society in ways sanctioned by traditional gender roles: neither as an independent worker nor as a mother or female nurturer (Crawford & Unger, 2004). Counselors may overemphasize or minimize a woman's disability, thus creating additional barriers to treatment. Even among feminist counselors, discrimination can occur if disabled clients are not able to embody an image of strong, self-sufficient women (Crawford & Unger, 2004).

In the addiction counseling community, these clients may fall victim to myths or stereotypes held about women with disabilities. For example, because of the disability, a female client is "entitled" to use alcohol or drugs to cope; thus, substance abuse is not a primary concern (Harley & Bishop, 2008). It is not uncommon for counselors to give top priority to the disability, making the addiction issue a secondary or tertiary problem (Stevens & Smith, 2009). In fact, disabled clients are in need of integrated and individualized services (just like any other client) that take into consideration the physical, mental, and cultural concerns of disability and addiction.

Persons with disabilities have specific risk factors that must be taken into consideration when conducting addictions diagnosis and treatment planning. These include (Harley & Bishop, 2008)

- Health and medical risk factors (e.g., using prescribed medications over a long period of time and medication conditions that may impact an individual's ability to tolerate or process substances)
- Psychological risk factors (e.g., enabling behaviors from family, friends, or health professionals, stress due to adjustment and financial problems)

- Social risk factors (e.g., isolation, few social connections, changes in support network)
- Economic and employment risk factors (e.g., expenses due to medical treatment, costs due to assisting equipment or transportation)
- Access risk factors (e.g., limited access to addiction counseling treatment due to mobility or speech/hearing/vision problems)

While taking into consideration these risk factors, counselors should strive to approach addiction counseling with disabled women from a strength-based perspective (Harley & Bishop, 2008). This is particularly important for disabled individuals, as much of their worldview and interaction with others may have been based on a perspective of weakness or lacking rather than one of strength and possibilities. While keeping in mind genuine limitations, counselors should make every effort to build on strengths, supports, and assets.

Issues of Poverty

Poverty is a painful reality for many women who struggle with addiction. Worldwide, women are generally more likely to be poor than men. In the United States, the ranks of women living in poverty are dominated by older women, women of color, and single mothers (Lips, 2006). In fact, two-thirds of all people living in poverty in the United States are women, and about half of households headed by a single mother are below the poverty line (Templeton, 2007). The term *feminization of poverty* was coined by Diana Pearce in 1978 when she observed that as the divorce rate rose, so did the number of women experiencing suddenly reduced household incomes, and thus poverty (Rosen, 2007). Perhaps because issues of poverty are largely a problem for women and people of color, it is one of the most neglected "isms" in the profession of counseling. Even as counselors and counselor educators embrace multiculturalism and social justice, poverty continues to be largely ignored in practice and in the research literature (M. Graham, personal communication, July 5, 2008).

Among women struggling with addiction, poverty can create formidable barriers to treatment. While lack of financial resources to pay for treatment, childcare, or transportation may make addiction counseling more difficult to access (Fendrich et al., 2006), there are subtler but equally detrimental forces at play. In recent decades poverty has become criminalized. As public policy responses to poverty have been decimated in recent years, the prison system has grown and expanded, with a disproportionate number of prisoners claiming poor or minority status. In fact, the War on Drugs in the United States has played a large part in fueling this growth, as penalties for simple possession of a controlled substance have gotten stricter (Templeton, 2007). With this perception of criminalization comes a subtle shift in our consciousness about poverty: We begin to judge people more harshly on the basis of being poor, often blaming them for their circumstances and assuming low moral character. The result is counselors and health care providers may treat clients living in poverty with "disrespect, stereotyping, coercion, and dismissive behavior" (Mulia, 2002, ¶ 3) rather than with respect and need-sensitive care.

As a result, clients may passively or actively resist counselor efforts in treatment, earning them the traditional addiction counseling label of "resistant" or "in denial" when these women may simply be fed up with disrespectful treatment from the counselor or counseling agency. However, resistance "refers to the adaptive strategies employed by aggrieved communities to avert, minimize, or overturn that which threatens their physical welfare and basic dignity" (Mulia, 2002, ¶ 7). In other words, for women living in poverty who encounter disrespectful treatment, resistance is simply a pull for dignity and control of their own addiction counseling experience. All too often, addiction counselors minimize or disregard a client's complaints if she is living in poverty, or may fail to include her in the treatment planning process. It is important to remember that client needs may be very different from counselor goals (Crawford & Unger, 2004). For example, a woman living in a shelter may be far more concerned with finding stable housing than in obtaining sobriety. In order to minimize client resistance (which in this case is really an indicator of a therapeutic rupture between counselor and client rather than true resistance on the part of the client), counselors must be aware of the "culture of poverty," which may include elements such as undereducation, under- or unemployment, poor health care and nutrition, linguistic barriers, poor housing, prejudice, and discrimination (Stevens & Smith, 2009). Addressing these complex issues may take priority over abstinence for clients. Additionally, counselors must contend with their own covert and overt biases about clients who live in poverty, and must be willing to engage in critical self-examination and transformation.

SUPPLEMENTAL OR ADJUNCTIVE THERAPIES

In our clinical experience, clients in addiction counseling report having formed a significant relationship with their drug or process of addiction. Similar to an actual human bond, once that relationship is over, clients feel a large hole or gap in their lives that they find difficult to fill.

Relapse often occurs because clients and counselors have failed to find a replacement for the lost "other," in this case, addiction. If clients have been using substances or processes to generate or manage emotions (as most do), then there is a much greater risk of returning to addictive behaviors posttreatment unless a replacement behavior is provided. There are multiple adjunctive therapies that both provide an alternative behavior to addiction and enhance the therapeutic process and alliance between counselor and client. In this section, three such therapies, acupuncture, bibliotherapy, and yoga, are discussed.

Acupuncture

Acupuncture is the use of tiny, disposable, sterilized needles to stimulate certain areas of the body. According to the World Health Organization (World Health Organization [WHO], n.d.), acupuncture has been shown effective in treating a number of physical and mental health problems, including reducing chronic and postoperative pain, nausea due to chemotherapy or radiation, panic disorders, depression, anxiety, and insomnia.

For women who experienced depression or anxiety prior to entering addiction treatment, and who used drugs, alcohol, or processes to cope with symptoms, relapse is likely unless alternative coping mechanisms are introduced. In fact, levels of anxiety and depression are likely to increase in the absence of addictive behaviors posttreatment (Courbasson, de Sorkin, Dullerud, & Van Wyk, 2007). A recent study of 300 women engaged in a 21-day residential treatment demonstrated that acupuncture helped reduce symptoms of depression and anxiety, enhanced problem-solving ability, reduced cravings, anger, and irritability, and enhanced calmness and confidence (up to three months posttreatment) in their ability to persist in high-relapse situations (Courbasson et al.). What is particularly interesting is that nearly all women in the program agreed to acupuncture when offered the choice, demonstrating perhaps women's interest in and willingness to try alternative methods of therapy.

Bibliotherapy

Bibliotherapy can be defined as "the guided reading of written materials in gaining understanding or solving problems relevant to a person's therapeutic needs" (Riordan & Wilson, 1989, p. 506). Addiction counselors might employ bibliotherapy in two different ways. First, the use of self-help books can complement counseling and can also include therapeutic writing or journaling. By engaging in these processes, the counselor–client team can accelerate learning and increase treatment impact, especially between counseling sessions. A second method involves the use of literature such as poems, short stories, and novels. With this method, counselors recommend works of literature to clients where similarities between clients and specific characters or situations can be found. This method can help clients find insight and new perspectives as they relate to the narrative. Literature can also provide clients with opportunities for emotional catharsis. Other benefits include enhanced insight and discussion about personal problems, reduction of perceived isolation, and generation of solutions (Briggs & Pehrsson, 2008). While there have been some mixed research results, many studies do demonstrate the effectiveness of bibliotherapy for a wide range of problems, including anxiety, geriatric depression, adolescents coping with mentally ill parents, stepfamilies in transition, and grieving children (Briggs & Pehrsson).

With regard to addiction, bibliotherapy has long been a component of the 12-Step movement in the United States. Alcoholics Anonymous introduced the Big Book to its members to provide advice, wisdom, and support for those struggling to understand alcoholism and attempting to heal their relationships hurt by their addiction. The Big Book, 4th Edition is currently available online on the AA Web site (AA, 2001). The Big Book is meant to supplement the group experience of AA, and to provide support for recovering alcoholics during times of need. Pamphlets and other materials are also available. Similarly, NA offers the Basic Text, pamphlets, and informational newsletters to its members. Though AA and NA do not engage in research, these organizations do promote the use of literature as an adjunctive experience for those in recovery.

Research literature has demonstrated some support for the efficacy of bibliotherapy for recovering addicts. Similar to methods used by AA and NA, self-help reading material used in addition to counseling or medical care for addiction has been found to benefit alcoholics more overall, as demonstrated by treatment outcomes and relapse prevention (Apodaca & Miller, 2003). Anecdotal evidence and clinical experience show that bibliotherapy (again, in the form of informational or self-help literature) might benefit women with process addiction, including sex addiction or eating disorders (Power, 2005). For adolescents, use of fiction is recommended to educate and assist in recovery from substance abuse and dependence. In this case, bibliotherapy appears most effective when there is a strong working alliance between counselor and client and when the client demonstrates low resistance to treatment (Pardeck, 1991).

Counselors interested in using bibliotherapy must keep the following caveats in mind. First, counselors should take great care in selecting literature, as some books may be developmentally inappropriate for clients or may reinforce negative patterns if clients project unhealthy motives and beliefs onto story characters. Also, clients with reading disorders, poor academic performance histories, or who are illiterate may be inadvertently harmed by counselors prescribing literature or self-help books. Finally, materials need to be selected with care to ensure they do not contain material that may be offensive to a particular client (Briggs & Perhsson, 2008).

Yoga

Yoga is a 5,000-year-old Eastern practice. Yoga incorporates exercise, breathing, and meditation to bring one into greater harmony with the mind and body. It is a physical and spiritual exercise intended in part to help practitioners develop greater respect for their body as a vessel for the spirit (American Yoga Association [AYA], n.d.). Yoga is used by health professionals to treat a variety of conditions, including arthritis, fibromyalgia, heart disease, chronic pain, depression, anxiety, and stress management (Godfrey, 2006). Though yoga is considered an alternative therapy and is not entirely embraced by the mainstream medical community, there is both anecdotal and empirical evidence that suggests it may benefit women struggling with addiction.

In particular, yoga teaches connection to the physical being; tolerance for stress, discomfort, and anxiety; living in the "now"; and reduction of stress. All of these tools would be of great benefit to addicted women, who frequently contend with difficult emotions, impulsivity, and a disconnection from their physical and spiritual selves. Overcoming addiction is difficult in part because the substance or process of addiction has been a tool for avoiding the pain of reality. An addict who harbors difficult memories of abuse, neglect, depression, or other emotional pain may find she has low tolerance for coping with the anxiety that emerges once the substance or process of addiction has been removed from her life. Yoga can offer an alternative, and can teach important lessons about staying present and allowing anxiety to emerge without reacting impulsively to remove or reduce it (Robertshawe, 2007; Stukin, n.d.).

Addicted women often find that once they begin to tend to their physical bodies, the idea of polluting the body with drugs or alcohol becomes less attractive: Once clients learn how good it feels to be healthy, the idea of returning to unhealthy behaviors loses its appeal. With yoga, once addicts realize how ingestion of substances (particularly smoking) impedes progress in the practice, it becomes easier to turn away from former addictive behaviors. In tending the physical body, practitioners of yoga also find brain benefits in that yoga releases the good chemicals in the brain that bring pleasure, relaxation, and peace to the mind and body. In other words, yoga can potentially replace the high previously sought through substance or process abuse and addiction. Other benefits of yoga include a supportive community and reduction of cravings, both of which can reduce the potential for relapse (Stukin, n.d.).

To date, there are few studies that specifically explore the use of yoga with addicted clients. Therefore, yoga should be applied by an experienced professional with care. However, preliminary studies and anecdotal evidence point to yoga as an effective supplemental therapy for addicted women.

CONCLUSION

Women face specific barriers to recovery when entering counseling. Socialized gender norms, traditional modes of addictions counseling, and lack of gender-specific services such as childcare all converge to reduce the likelihood of treatment success for women. However, it needn't be this way. If addictions counseling agencies are willing to look beyond traditional attitudes and theoretical orientations, they will likely increase women clientele attendance and treatment success. By adding childcare, assisting with medical care and case management, and utilizing empathic counseling interventions, agencies could better facilitate women clients' success. Adjunctive therapies such as acupuncture, bibliotherapy, and yoga may also add value to counseling programs.

Case Study

Sheila has reached the end of her rope with her prescription medication and alcohol abuse issues. In addition, she struggles with depression and feels alienated from her family. She seeks treatment but feels frustrated by the process. She received an assessment at a local private nonprofit agency based on the 12-Step model. At the assessment, the counselor insisted she accept the label of "addict" in order to begin treatment. She did not feel the counselor was truly interested in hearing her story, and felt her concerns about past sexual assault and current relationship problems were minimized. Sheila feels strongly that all her current problems are equally important: She knows her substance use is related to her past trauma and she uses to feel relief from her pain. When she informed her assessment counselor of her intention to seek counseling elsewhere, she was labeled as "resistant" and told to come back to counseling when she was truly ready, after she had hit rock bottom. Sheila hopes to find another counselor who understands the connections among all her current concerns. She also seeks treatment at an agency with quality childcare and adjunctive psychological services. Most of all, Sheila wants to be heard and understood. She has felt alienated from others for so long, she craves a genuine connection with her counselor.

The multiple layers of Sheila's concerns are a perfect example of the need for comprehensive counseling services for women seeking addictions treatment. Sheila is far more than her addiction: She is a survivor of sexual assault, a wife and mother, and an African American woman in a country where racism is still a potent force. To ignore these realities is to disregard the core of Sheila's being and to alienate her from the counseling process. While Sheila does indeed need effective addictions counseling, she is also in need of marital counseling, and effective treatment for her ongoing sexual assault issues. Until these emotional wounds are tended to, Sheila is at risk of seeking solace and relief from alcohol and pills. Sheila needs to replace chemical solutions with healthier ones, so identifying alternatives such as exercise, yoga, meditation, or hobbies may be beneficial.

DISCUSSION QUESTIONS

1. Traditional ideas about addiction, including "breaking through denial," abstinence, and criminalization, are entrenched into the American psyche. What kinds of reactions did you have when reading about alternatives to these traditional attitudes? In particular, what are your initial reactions to harm reduction as a treatment alternative?
2. Binge drinking is often perceived as a typical part of the maturation process for women in their early 20s. Paired with these drinking behaviors are frequent displays of oversexualization (think *Girls Gone Wild*) or risky sexual behaviors. If you were to design an educational or prevention program, what would be the most important components to include?
3. Acupuncture, bibliotherapy, and yoga were suggested as adjunctive therapies to talk therapy. What are some other activities that might be helpful to clients struggling with addiction?

7

ADOLESCENTS

The previous chapter explored the unique treatment considerations for addictions counseling with women. As women have unique addictions counseling needs, so do adolescent girls. Many of the addictions counseling modalities that are appropriate for women are also appropriate for adolescent girls, but there are unique areas that addictions counselors should be cognizant of. Girls have process addictions and developmental needs that are different from those of women. This chapter will review some specific interventions for working with adolescents.

Adolescent girls are closing the gender gap in the use of most substances, including alcohol, cigarettes, marijuana, cocaine, and other illicit drugs (Guthrie & Flinchbaugh, 2001). In some instances they are passing adolescent boys, including the use of tranquilizers and amphetamines (Guthrie & Flinchbaugh). With process addictions such as eating disorders and self-harm, girls lead the way. The risk factors for addiction include issues of access to substances (Lysaught & Wodarski, 1996), family dysfunction, and chronic mental health issues (Kulis, Nieri, Yabiku, Stromwall, & Marsiglia, 2007). Also, social struggles of trying to fit in and have a sense of belonging are critical components of girls' social development: Girls with high self-efficacy and self-esteem have lower levels of substance abuse than girls who lack self-esteem (Guthrie & Flinchbaugh, 2001). While relationships may bring girls to substance use, through peer pressure and a desire to be like their friends, strong relationships may also protect girls from problematic use of substances or behaviors. It is a journey that they must learn to navigate.

In addition to social considerations, mental health symptoms are also significant contributors to adolescent addiction. As discussed in

Chapter 4, girls with undiagnosed depression, anxiety, or histories of abuse are much more likely to become addicted than girls who do not have a mental health issue. This is true for both substance and process addictions, with depression or anxiety being the most common underlying diagnoses. Treatment then is more effective when addressing both concerns. As Lysaught and Wodarski (1996) stated, "Due to the cyclical nature of depression and alcohol, e.g., alcohol being used to alleviate the symptoms of depression or alcohol abuse promoting depression symptomatology ... address both clinical issues simultaneously rather than treat only one problem" (p. 58). Yet, this is what many of the treatment centers do, treat one issue, the addiction, without looking at what else might be occurring, doing girls a tremendous disservice.

DIFFICULTY IN DIAGNOSING ADOLESCENTS

Conducting an assessment and diagnosing adolescents can be very difficult. Something that would be symptomatic in an adult may simply be a normal developmental hurdle for an adolescent (Erk, 2008). It has been reported that half of all lifetime cases of mental illness begin by age 14, and it often takes several years between the onset of symptoms and the beginning of treatment (Erk). Part of why it may take years for treatment to begin has to do with developmental considerations, as individuals may not know if the symptoms are indicative of normal development or truly problematic. There is no clear explanation about why or how mental illness occurs in children; there are several models that attempt to explore its occurrence. The first is the biological model. This model considers issues such as neurobiological health and genetics. The next is the psychological model. Issues like attachment, inborn drives, and personality structure are considered with this model; this is our traditional model of looking at mental health. Next we have the behavioral models, where mental illness is externally influenced and inadequate or maladaptive reinforcement was involved in a child's learning. The cognitive model looks at the pattern of thinking, such as irrational and negative self-statements. Parent-child interaction and vicarious learning are also a part of this model. Next, the school model speaks to how the child is functioning in school in terms of peer relationships, teacher-student relationships, and the conditions at the school. Finally, the family model: Family systems, cycles, and parenting structures are all considered in this model (Erk). All of these models have their strengths and weaknesses, but in general, they have provided the foundation for how we have conceptualized child and adolescent mental illness. An emerging approach is to integrate the models. By integrating the models, counselors can use elements from different models that more fully explain adolescent clients' maladaptive behavior (Erk). This paradigm allows for a more holistic and open practice of diagnosis and assessment and is important to addictions counselors, as part of the work should be ferreting out the mental health concerns and the addiction. This diagnostic portion is critical to successful addictions treatment.

HOLISTIC PRACTICES

One struggle in assessing adolescents is determining what is normal and what is not normal. With substance abuse, high-risk behaviors may include deviant behavior, sensation-seeking behavior, and using drugs or alcohol with peers. What is difficult is that these are also all behaviors that could be expected in a normal transition from pre-adolescence to adolescence (Lysaught & Wodarski, 1996). As Vernon and Clemente (2005) expressed, having an understanding of age-appropriate behavior as well as developmental differences is critical in deciding whether a child's behavior is normal or abnormal. A critical component for child and adolescent counselors is their level of understanding of human development (Erk, 2008). The first component to treatment with adolescents is to conduct a developmental assessment. It is only then that counselors can begin to know if clients' behavior fits within what is considered normal or not. Within this framework counselors can create a treatment plan that will be effective for each individual client. Mood swings in adolescent girls may be a completely normal part of development, and should not automatically be categorized as pathological.

In conducting a developmental assessment it is critical that adolescents are assessed for development in the areas of social, emotional, physical, cognitive, and moral development. There are a variety of tools that can be used to measure this development, items such as incomplete sentence blanks, the social recognition skills checklist, the draw-a-person and other projective drawing tests, and the Denver Developmental Screening Test II (Vernon & Clemente, 2005). What is most important is that the assessment tools that are chosen are used appropriately, and are part of a larger screening process. It is also critical that the practitioner have a strong understanding of the stages of development, and of multicultural aspects of development before doing these assessments. "Ignoring the importance of culture during the assessment processes can be detrimental to the psychological and educational progress of a young ethnically diverse client" (Vernon & Clemente, p. 66).

IDENTITY DEVELOPMENT FOR GIRLS

When determining what may be typical for adolescent girls it is also critical to consider developmental theories that are inclusive of adolescent girls. The primary social development theory in the field of counseling and psychology is Erikson, yet his theory has been criticized for its majority-culture, male perspective. According to Erikson's theory, the developmental goal is autonomy, which does not allow for the connection and relationships so critical for girls (Wastell, 1996). One of the first criticisms of stage theories, such as Erikson's, was the exclusion of girls from the studies. Gilligan, Ward, and Taylor (1988) stated, "To reconsider adolescent development in light of the inattention to girls and women is to hold in abeyance the meaning of such key terms as 'self' and 'development' and perhaps above all, 'relationship'" (p. xi). They found that girls define themselves not, as Erikson believed, by reflecting back what others see, but by their relationships with friends and family. Gilligan et al. (1988) described girls and adolescents as moving toward connectedness with others. This perspective of identity development allows for self-definition by the adolescent who is finding her voice and connection. This understanding would not have surfaced had researchers continued to conduct research with only male participants.

Stern (1991) further demonstrated the difference between stage theory and feminist theory when she described her work with girls in the process of adolescent growth. Stern stated that all psychological theories of development point to the critical role of relationships in either enhancing or inhibiting development. For feminist theorists the emphasis is on the significance of relationships in every aspect of a girl's development. Erikson's theory of development explained that detaching from relationships forms that self-identity; this view was considered inaccurate for women (Gilligan et al., 1988; Stern, 1991).

Within the literature, the traditional view of identity development and the feminist view of identity development differ dramatically. The primary difference is the feminist researchers' use of girls to conduct research, opening up a new understanding of girls. Feminist researchers found that girls form their identity in connection to relationships of family and friends. This finding diverges significantly from traditional theory that found that individuals move into more autonomous and independent states as completion of their identity development. From the feminist view, for adolescent girls to develop a self-concept, they come to understand the relationships that are most important, develop a voice in relation to others, and understand self not in terms of male standards of independence, but in terms of fit with society (Gilligan et al., 1988; Kerr, 1994; Stern, 1991). For addictions counselors, having an understanding of the differences in the ways in which girls develop their identities and self-concepts is critical when assessing or creating treatment plans.

The rest of this chapter will look more closely at treating adolescent addiction, beginning with a discussion of process addictions, and then looking at treatment planning for any addiction.

PROCESS ADDICTIONS

Eating Disorders

For adolescent girls the struggle to fit in and look the way they think they should can be very arduous. It is difficult to know how many girls struggle with their weight, but there are some data. Ackard, Fulkerson, and Neumark-Sztainer (2007) conducted a study to examine the prevalence of eating disturbances that could be categorized by the *Diagnostic and Statistical Manual*, 4th Edition (DSM-IV) criteria as anorexia nervosa (AN), bulimia nervosa (BN), or binge eating disorder (BED). In their survey of 4,746 adolescents, they found a large number of students had weight concerns, or some type of disordered eating symptoms, but they were not severe enough to meet the criteria for a diagnosis. While they may not have met the criteria for an eating disorder, they certainly are engaging in the behaviors. They found that 16% of the girls reported engaging in physically harmful behaviors such as binge eating, self-induced vomiting, laxative use, and excessive exercise. They also found that one-third of the girls reported that their body shape and weight had an effect on how they evaluated themselves, with some of these girls reporting eating disorder behaviors. With so many participants engaged in dangerous behaviors, and so few meeting the diagnostic criteria, there is clearly a disconnect that this study demonstrates. This has clear implications for potential treatment options. If girls are not meeting the criteria for eating disorders, then they are not receiving services for those disorders. However, there are numerous girls headed down a dangerous path who could benefit from counseling services that assist with their disordered eating; they just may not be recognized. What this study also did was begin to demonstrate the large numbers of adolescents that do describe body-shape perception issues, low self-esteem related to body size, and the ways that they are behaving to compensate for those feelings.

Part of the reason so many adolescent girls struggle with their body image is the pressure to fit in and attain a perfect body that they believe they must look like. There is pressure to be thin from peers, family, the media, and for girls who are not thin, or just don't believe they are thin, they begin to diet (Stice, Presnell, & Spangler, 2002). Most eating disorders begin with a simple desire to diet, to lose just a few pounds to fit in more, or to go along with the social pressures to diet; to diet because everyone else seems to be dieting. Yet, for some, there is a point where the dieting cannot stop. In fact, elevations in dieting, along with body mass, body dissatisfaction, appearance overvaluation, a perceived pressure to be thin, and modeling of eating disturbances, along with depressive symptoms, all put girls at higher risk for binge eating behaviors (Stice et al.). Many of these triggers are likely to be found with peer interactions. Peers may add to pressures girls experience about not being thin enough. Girls may binge together or talk about the unhealthy behaviors they are each doing to keep their weight down. Girls with higher levels of depression are at a much higher risk for addiction; this dual diagnosis holds true for eating disorders as well. Appearance overvaluation is almost a group norm for adolescent girls that is said not to minimize the experience, but to normalize the developmental process of evaluating and critiquing the physical body. Much of girls' time is focused on what to wear and how to look, which creates a world of constant critiques of one's own body. It is easy to see how the risk factors for an eating disturbance are really very much a part of an adolescent girl's typical experience. To add to the complexity, there is research that supports the relationship between binge eating and coping with depressed moods (Bradford & Petrie, 2008). This research finds that young women often internalize the sociocultural pressures that they face, internalization contributes to depression, and binge eating may be utilized to help treat the mood disorder.

For adolescent girls suffering with an eating disorder, or more common, disordered eating behaviors, it is most likely due to social pressures. Disordered eating behaviors tend to worsen and are usually associated with other issues, such as depression, low self-esteem, substance abuse, and high-risk sexual activity (Colton, Olmsted, & Rodin, 2007). With binge eating behavior hallmarks include a loss of control, feelings of guilt and shame, and the bingeing becoming a habit. Marcus and Kalarchian (2003) reviewed several studies related to binge eating in children and adolescents and found that girls were more likely than boys to "be embarrassed about binge eating, to fear that binge eating had become an involuntary habit, and to be depressed or self-critical after a binge" (p. 550). They also found evidence that binge eating is significantly more common in girls, particularly when linked with issues related to loss of control.

Loss of control, hiding behaviors, increased risk taking, and dual diagnosis may sound similar to other addictions, yet for girls who are suffering with an eating disorder, the inability to cope with the issue on their own is significant in that eating disorders have unique components. For example, their experience is the same as if they were addicted to alcohol; however, the treatment cannot include abstinence. Treating an eating disorder is a balancing act between treating the underlying issue and working to ensure medical needs are cared for. In fact, many of the needs of girls suffering from eating disorders are outside of the scope of this text. However, the primary issue for addictions counselors is to recognize that in many ways disordered eating is like other addictions and the link to mental health symptoms and self-esteem is significant. When counseling girls with disordered eating behaviors counselors should be sure not to minimize or negate the cause of the addiction.

Self-Harm

Girls who harm themselves typically do so to cope with some type of undiagnosed mental illness, most often depression or anxiety. Self-harming behavior includes cutting with any sharp object, or burning one's self, hitting, scratching, pulling hair, or extreme nail biting (Svirko & Hawton, 2007). Individuals cause harm to their bodies during a psychological crisis, but they are not suicidal. This is an important point to remember. There have been some links to self-harm behaviors and eating disorders, and Svirko and Hawton conducted a review of the literature that examined the possible reasons for the association. Two of the natural reasons for the association are that they both primarily occur in women and they both begin in adolescence. They also found some very interesting connections in the research literature, primarily that the reported prevalence of both an eating disorder and self-harming behavior ranged from 54% to 61%. While they only found two studies directly reporting the connection, they both had similar figures, showing some association between the two.

Svirko and Hawton (2007) found that impulsivity was perhaps related to eating disorders and self-harm behaviors. There were also findings linking obsessive compulsive disorder (OCD) with both eating disorders and self-harm, although there were mixed findings about how these connected. For cutting and burning, two of the more common types of self-harm, Favazza and Simeon (1995) found those tend to be impulsive and fit into a category with substance use and addiction. That type of self-harm behavior tended to be reactive, either to an external event, a fight with a friend, or a feeling of being overwhelmed. It is also a more impulsive reaction than some of the other, more obsessive, or planful self-harm behaviors, such as nail biting, which one may think about all day.

Another interesting aspect is related to affect dysregulation. While there certainly is some research to demonstrate that self-harm behavior is a method to regulate feelings, there was inconsistency about how that connected to eating disorders, or if it did. There was a mention that eating pathology makes individuals who self-harm more susceptible to depression, but nothing to sustain that hypothesis (Svirko & Hawton, 2007). Svirko and Hawton found clear evidence of the need for control in eating-disordered subjects. Many individuals who self-harm do so to take back control, but there is no connection between individuals with eating disorders and participation in self-harming behaviors as a means of control. They also found very high connections between childhood abuse and unstable families and higher rates of self-harm and eating disorders. This fits with the idea that children with histories of sexual or physical abuse, or unstable homes have higher rates of psychological trauma and mental health needs. Mental health needs increase the rates of both eating disorders and self-harm behaviors.

So, why share all of this in an addictions book? Here is the connection: Adolescent girls who harm themselves often do so because they feel overwhelmed. This is an impulsive act, and often the first time they don't think it through, but then they feel better after they have done it. Girls who cut often report feeling better after they do it; however, cutting only once does not work. So, they will cut more than one time to feel the same release that they used to get with only one cut. They hide what they are doing from their family and friends. They often cut where people cannot see it, at first on their arms, then even on their legs, between their toes. Eventually, they cannot really cope well with any type of emotion without cutting, and feel they need to do this more and more often. Sound familiar? Self-mutilation also shares similarities with drug or alcohol addiction in that girls often talk about feeling guilty after they have been cutting, wanting to stop but not being able to, and feeling out of control and not knowing what to do about it.

Girls who are engaging in self-harm behavior, in general, tend to have characteristics similar to those of girls who have disordered eating patterns, which is probably why so many of them have both. They tend to strive to be perfect, they want to be organized, to fit in, and seem to have things going their way. They strive to be in control. They tend to be some of the best students, some of the more popular girls, the ones other girls want to be. Yet, they have given up their real self in order to possess the perfect image and they are lost. These girls have higher rates of depression and anxiety because of their drive to be perfect, so they often hide any symptoms they may be experiencing and are left to cope alone. They do not turn to substances because substance abuse would get in the way of their goals. Instead, they self-harm and engage in disordered eating. Under this perfect image is a deep need for help.

Often, once parents find out, they become confused. Parents may fear their child is suicidal. It is important for counselors to help parents understand the dynamics of self-mutilation and then to counsel girls to treat both the behaviors and the mental health issue behind the self-harm, just as with eating disorders. Self-mutilation is about more than the cutting, just as disordered eating is about more than food alone.

Internet Use

Internet addiction is the newest addiction to develop. In recent years computer use has grown in homes and schools to the point where it has become our norm. We are a society that moved from phone calls to e-mail to text messaging. But becoming preoccupied with the Internet can interfere with daily life, and can be damaging in a way that is similar to gambling (Ko et al., 2006). Some of the characteristics of Internet addiction include a preoccupation with the Internet, uncontrolled impulse while online, longer than intended use, building a tolerance, impairment of control, excessive time and effort spent on the Internet, and impairment of decision-making ability (Ko et al.).

Part of the appeal of the Internet is online gaming, which allows individuals to create a social world without having to meet anyone face-to-face. For adolescents who are struggling socially, these fantasy games let them escape to be someone else and develop an entirely different social world. However, this is a double-edged sword for adolescents.

> Role-playing games may offer beneficial outlets to adolescents and young adults but also present substantial risks. Although the addictive component in some cases is striking, they also provide an experience of a virtual community, ameliorate social anxiety and loneliness, allow the "trying on" of new identities, and assist in the developmental task of forging a sense of identity apart from one's family. (Allison, Wahlde, Shockley, & Gabbard, 2006, p. 385)

The Internet may allow for adolescents to practice new roles, but it may also serve "as a way of avoiding intimacy with peers and the expansion of [an] identity in the outside world" (Allison et al., p. 384). The Internet may also be used as a primary method of meeting people, or having entertainment and social needs met, which can be problematic (Beard, 2005).

Adolescent girls are dependent upon real in-person relationships to learn about themselves. The Internet, therefore, is not enough for those critical developmental stages. Part of their social relationships can be supported through the Internet via social network pages; however, without the face-to-face contact, girls may not be able to develop authentic relationships. Facebook is one of the current social network pages girls use to connect with friends, both ones they know and ones they have never met. Girls may spend hours on Facebook making sure that their page looks the way they want it to, putting notes on their friends' "walls," and keeping up with what is going on. This is the new way that they communicate. There is a dearth of research about how this may ultimately affect relationships and self-esteem, but for girls who use this to hide their true identity, who do this instead of spending time with others, and who are on the computer at the expense of schoolwork and relationships, it may become problematic, just as disordered eating or self-mutilation. It is just a matter of time before the research catches up with the technology.

TREATMENT PLANNING

In some ways treating adolescent girls for addiction is much like treating adult women, and many of the methods mentioned in the previous chapter can be employed when counseling girls. Methods such as motivational interviewing, cognitive behavioral therapy, harm reduction, and of course, the use of the relational-cultural model are all effective models with adolescent girls for the same reasons that they are effective with women. They are more open models of addiction, allow room for relationships to develop, provide an opportunity for an exploration of social and emotional needs, and are not based on giving up their already limited power. However, there are some issues unique to treating adolescents, primarily due to their developmental needs. Counseling methods that may be used include adjunctive and stand-alone methods and will be discussed here.

Before beginning any treatment plan, there are a few basic considerations when working with adolescents with addiction issues. Burrow-Sanchez (2006) summed these up in what he described as *four key clinical areas for counselors* (p. 285). These areas are (1) creating a working relationship, (2) assessing the severity of the problem, (3) identifying a treatment plan, and (4) acknowledging the potential for relapse. These are the most critical components of working with adolescent girls. Without these four, regardless of treatment methods, it is likely that treatment will be unsuccessful, regardless of the addiction issue.

The first, *creating a working relationship*, goes to the heart of counseling and feminist thought. Adolescent girls often arrive in the counselor's office, just as Burrow-Sanchez (2006) described, through the courts, the schools, or the parents. Adolescents are rarely self-referred, although they may be to school counselors, but only if that relationship is already in place. By the time they get to a counselor for substance abuse or process addiction issues adolescent girls may have heard from many adults who argue with the girls to stop the behavior. It may be hard for them to trust a new adult. Addiction counselors must build a relationship first or there will be no effective counseling and no honest communication. Counselors must create a supportive, nonthreatening environment without blame by listening to what adolescent girl clients have to say (Burrow-Sanchez). Fundamental counseling skills learned for treating mental health issues are essential. Remember, addictions typically occur as a result of an underlying issue; thus, counselors' responsibility is to work with girls to learn about both the addiction and the underlying issues. There is nothing more important than relationships. Thinking about the relational-cultural model and the importance of building that empathetic and shared space is critical for addiction counseling with girls. This not only supports the current counseling relationship, but also models a supportive, nurturing relationship for outside of the counseling sessions.

The second of these four key clinical considerations is *assessing the severity of the problem*. Developmentally, it is appropriate for adolescents to experiment with substances, the way they look, and Internet use. For counselors, it is critically important to sort out what is typical behavior and what might be a dependence or addiction. Only in doing so can they determine the correct level of treatment, whether it is some basic psychoeducation or an inpatient program (Burrow-Sanchez, 2006). There are many different assessment tools available for substance use, eating disorders, and self-harm. There are a few important issues when assessing individuals. The first is to ensure familiarity with the assessment tool, how to score it, and how to interpret the results. Counselors should also make sure that the tool is appropriate for the individual to whom it is administered (Hood & Johnson, 2007). These are two essential ethical issues to consider when giving assessments.

After assessing for the addiction issue itself, counselors must uncover other reasons for the substance or process addiction (Burrow-Sanchez). Consider comorbidity issues (see previous chapters) to determine why adolescent girls begin to use substances, engage in disordered eating or self-harm. The second phase of the assessment is to assess for mental health issues. This is an area where the needs of the clients and the training of the addictions counselors or mental health counselors may be in sync. Substance abuse counselors are rarely trained for mental health screening, and mental health counselors very often have limited addictions training. This is a systemic problem, but nonetheless, these girls need the mental health screening. Counselors must advocate for mental health–trained counselors at addiction facilities and vice versa. It is critical to provide both. Without the proper screening, counselors cannot determine the best treatment approach.

The third component is *identifying a treatment plan*. As discussed in the previous chapter, there are currently three main types of treatment: outpatient, inpatient, and longer-term residential. As previously discussed, most addiction counseling is based on the 12-Step or Minnesota model of addiction, which is generally less effective for girls and women. While there is some evidence that some traditional methods of counseling are better than no treatment at all (Burrows-Sanchez, 2006), outcomes are poor. Counselors can do better than *some treatment is better than no treatment*. Some of the models that currently seem to be more effective are motivational interviewing, cognitive-behavioral, and harm reduction. In addition, adolescent girls may benefit from family-based models, art and music therapy, and gender-specific group therapy.

Finally, *acknowledge the potential for relapse.* Among counselors there are a lot of opinions about how to address relapse and whether relapse is a healthy part of recovery. Burrows-Sanchez (2006) describes a way of using the potential of relapse as a way to talk about follow-up care with clients. Sharing with them the high rates of recidivism and the resources available to them and encouraging them to continue with whatever group or supportive services seem a critical part for adolescent girls. They are back in their environment, with their friends and other relationships that may have contributed to their addictions. Unlike adults, who can make a choice to move or change jobs if needed, adolescents cannot make these choices. Most often they are right back into their routines, and helping them find ongoing support is critical.

It can be very difficult to attempt to determine which program might work the best for adolescent girls. The bulk of the research in the field of addictions was conducted with male participants. Then, over time, counselors began to get more information about women and what would be helpful interventions for them. In the 1990s, with the help of priority funding from federal agencies such as the National Institute on Drug Abuse (NIDA) and Substance Abuse and Mental Health Services Administration (SAMHSA), there were some advances in gender-specific programs for women (Blake, Amaro, Schwartz, & Flinchbaugh, 2001). In 1995 the Center for Substance Abuse Prevention earmarked money for studies related specifically to adolescent girls and the gender differences for this population. Little has come of this research; some of the studies are still coming in, but few were funded (Blake et al.). This explains the dearth of research on intervention with adolescent girls, and how to best support this population. What we will offer you here is what is in the literature along with our own experiences and those of our colleagues.

Family-Based Model

Family-based models of treatment are among the most widely used, and among the most widely studied models of treatment in the field of adolescent addictions (Ozechowski & Liddle, 2000). This makes a great deal of sense given the importance of family dynamics when working with adolescents. Families are often incorporated into the treatment of their adolescents in some manner, and this model of treatment is one that for adolescent girls can be critical, depending on the family. For adolescents, parent substance use, parent divorce (Lysaught & Wodarski, 1996), domestic violence, and physical or sexual abuse in the home (Chen, Tyler, Whitbeck, & Hoyt, 2004; Harrison, Fulkerson, & Beebe, 1997) are all contributing factors for substance use. For girls from a stable and nurturing home, having the family involved in the treatment can be effective and extremely helpful. However, for girls from an abusive home, family treatment may perpetuate any abuse and continue their addictive patterns.

In family-based treatment, the addiction is viewed as a systemic issue passing through generations of the family, or from dysfunctional relationships. Another key component is that the adolescent's substance use and overall functioning is seen in relation to her parents/guardians, siblings, and extended family (Ozechowski & Liddle, 2000). Their patterns of communication and relationships are examined and the addictive behavior is seen as a symptom of poor relationships, or general family dysfunction. Through traditional family therapy techniques, the family works together to discover the systemic root of the problem and then works to help the adolescent find alternative ways of coping, simultaneously working on the relationships and communication patterns in the family.

The benefit of this model is that an adolescent is not alone in this process and the family is part of the recovery, which for girls is very important. Adolescents should feel supported and not blamed. Families who participate in family-based treatment report some drug use reduction and behavior changes that last 6 to 12 months beyond terminating treatment (Ozechowski & Liddle, 2000). Ozechowski and Liddle also reviewed family functioning following family-based treatment for adolescents with substance use issues, and while the research is limited, they did find that family functioning improved. This is important because if families are functioning at higher levels, communicating well, and have strong relationships, then their adolescent's drug use should subside. One interesting finding is when split by gender using pre–post test measures, the girls treated with family-based models had deteriorated. We have some thoughts about that.

In general, a downside to using a family-based model is that if the family is not stable, the girl with the addiction issue my ultimately take the blame, particularly for any relationship issues. Basically, a counseling session easily becomes the parents blaming their daughter and her addiction for their problems. Even well-trained counselors have difficulty helping girls not feel worse after that. Additionally, if there has been any abuse that has not been disclosed, this type of therapy may make issues worse. From a feminist perspective, family therapy may also not be the best fit. At best, it does not address gender issues within a family; at worse, it minimizes and patronizes an oppression the adolescent may be feeling in her home due to her gender. Family therapists often align with the father, the typical head of household, and the mother is often silently blamed (or takes on the blame) in family sessions (Enns, 2003). While this can be modified, it must be done deliberately and consciously. If family therapists are able to talk about gender roles in the family, allow for clients to share feelings, and advocate for a balance, then this may be an appropriate model, particularly with a supportive family who is interested in being involved. If not, then there are other more individual or group treatment modalities available.

Art Therapy

Interventions with girls tend to be more effective if they are focused on social skills training and social norms (Blake et al., 2001). This fits with what others have found about teen girls' need to fit in, make connections, and learn about who they are in relationship to others. Guthrie and Flinchbaugh (2001) found interventions were effective if they connected to girls' self-efficacy (a perception that one can control her own motivation, which helps to control behavior). For girls, having self-efficacy "creates an essential bridge between her thoughts and her actions—especially as the thoughts and actions relate to engaging in health-promoting skills and the ability to actualize these skills in vulnerable situations" (Guthrie & Flinchbagh, p. 361). Interventions that help develop self-efficacy and self-esteem and help girls to understand the social construct that has minimized their value all help promote better choices. The use of art with adolescent girls allows for this development.

Much of the art therapy literature that connects to addiction work does so in relation to the 12-Step model (Horay, 2006), and is dedicated to a body of artwork that is focused on powerlessness and hopelessness. Not what is typical for art therapy. Horay began to connect art therapy with motivational interviewing and the stages of change model and found an increase in self-efficacy and engagement in sessions with his client. During the sessions he used collage, hypothetical greeting cards, and a check-in drawing each session. He found that his client was able to explore his own ambivalence about his addiction and recovery, that the counselor was able to be flexible in his work with the client, and that there was growth in unexpected ways. While this study is with an adult man, it is similar to the work that can happen with an adolescent girl. Hartz and Thick (2005) described the use of art with girls as "minimizing resistance and offer[ing] many avenues for positive identity development" (p. 73). Their research found that art therapy and factors related to improved self-esteem were connected; themes such as identifying feelings, experiencing safety, and feeling comfortable in self-expression are all important steps in growing and developing a sense of self. While there was little direct research on art therapy with adolescent girls suffering from addiction, the idea of art supporting the development of self-esteem, self-efficacy, and connection to self is important in addictions work.

Some of the techniques that can be used in art are as follows:

- Collage work: Creating collages that show self-esteem (choosing items that speak to them), show life pre- or postaddiction (identify what their addiction "looks like" and "looked like"), or identify *my favorite things*.
- Self-portrait: This allows the counselor to see how clients see themselves. This can be very difficult for some girls. In groups individual clients can be asked to describe themselves. Then the other girls share how they see her. In addition, counselors can ask clients to write on the back of the portrait what they keep private versus what is shown the world. This gets at the real self/false self issues.
- Family portrait: Allowing them to put any members in. This lets counselors see how clients see themselves in relation to their family—who is there, who is not.
- Use of clay: Use a guided image and have clients sculpt their reaction to that guided image.
- Free draw: Let clients draw anything they like, then ask them to discuss it. Choice of color, image, shape, or size may all be revealing.

There are many other options. One strong word of caution: It is unethical to diagnose or base an assessment on one drawing, especially if counselors are not licensed as an art therapist. These ideas are to supplement current practice. Counselors should ask adolescent girl clients to discuss their artwork without making assumptions about a diagnosis or history based on one picture alone. Art therapy can be powerful, so use these as strengths-based tools to add to the relationship building and to the counseling you are already doing. If it seems effective, seek training in art therapy.

Music Therapy

Music therapy has been described as the use of music as a therapeutic tool that can help improve psychological, mental, and physiological health (Camilleri, 2000). Camilleri described music therapists as combining their traditional counseling paradigm, such as humanistic, behavioral, cognitive, and so forth, with the use of music. By doing this, an experiential component to the counseling session is created, allowing for personal growth. "Music therapy capitalized on the familiarity and accessibility of music to help people recover, cope, learn and grow" (p. 185).

In the early 1990s music therapy began to find its way into a small number of recovery programs (Gallant, Holosko, & Siegel, 1997). The use of song writing was found to be an important part of the therapeutic process. When clients write their own songs, as you can imagine, the counselor is able to get a small glimpse into what they are experiencing. For clients, unlike journaling, this activity asks them to tell a story, with a purpose. Also, asking clients to listen to music "is likened to choosing a pathway to reach out to one's emotions, issues, concerns, in search of one's spiritual soul" (Gallant et al., p. 44). What song was chosen? What did they say about it? How does it affect them? In discussing the chosen song, another door to their experience opens up.

For adolescent girls, much of their social lives revolves around music. You may have a client who, like most girls, likes to listen to music, or you may have a client that plays an instrument, is involved in dance or other activities around music. There is something very natural about using music in therapy with girls. We like the following:

- Ask clients to bring in a favorite song: Play the song (ask for the lyrics also) and talk to the client about why this song speaks to her. What does it mean to her? When does she play it? How does it affect her? This can also be done in a group.

- Song writing: Ask a client to write a song. This will often reflect how she is feeling about herself, or her counseling experience.
- Use of instruments: Bring any rhythmic instruments to a session and play together, or in group.

These are only a few of the many music therapy techniques that can be used to supplement counseling work. Just like art therapy, as counselors evaluate clients and their music, be cautious and remember this is only one piece of information. Also keep in mind that much of what adolescents listen to is violent and aggressive. It is critical to talk about the messages about gender and what it means to be a female and male and what social roles are in the songs, but many girls listen to sad songs to elicit those feelings. Talk to them about how they react and, when they listen to music, refraining from assumptions.

GROUP COUNSELING

As with women, group counseling is one of the foundational pieces of addictions work. Much of the recovery process for girls happens in groups, and groups have the power to be empowering or dejecting. Empowerment groups provide girls the opportunity to find their voice, their sense of self, and their purpose. They also learn in what ways they have been oppressed, victimized, or manipulated (Toporek, Lewis, & Crethar, 2008). Part of that empowerment process is teaching clients to advocate for themselves and for what they need. As they learn this skill, they will be better able to heal, and navigate the social system that contributes to their addiction. There are three principles that have been related to self-advocacy in counseling: self-determination, empowerment, and social justice (Astramovich & Harris, 2007). As group leaders, in order to promote and teach self-advocacy, counselors must first teach members to be self-determining individuals. It is critical to teach group members to be more aware of their own needs, and develop skills for effectively communicating those needs. They must also learn to have their needs met without compromising the dignity of themselves or others (Astramovich & Harris). According to Astramovich and Harris, acquiring self-advocacy skills, particularly for clients of nondominant groups, means

a. value one's cultural identity,
b. identify personal and educational needs,
c. recognize the influence of social power structures in meeting needs, and

    d. assert and negotiate for one's needs in ways that promote the
      dignity and self-respect of all people. (p. 272)

What this means for group workers is encouraging group discussions, or perhaps activities that promote growth in individuals' cultural understandings, social issues, and of course, communication skills.

For groups with girls who are suffering from addiction, it is critical when running the groups to help the girls begin to see that their addiction is not a single affliction, but a symptom of many different issues. These issues will be different for each girl, but may include mental health concerns, peer relationship issues, family issues, pressures to fit in, and confusion over social roles and cultural concerns. The group process can allow for girls to begin to sort out the issues and learn the interplay between the components of their lives and their addiction. The group process can also help girls learn how to communicate and advocate for their needs, without damaging relationships.

One important point is group composition. In the previous chapter we discussed the importance of having single-gendered groups for women, and single-gender groups are critical for girls with addiction issues as well. Girls, like women, are socialized to act differently around adolescent boys, to be less open and to attempt to impress boys, or other girls in front of boys. Consideration should also be made for the high rates of sexual abuse and physical abuse that girls who suffer from addiction face, and most of those attackers are men. The sense of safety would not be the same in a mixed-gender group.

TREATMENT OUTCOMES

The literature on treatment outcomes for adolescent girls is sparse. According to SAMHSA (2007) in 2005 adolescent girls accounted for about 34% of the admissions for substance abuse treatment (they do not keep statistics on process addictions), and they were much more likely to enter treatment for alcohol abuse than for marijuana, which was adolescent males' drug of choice. They were also diagnosed as having a concurrent mental health concern at higher rates (18 to 23% higher than their male counterparts). What has been repeated in the literature is that the only thing we seem to know so far is that treatment for adolescents does seem better than no treatment, but is that effective treatment?

Part of the issue for adolescents is access and points of referral. Adolescents tend to receive referrals for treatment through either a court order or a member of the juvenile justice system. It then falls to those individuals to determine if an adolescent should receive substance abuse treatment or mental health treatment (Libby & Riggs, 2008). We have already discussed the importance of addressing both. For girls, it is not enough to only address the addiction and not look at the mental health and social system that brought them to that place of addiction. This is why the recidivism rates are so high. Treatment facilities that do both, and do them at the same time, tend to be much more effective. "Progress in research over the past decade indicates that the treatment of adolescents may be most effective when it addresses substance abuse, medical problems, psychiatric comorbidity, and psychosocial and family problems with an integrated or tightly coordinated approach" (Libby & Riggs, p. 446). While more research is needed, especially gender-specific research, there is progress being made toward understanding how counselors might best begin to help.

RELAPSE PREVENTION

Similar to the addictions process itself, there is very little research related to relapse in adolescents. In fact, Maisto, Pollock, Cornelius, Lynch, and Martin (2002) stated: "Although there has been a substantial amount of research on alcohol and drug relapse in adults in the last 20 years, there has been virtually no systematic research on relapse in adolescents" (p. 449). Some assumptions can be drawn based on what has been learned about why girls begin to use substances or engage in self-harming behaviors through either food or cutting behaviors. These addictions tend to occur, at their root, because girls are in need of connections to find their identity trying to fit in. This normal developmental struggle for some girls can lead to depression, anxiety, and addiction to cope. Like women, girls are brought to addiction through others, and providing that connection, that support, and resources to help them once the more intensive treatment has ended will be critical to preventing relapse. It is also important, like for women, to educate girls about the possibility of relapse, and that it is not the end of treatment but a signal to get help again. Let them know ahead of time that addiction does not mean failure and have systems in place to help support adolescent girl clients when needed.

LESBIAN, BISEXUAL, AND TRANSGENDERED GIRLS

For many adolescent girls the struggle to move into adulthood can be difficult, and some struggle more than others, but for one group of girls the struggle can be even more difficult. Adolescent girls that identify as lesbian, bisexual, or transgendered (LBT) have a unique set of issues that for many make coping with normal transitions very difficult. Adolescents with a marginalized sexual identity are at a higher risk for developing problems with substances than adolescents who have a dominant sexual identity (Jordan, 2000). This is likely due, in part, to the heterosexism that surrounds LBT adolescents (Jordan). Many of the risk factors are the same for LBT girls as they are for non-LBT girls; however, LBT girls do have some unique risk factors that Jordan described. These girls may feel marginalized by society and their peers, which may lead to feelings of depression and isolation, which may contribute to substance use for self-medication purposes. Similar to adult women, adolescent girls may also find themselves as part of the LBT youth culture, much of which is located around bars and clubs and supports the use of substances. In addition, LBT students may find themselves victimized at home or school.

A lack of safety at school has become a recent theme in the literature around LBT youth, and it is described by youth as very difficult. Girls often feel afraid all the time at school. They don't feel safe with other students, but they also do not feel safe with many of the teachers or administrators either. Imagine attending some place day after day being harassed, hit, threatened over and over with no one willing to put a stop to it because of your sexual identity. For many girls, the fear and stress lead to substances or self-harm behaviors in order to cope with the day-to-day pain.

For counselors working with LBT adolescents, the process is similar to that with LBT women, save one piece. Many times there can be a belief that adolescents cannot know that they are lesbian, bisexual, or transgendered. For some counselors, the instinct is to assume that they are experimenting and that they will outgrow these feelings. Teens are more than capable of knowing their sexual orientation at this age, and to discourage this, or tell them they will outgrow it, is demeaning and based on a heteronormative perspective that an individual is straight. Support them in learning about sexual identity, and when they talk about not feeling safe or supported at school, know that this is true and then strive to figure out how you can help.

CONCLUSION

Treating adolescent girls with addiction, whether it is substance addiction or process addiction, requires unique attention. It is critical that counselors consider the full picture of what is happening in the adolescent girl's life and the contributing factors to the addiction, then design a treatment plan and interventions that make sense for each individual client. Utilizing art or music can be a critical component of work with adolescents, as they both allow for a freer expression of emotion. Knowing when and how to involve the family is also a critical difference in treating adolescents. Most important is understanding that no matter if the addiction is food, self-harming behaviors, Internet use, or substance use, the treatment must start with what facilitated the addiction, helping girls reconnect to themselves and building that sense of self-efficacy.

Case Study

At age 17, Sheila often struggled to fit in. As an African American girl in a predominantly Caucasian school she had difficulty determining what type of clothes she should wear and what she should look like. She struggled with her body image, which was something new to her parents. Her mother never had an issue with her body image, as she grew up in a country where women were valued for being a healthy size and thinness was a sign of malnourishment. Sheila did not want to emulate the Caucasian ideal of thinness, but she also wanted to fit in with her friends. She began to diet, just like her friends. She also tried using laxatives to lose weight. After Sheila was raped, she decided that she did not want to be small; in fact, she decided that bigger was better. She wanted to make herself as unattractive as possible so that she would not be raped again. She began to eat as much as she could until she made herself sick. She often felt anxious around food and then around her family. She struggled to fit in anywhere.

Sheila's struggle to fit in with her peers is a process that many adolescent girls experience during high school. Yet, for girls who are of a nondominant culture, this process can be more difficult. Her attempt to balance between two cultural worlds and the messages about how she should be and look are quite daunting. Ultimately, like many adolescent girls, she chose to follow her friends. She found herself attempting to fit in to a cultural norm of thinness that is virtually unattainable, all the while putting her health at risk. This changed once she was raped. For many individuals who experience sexual assault or ongoing abuse, weight becomes a way of self-protection— a protective shield. Once again, she found herself in an unhealthy relationship with food and struggling between two cultures.

DISCUSSION QUESTIONS

1. How might you conceptualize Sheila's relationship with food. How does she utilize food to either cope, fit in, or defend herself? And how does her culture affect her disordered eating behaviors, or the way she might feel about her behavior?
2. In counseling Sheila, how might you think about her development, her mental health, and her social and cultural concerns? How might you balance all of them?
3. What difficulties might you have in working with Sheila at this point in time?

8

WOMEN IN LATE ADULTHOOD

Just as men's addiction has received more attention in the research literature than women's, older women receive far less attention in the literature than women under the age of 60. We are delighted to dedicate an entire chapter of our text to the addiction treatment needs of older women. In this chapter, we review the developmental and life span needs of women over the age of 60. We discuss specific concerns with regard to substances and processes of addiction, in particular alcohol, prescription medication, and gambling addictions. Finally, we offer specific treatment planning and relapse prevention recommendations for this population.

Older Americans are increasingly a significant percentage of the total population. In fact, this fastest growing population in the United States makes up 20% of the total population, and is expected to double by 2030 (Campbell, 2000). In 1994, Americans over age 60 numbered 33 million. Due to the aging of the baby boomer generation, this number is projected to reach 80 million by 2050 (Substance Abuse and Mental Health Services Administration [SAMHSA], 1998). And as the number of Americans over 60 increases, life expectancy is also on the rise. In 1970 life expectancy average was 68 years. By 1991 it was 72 years for men and 79 years for women (SAMHSA). In 2003, life expectancies for African American men and women were 69 and 76 years, respectively; for Caucasian men and women, 75 and 80 years (Arias, 2007). As more Americans live longer, and women outlive male partners, the number of older Americans experiencing addiction problems is likely to increase.

However, research literature about older Americans and addiction has lagged behind the population growth. Very little information exists about older women and drug or process addictions. What we do know is alcohol use and problems related to drinking appear to decline with age, and women in particular seem to be more likely to abstain from alcohol use in older age (Moos, Schutte, Brennan, & Moos, 2004). While this certainly bodes well overall for older women, it would be a mistake to assume that addiction problems are not worthy of concern for older women. With regard to alcohol, physical and psychological problems can occur even with smaller than expected amounts consumed. For example, "Average consumption of more than one drink per day predicted alcohol-related symptoms among adults over age 55" (Moos et al., p. 830).

LIFE SPAN DEVELOPMENT PERSPECTIVES

From a life span development perspective, life after age 60 is a time of "gradual disengagement and of cathexis with an earlier period; it is a period of aligning one's focus" (Campbell, 2008, p. 428). Traditional life span development theorists, including Erik Erikson, assert this is a period hallmarked by integrity, learning to live with life's successes and failures and to recognize the inherent dignity and worth of one's life (Campbell). For all the strengths of Erikson's developmental theory (and there are many), it must be remembered that his theory was developed from a male, heterosexual, Eurocentric perspective. Thus, Erikson's theory may have limited usefulness for women, particularly for women from non-Western cultures.

Carol Gilligan and other feminist critics assert that the process of developing intimacy takes far longer than its appointed stage period, and is perhaps more important for women's development than for men's. Furthermore, Gilligan states that connectedness rather than autonomy is particularly important for women (Wastell, 1996). So in working with older women, it is important to remember that many of the traditional assumptions about human development taught during a counseling program may possess limited application toward women clients. As with women clients of any age, addiction counselors should hasten to understand each client's personal and cultural worldview before, during, and after creating treatment goals and programs.

Feminist theories of development exist that shed light on women's specific developmental tasks in later life. Conarton and Kreger-Silverman describe the developmental stage of late life as a time of integration, when women become teachers and healers, maintaining both an inward and outward focus as they attempt to heal the damage caused by societal oppression (Wastell, 1996). In general, feminist developmental theories tend to focus on helping women rediscover their voice in a patriarchal culture that may not honor or nurture a woman's way of being. For older women, conceptualizing recovery from addiction as a process of self-healing is one way addiction counselors might implement these feminist concepts into the counseling relationship.

In the presence of increasing losses, older women may find it difficult to remain motivated and fully engaged in life. Losses include people, family, friends, and life partners as well as material things, such as income or independent housing. Reduction of independence and autonomy can significantly reshape the way older women perceive themselves. And for women in particular, loss of a youthful identity and the physical indicators of youth may be particularly difficult, as older women are burdened with negative perceptions from self and others in U.S. culture.

Due to these losses, self-motivation for healing and recovery may be difficult to maintain. Self-motivation is maintained through the satisfaction of three primary needs: competence, relatedness, and autonomy. These needs can be met through tasks, including ongoing community involvement via expression of personal abilities, developing and maintaining involvement with friends, family, and the larger community, and maintaining self-control as much as possible, either independently or with support (Campbell, 2008). As discussed previously in this text, developing client motivation and self-efficacy for change is an essential counselor task in the treatment of addiction. Thus, older adults may be handicapped in treatment if they feel their worth and value have been compromised by age. Neglecting this important counseling task can minimize or negate the positive impact of addiction counseling.

SOCIAL CONSTRUCTION OF AGE

In this text, we have discussed extensively issues of oppression experienced by women in general. Older women experience oppression because of age as well as gender. Similar to gender, roles and norms expected of older women are socially constructed. For example, in some cultures, such as Native American or traditional Japanese cultures, women are viewed as wise, powerful, and creative as they age, liberated from cultural sanctions placed on them as younger women (Crawford & Unger, 2004). However, in most Western cultures, including the United States, images and attitudes toward older women are not so positive.

While writing this text, one of the authors asked her 63-year-old mother how best to refer to women over the age of 60. After an eye-roll, she replied, "Just don't call us 'elderly.'" The mere mention of being aged is stigmatic and is cause for concern. Euphemisms such as "golden oldie" are used to lighten the burden of age. Even as women in our mid-30s, we (the authors) frequently encounter situations among peers where age is reluctantly discussed. It seems that aging is coupled with the burden of irrelevance, as though women stop being viable after the age of 35.

The stigma surrounding aging appears more significant for women than for men. In examining terms used to describe older people, those assigned to men imply tenacity and endurance, such as *old salt* and *old duffer*, while those assigned to women are less gracious: *crone* and *old hag*, for example (Crawford & Unger, 2004). When women internalize these names and concepts the aging process becomes stressful and one's sense of self-concept is diminished with the passing years.

Underneath the stereotypes aging has the potential to be a positive experience for some women. Studies demonstrate that women feel more certain about their identity and power in their 40s, 50s, and 60s than they did in their 20s. The only negative concern for aging women was concern about aging (Crawford & Unger, 2004), mirroring Roosevelt's famous quote, "There is nothing to fear but fear itself." In fact, many women report relief as they reach middle age, reveling in the freedom that comes from liberation from societal expectations regarding attractiveness and sexuality (Lips, 2006). So it seems that while stereotypes may not bear out in reality, belief in the stereotypes can create concern tainting the aging process before it has even begun.

These negative stereotypes can be defined as *ageism*, or "negative attitudes and behaviors targeting older people" (Crawford & Unger, 2004, p. 399). Some typical stereotypes for women include loss of attractiveness and sexuality, loss of perceived value, and loss of intelligence and capabilities. As a result, aging women are often treated with less care and attention in medical and counseling communities than younger women. For example, physicians may be more dismissive of symptoms reported by aging women than they would be of younger women with similar symptoms. With regard to addiction counseling, lower quality of life standards for those over age 60 may result in ignoring or minimizing the problem. Attitudes such as "What's the big deal? She's lived a long life, let her enjoy her cocktails/slot machines" may assist families or others in masking or minimizing a potentially problematic situation. Since some symptoms of addiction mimic other medical problems, physicians may fail to ask about substance abuse during examination, assuming the problem is medical and not addiction related (SAMHSA, 1998). An older woman feels liberated to "drink too much, use forbidden language, or dress in a way that pleases her ..." (Ward, 1996, as cited in Lips, 2006, p. 382). As with most aspects of addiction, there are positive and negative sides to this freedom. While liberation from social stigma around certain behaviors can certainly bring relief, liberation to drink to excess can have negative effects on older women because of biological changes that raise risks for health concerns.

Furthermore, research shows us many of our perceptions and assumptions about older women are culturally based. While women in the United States tend to perceive a loss of power and status as they age, women in other cultures (specifically, non-Western societies) enjoy seniority status, new roles, permission to participate in traditionally male-dominated decision-making processes, greater respect, and authority (Crawford & Unger, 2004). Clearly, what are assumed to be normal processes of aging in the United States are culturally specific and not shared by all cultures worldwide.

Even within the United States cultural norms about aging are not consistent from one generation to the next. When counseling older women, cohort experiences must be considered. Many assumptions about women's roles and social expectations are formed based on the generation in which they came of age. To demonstrate, consider the following contrast. Women in their 80s were born in the 1920s and came of age during WWII. These women may have worked in factories during the war, and experienced some level of self-sufficiency during that time. This was a period of migration from rural to urban life, so family and social networks may have been fractured in ways not experienced by previous generations. It is likely their work history was uneven due to shifting gender and family roles, resulting in lowered pension or social security payments. Conversely, women in their 60s who came of age during the 1960s (baby boomers) experienced a very different reality. Women of this generation had access to birth control and abortion, were better educated than previous generations, and likely had steadier career paths (Crawford & Unger, 2004). Similarly, alcohol use (for example) was very different from generation to generation: Use was less common in the 1930s to the 1950s than in the 1960s. Understanding cultural norms and values within and among generations is essential to accurate diagnosis and treatment planning (SAMHSA, 1998). Additionally, women had different cultural experiences based on their geographic location. Women coming of age in the 1960s living in Greenwich Village, New York City, had a very different experience than women living during the same time period in rural Illinois. All of these factors can have a significant impact on how women experience themselves and perceive their addictive behaviors.

SOCIAL DIFFICULTIES FOR OLDER WOMEN

Poverty issues are a significant stressor for many older women. "Thirteen percent of adults 65 or older are poor, and nearly three-quarters of this group are women" (Crawford & Unger, 2004, p. 420). Women are more likely to suffer from poverty in their later years than men for a variety of reasons: Gender roles generally favor men as family financial planners and breadwinners over women, women tend to outlive their male partners, and women tend to save less for retirement. In fact, widows have the lowest income of any group in the United States (Crawford & Unger). Lesbian couples and widows are further impacted by poverty as they lack civil and legal protection afforded heterosexual couples. Older women who are members of a racial or ethnic minority group are more likely to be living in poverty as well. Latino, African American, and Asian American older women are all more likely to be living in poverty than their Caucasian counterparts (Crawford & Unger).

Older women who lose a spouse through divorce or death, or who find themselves with an empty nest after the children leave home, may find themselves either on the cusp of potential self-discovery or entering a period of hardship. On the one hand, some women find this time in life to be a chance to redefine themselves, to accomplish personal goals and dreams without the encumbrances of family. However, women with fewer options or possibilities due to financial, social, or other limitations may simply feel a loss of identity and community (Lips, 2006). For these women in particular, addiction is a risky possibility, as older women may abuse substances to cope with loneliness. For older women coping with loneliness and addiction, supports within the community may provide benefit. For example, church and volunteer activities can provide a sense of generativity and community for older women. Extended family networks and support can also be an excellent resource for counselors, especially for women from ethnic minority groups who tend to value interdependence more so than Caucasian women (Crawford & Unger, 2004).

SUBSTANCE ABUSE PROBLEMS

Substance abuse among adults aged 60 and older has been described as "one of the fastest growing health problems facing the country" (SAMHSA, 1998). While most older women do not abuse illicit drugs, alcohol or prescription drug misuse, abuse, or dependence are of particular concern (National Center on Addiction and Substance Abuse [NCASA], 2006). Estimated as effecting 17% of older adults, substance abuse issues within this population were not discussed in the research literature until recent years (SAMHSA, 1998). This lack of attention is linked to ageist attitudes about older Americans. The assumption that "sweet old ladies" don't drink, use drugs, or gamble to excess flavors the interaction of doctors and counselors with their patients. Since older women experience increased internal and external stigmas about addiction due to both their age and their gender, they are less likely than younger women to admit they may have a problem. Finally, ageism is reflected in treatment attitudes overall for this population: that because they are older, women over 60 are not worth the time and money for treatment due to their shorter duration of life, and that addiction treatment for this population is ineffective and destined to fail (SAMHSA). Another way ageism surfaces in interactions with doctors and counselors is in professional dismissal of physical symptoms. In older women physical symptoms that mirror natural progression of aging, including tremors, memory loss, or sleepiness, may actually be symptoms of addiction (Campbell, 2008). Professionals may be quick to write off these symptoms as the natural progression of old age rather than an indicator of a more serious problem, such as addiction. All of these factors act as barriers for older women struggling with addiction issues.

Older adults experience depression and anxiety just as younger adults do, and these mental health concerns may be further complicated by the life circumstances that accompany age. Isolation, dwindling family and social networks, limited mobility, and fewer financial resources may compound concurrent disorders. Similar to younger women, older women may self-medicate using alcohol or other drugs in order to deal with negative feelings. Those who do are more likely to report greater isolation and lower life satisfaction (SAMHSA, 1998). Losses of community and autonomy may be predictors for addiction problems, as older women withdraw from normal routines and relationships that act as a natural monitor for problems (Campbell, 2008). For example, many addicted individuals are "found out" by coworkers, bosses, family members, or friends in religious communities. In the absence of these interactions, addiction problems are more likely to go unnoticed.

Alcohol

Alcohol abuse and dependence are the leading substance abuse concerns among older adults. While exact numbers are difficult to determine, approximately 37% of women aged 60 to 85+ engage in alcohol use (Stevenson & Masters, 2005). Up to 10% of older Americans engage in heavy or problematic alcohol use, while 2 to 4% meet criteria for alcohol dependence (Brennan, Schutte, & Moos, 2005). About 12% of older women engage in drinking behaviors that exceed the limits (one drink per day) suggested by the National Institute on Alcohol Abuse and Alcoholism (NIAAA; SAMHSA, 1998). In spite of data that indicate that drinking among older Americans presents a significant public health problem, older adults are less likely to receive the diagnosis of alcoholism than younger adults (SAMHSA). Additionally, nurses and doctors who are often the first line of contact for older women experiencing alcohol problems are often uninformed about detecting alcohol problems (Stevenson & Masters, 2005). This oversight can occur for many reasons, including perceptions of older adults as nonsubstance users and misdiagnosing side effects of alcohol use as normal indicators of aging.

Another reason drinking in older women is often overlooked is because women tend to drink less than men overall; in fact, women drink only about 50 to 60% as much alcohol as men (Stevenson & Masters, 2005). One study demonstrated that in a mixed-gender study of older-aged drinkers, when a decline in drinking was documented among study participants, the decline was attributed solely to the women participants (Moos et al., 2004). This indicates that older women are more likely to naturally reduce alcohol consumption or to abstain altogether from drinking once they reach age 60. While these data certainly inform, they are somewhat dangerous, as counselors might assume this means alcohol abuse or dependence is not necessarily problematic for older women clients. As previously mentioned, the current cohort of older adults was born shortly after Prohibition. Thus, these women entered adulthood during the 1950s and 1960s, as alcohol use grew increasingly acceptable. Due to this shift in social norms regarding alcohol, these women may be at greater risk for alcohol problems (Moos et al.).

There are several predictors for possible alcohol addiction counselors should consider when treating older clients. These include being male, earlier problem drinking behaviors, a community that supports drinking, multiple social stressors, financial problems, loss of a friend or spouse due to death, and use of avoidance as a primary coping mechanism (Brennan & Moss, 1997; Moos et al., 2004). Among older women, a history of heavier drinking, and having a partner, family, or friends who support drinking behaviors are likely to be linked to alcohol problems. Additionally, women who use psychoactive medications, who self-medicate with over-the-counter medications, who drink excessive amounts of coffee, who use alcohol to fall asleep, or who smoke cigarettes are also more likely to engage in problematic drinking behaviors (Moos et al.; Stevenson & Masters, 2005).

One of the most important considerations when assessing alcohol use in older adults is whether their drinking behaviors are early-onset or late-onset. While overall drinking behaviors seem to decline for most aging adults, for some problems become apparent after age 60. Age of onset is a particularly important consideration for women. Although most men with problematic alcohol use behaviors begin abusing alcohol around age 17, for most women, age of first alcohol abuse is after 30 (NCASA, 2006). Thus, women are more likely than men to develop alcohol problems well into adulthood. Most older adults who experience alcohol problems are early-onset problem drinkers, and experience problems related to their alcohol consumption for most of their adult lives. Their alcohol use evolves into a lifelong coping mechanism and often pairs with a mental health diagnosis. Early-onset problem drinkers who engage in problem drinking into adulthood will likely continue into old age. On the other hand, late-onset problem drinkers (more likely to be women) typically drink in response to one discrete life stressor, such as the death of a spouse. As opposed to early-onset problem drinkers, late-onset drinkers do not have a lifetime history of alcohol use as a coping mechanism. These individuals tend to be more physically and psychologically healthy than early-onset problem drinkers, and often their drinking behaviors resolve themselves without formal intervention (SAMHSA, 1998).

Care and attention are needed when diagnosing late-onset problem drinkers. Often, late-onset problem drinkers are overlooked because they appear too healthy to be alcoholics. However, late-onset problem drinking is a significant problem in particular for older widowed women who are more likely to be isolated from community. While older men are more likely to have early-onset problem drinking and a history of treatment or legal intervention, older women who are late-onset problem drinkers suffer in isolation without receiving appropriate counseling (SAMHSA, 1998). It is important to note that telescoping occurs in older women populations just as it does in younger women: So even though older women may begin drinking later than their male counterparts, they may develop problem drinking behaviors and related health outcomes more quickly (Satre, Blow, Chi, & Weisner, 2007).

Alcohol can have a greater negative impact on older women than on younger women due to changes in body composition (lower water ratios) and decreasing ability to metabolize alcohol in the digestive tract. Consequently, older women have increased sensitivity to the harmful effects of alcohol consumption on organs, including the liver, heart, and brain. Older women also have heightened sensitivity to the effects of alcohol and lower tolerance, resulting in falls and accidents (SAMHSA, 1998; Stevenson & Masters, 2005).

In addition to these general concerns, alcohol has other deleterious effects on older women. First, when alcohol is combined with prescription medications, it can enhance or diminish the effects of these medications. Similarly, alcohol consumption concurrent with existing medical problems can exacerbate symptoms and worsen medical conditions. These conditions include heart problems (e.g., hypertension or myocardial infarction), stroke, immune system deficiencies, liver disease, weakened bone density, mental health problems, gastrointestinal bleeding, and malnutrition. Thus, screening older women clients for alcohol use and abuse can assist in managing other medical problems that may already be present. Finally, chronic, long-term alcohol use can also have a negative impact on the older brain, preceding such conditions as cognitive impairment, alcohol-related dementia, Alzheimer's disease, sleep disturbance, and suicidal behavior (SAMHSA, 1998; Stevenson & Masters, 2005).

Alcohol may be used to manage pain. Older adults may self-medicate in order to deal with the physical pain as well as the stress it causes. One study demonstrated that among older Americans with problem drinking, about 57% used alcohol to manage pain, compared to only 21% of nonproblem drinkers (Brennan et al., 2005).

It is important to note that in spite of the many negative effects of alcohol use on older women, there are some small benefits of drinking for this population. Namely, moderate alcohol consumption seems to improve high-density lipoprotein (HDL) levels in women, and may have cardiovascular benefits, though further study is warranted (SAMHSA, 1998). In spite of these benefits, women who have a history of substance abuse or addiction, or who appear to be experiencing negative side effects from alcohol consumption, should drink with great care.

In addition to biological antecedents and consequences, certain social conditions can exacerbate older women's alcohol use. Older women with alcohol problems are more likely to partner with a male who also experiences problem drinking, to be a widow, to experience depression, and to suffer injury in a fall (SAMHSA, 1998). This information parallels that of women in other age groups who often feel influenced by their male partner's addictive behaviors and who experience accidental injury as a result of their behaviors. Finally, moderate alcohol consumption appears to have a social benefit for women in that it offers an option to engage in community with others (SAMHSA, 1998). Older women might engage in drinking behaviors in order to feel connected with others in spite of negative consequences.

Personal and environmental factors interact in complex ways to create conditions for problem drinking in older women. Women who tend to deal with stressful events or problems through avoidance, who are dealing with negative life situations, and who live in an environment where drinking is encouraged and alcohol is available may fall victim to problem drinking behaviors (Brennan & Moss, 1997).

Prescription Medications

Prescription drug abuse and addiction are growing public health concerns in the United States, and older adults are the most vulnerable population within this trend (National Institute on Drug Abuse [NIDA], 2005). Among older women, prescription drug abuse and dependence are the most significant substance use problems (NCASA, 2006). Older adults are at risk for developing an addiction to prescription medication for several reasons. First, older adults are much more likely to be prescribed psychoactive medication than their younger counterparts. Adults over age 65 are the leading consumers of prescription medication in the United States. Eighty-three percent of adults over aged 65 take at least one prescription medication, and 30% of these adults take eight or more prescription medications (SAMHSA, 1998). Women over the age of 59 take an average of five prescription medications simultaneously. In a recent survey, physicians estimated that among their older women patients, approximately 11% misused or abused prescription medication. While rates of addiction are relatively low for this population (0.2% for women and 0.4% for men), women over age 65 do seem slightly more likely to have misused or abused prescription drugs than men (3.9% vs. 2.9%) (NCASA, 2006). With increased drug use comes increased likelihood of drug interaction, adverse medical effects, abuse, and addiction. Side effects may include confusion, depression, memory loss, an increased likelihood of accidents, and drowsiness (NCASA, 2006), all of which may be written off by doctors and family members as the natural effects of aging. As described previously, this population is particularly vulnerable because social isolation can make it difficult for loved ones or medical providers to determine whether substance abusive behaviors are taking place.

A second reason older adults are more likely to experience prescription drug abuse or dependence is because many drugs prescribed to this population are mood altering or psychoactive. Prescription medications for sleep disorders, chronic pain, or mood disorders often carry the risk of abuse or dependence if used incorrectly. For example, about one-quarter to one-third of all tranquilizer prescriptions are written for older adults. Once prescribed these medications, older adults are more likely to use them over longer periods of time than their younger counterparts, increasing the likelihood of addictive tendencies (SAMHSA, 1998). In summary, the frequency, type, and duration of prescription medications all create a vulnerable and potentially dangerous situation for older adults.

Generally, older adults who abuse or become addicted to psychoactive medications do so unintentionally. Problems emerge for two primary reasons. First, patterns of use can lead to problematic use. Unlike younger people, older adults do not tend to abuse prescription drugs for recreational use. Instead, misuse occurs because older patients may not understand directions for dosage, have multiple physicians who are unaware of other prescriptions, or take more than necessary for longer periods of time in order to achieve the desired effect. Since older adults are often more vulnerable physiologically than younger adults, adverse affects of abuse or dependence may emerge more quickly. "In other words, [older] adults can become dependent on psychoactive medications without realizing it" (SAMHSA, 1998, p. 31). Likewise, there are differences within older adults: Medication that is appropriate for a 65-year-old may not be appropriate for an 85-year-old (Young, 2002).

A second reason older adults are at risk for developing addiction to psychoactive medications is systemic problems within the medical community that may result in improper medication management. Specifically, doctors may order medications without completing a thorough diagnostic exam, order too high a dosage for too long a period of time, fail to fully inquire about medications already taken by a patient, prescribe unnecessary medication, or not clearly explain the regimen for medication administration (DATA, 2006; SAMHSA, 1998). Similarly, many physicians lack training in geriatric medication management, and might unwittingly prescribe medications harmful or inappropriate for aging patients (Young, 2002). Another risk is that signs of addiction (alcoholism or prescription drug dependence, for example) among older patients can often mimic signs of depression. Thus, physicians who have not fully explored the likelihood of addiction in older patients may prescribe an antidepressant to manage symptoms, exacerbating the substance abuse/dependence problem (NCASA, 2006).

There are specific risk factors that may exacerbate the likelihood of prescription medication abuse or dependence. In particular, old age, declining physical health, and being female all potentially contribute to problematic use. Older women are the demographic group most likely to be prescribed psychoactive medication, to take medications for long periods of duration, and to be prescribed more than one medication at a time (NCASA, 2006). For example, older women are twice as likely as older men to be diagnosed with an anxiety disorder, occurring in part because of bereavement and loneliness following the loss of a spouse. Lowered economic status and social supports can further contribute to anxiety disorders. Once diagnosed, older women with anxiety disorders may be prescribed psychoactive medications that can ultimately be misused. Furthermore, "among older women, use of psychoactive drugs is correlated with middle- and late-life divorce, widowhood, less education, poorer health and chronic somatic problems, higher stress, lower income, and more depression and anxiety" (SAMHSA, 1998, p. 32). A mismanaged psychiatric diagnosis is one example of how older women may be overprescribed dangerous drugs.

Drugs of Abuse

Very little research has been done on older adults who abuse or become addicted to substances. This section will present a brief overview of some of the major categories of prescription drugs. For a fuller description, readers are directed to the SAMHSA publication *Substance Abuse Among Older Adults* (1998).

Benzodiazepines, or central nervous system (CNS) depressants, entered the health care scene in the 1950s and have gradually come to partially replace their older, more addictive predecessors, barbiturates. The SAMSHA report on substance abuse among older adults (1998) cites benzodiazepine use/abuse/addiction as an area of particular concern for counselors and the medical community due to frequency of prescription for older adults, who have greater physiological vulnerability for abuse. A recent NIDA report supported these findings, and found that benzodiazepine abuse and dependence continue to be significant public health concerns (2005). There exists particular risk for women, as long-term users (more than one year) of benzodiazepines are likely to be over age 45 and female. Long-term effects of use include impaired memory and concentration, lowered motor and cognitive functioning, and increased risk for accidental injury (SAMHSA, 1998). Long-term benzodiazepines use can result in dependence, and withdrawal can be painful and dangerous, especially for older adults. Withdrawal symptoms can mimic the original symptoms that resulted in the prescription of the medication, including anxiety, sleep disturbance, and panic. Tapered withdrawal over several weeks or months is recommended to minimize the effects of withdrawal, though withdrawal symptoms often persist regardless (SAMHSA, 1998).

Sedatives may be prescribed to help older adults deal with insomnia. Sleep patterns naturally alter as people age, often resulting in fewer hours of quality, deep sleep. Once again, women are more likely to experience sleep disturbance than men, and thus are at risk for overusing sedatives. The most prescribed sedatives include benzodiazepines, imidazopyridine (Ambien), or antihistamines, often found in allergy medications or nighttime pain relievers. Even over-the-counter medications can become dangerous or addictive if used too frequently or for too long a duration. Therefore, information and education about good sleep hygiene can benefit older clients (SAMHSA, 1998).

Opioids, though rarely prescribed for chronic pain management, are still worthy of attention because of their addictive properties. In particular, these medications may be prescribed to treat pain related to cancer or other advanced diseases. Once again, older adults are more vulnerable to side effects and addiction because of developmental physiological changes. Withdrawal from opioids, though less severe than withdrawal from benzodiazepines, may include flu-like symptoms, such as nausea, vomiting, fever, muscle aches and diarrhea, insomnia, restlessness, and dysphoric mood (SAMHSA, 1998). While opioids can be used to successfully manage long-term pain problems, patients and clients should be educated about side effects and risks of addiction via misuse.

PROCESS ADDICTION PROBLEMS

Gambling

Very little research exists about the effects of compulsive gambling behaviors on older women. In fact, much of the research that does exist shows minimal or no particular negative effects for older women when compared with their younger counterparts. However, several compelling reasons to consider the potential negative effects of gambling on older adults exist. First, the percentage of older Americans has grown significantly over the past several decades, and growth will continue as the baby boomer generation moves into retirement. In 2000, 12.6% of Americans were over the age of 65; by 2010 this percentage will have risen to 13.2%, and by 2020, 16.5% (Stitt, Giacopassi, & Nichols, 2003). In addition to growing numbers, older adults are also enjoying longer, healthier lives than any other generation in American history. Thus, older adults will increasingly become a focus of counseling literature, research, and theoretical practice. Understanding potentially destructive gambling behaviors needs to be a part of that ongoing discussion.

Second, gambling is more accessible than ever before. Forty-seven states have legal gambling; lotteries exist in 37 states, off-track betting sites in 40 states, and casino gambling in 28 states (Stitt et al., 2003). With accessibility comes greater potential for compulsive use.

Additionally, gambling institutions have specifically targeted older adults as a rich customer base, offering free bus transportation, hotel and dining discounts, entertainment discounts, and discounts on prescription medication, marketed in community living environments for retired Americans. These tactics make gambling even more accessible for older adults. Among this population, women make up a higher proportion of gamblers than men (Stitt et al.).

Often, older adults who gamble began gambling later in life, and thus may develop compulsive gambling behaviors without detection from friends or family members. Additionally, these older adults may have limited life experience with gambling, and may be less able to note compulsive behaviors in themselves. Older adults may also experience specific health and psychological problems related to problem gambling. These include health consequences of sedentary activity (such as sitting at a slot machine for hours at a time) and secondhand smoke present in some casinos. Other physical consequences include cardiovascular symptoms, musculoskeletal problems, and gastrointestinal issues. Psychological problems include depression, anxiety, and substance use disorders, though at lower rates than in younger problem gamblers (Erickson, Molina, Ladd, Pietrzak, & Petry, 2005).

Gambling is often the primary recreational activity for older adults, particularly for women who have been widowed or who lack community connections (Moufakkir, 2006). These gamblers often have a fixed life savings that may be in jeopardy if gambling becomes problematic ("Problem Gambling Shown to Affect All Ages," 1994). While documented rates of problematic gambling among older adults indicate it is still rare in the United States (ranging from 0.4 to 0.7%), there are still conditions that indicate problematic gambling is an area worthy of clinical attention. Between 1975 and 1998, the rates of individuals 65 and older who reported having gambled rose from 35% to 80% (Erickson et al., 2005). As access to gambling increases, the proportion of older adults in the United States increases, and as marketing to older adults becomes more sophisticated, the rates of problem gambling among older women may increase.

TREATMENT CONSIDERATIONS FOR OLDER WOMEN

Even though addictive behaviors cause significant negative impact to older women, fewer than 1% of the 2 million older women who might benefit from treatment for alcohol disorders actually receive help (NCASA, 2006). In addition, the unique needs of older women may be neglected in treatment programs, as only 20% have services specific to older adults, and fewer still specific services for older women. This is problematic because:

Particularly relevant for treatment programs, older women may have differences in clinical characteristics and outcomes compared with older men. As with other age groups, older women often have later onset of alcohol problems, more vulnerability to addiction stigma, and greater use of prescription drugs. (Satre et al., 2007, p. 216)

Thus, as we've determined for women across the age spectrum, specializing service delivery for older women is critical to their success in addiction counseling treatment.

Doctors and physicians are often the first line of defense for older women who are experiencing addiction issues. Due to the social stigma that exists for older women who drink, use drugs, or engage in process addiction, these women may experience reluctance in seeking help from an addiction counseling agency or may feel out of place if that agency does not have services specific to older women. Consequently, a doctor's assistance may be sought to deal with the physical ramifications of addiction. However, those in the medical profession may not be trained to screen for addiction issues. For example, among women over age 65, only 17% were asked about their alcohol consumption during routine checkups (NCASA, 2006). Doctors are also less likely to invest time educating older women patients about the dangers of smoking, alcohol use, or prescription medication abuse. Therefore, even generally well-informed women may be ignorant of the dangers inherent in addictive behaviors.

For counselors, screening can be a difficult task, as many of the criteria for substance dependence as outlined by the DSM-IV-TR do not correctly identify symptoms of older adults. Common examples of how symptomology becomes more complicated for older adults (SAMHSA, 1998; Turner, 2003) include the following:

- Tolerance is more difficult to track as older women may have particular sensitivity to substances, more so than younger women or men.
- Withdrawal symptoms may not manifest because often late-onset addicts do not develop physiological dependence.
- Taking larger amounts than intended may happen not because substance dependence has developed, but because cognitive impairment limits ability to monitor substance intake.

- Older adults who spend excessive amounts of time obtaining substances and recovering from the effects of substance may be experiencing these negative effects at lower doses relative to their younger counterparts.
- Giving up activities due to use is a common symptom of addiction; however, older adults may have fewer activities to give up and fewer people to interact with, and thus detection may be difficult.
- Many addicts continue to use substances despite negative physical or psychological effects. Medical personnel may misdiagnose older adults, mistaking symptoms of addiction for other medical problems. As a result, these clients may be unaware of the side effects of addiction.

Since social networks are so influential for older women, finding a network of friends and companions who do not support the use of alcohol can be integral to assisting women in reducing alcohol use or abstaining from use altogether. Informal networks (such as help from family and friends or community groups such as Alcoholics Anonymous [AA] or Women for Sobriety) may be more effective for this population than formal services (Moos et al., 2004).

If older women have late-onset addictive behaviors (rather than lifelong problems), then brief, motivationally oriented interventions may be most effective (SAMHSA, 1998). Since these women tend to be more psychologically healthy than lifelong substance abusers or addicts, they are more likely to respond favorably to social pressure to alter behavior, thus shortening the course of treatment.

Recommendations for counselors providing addiction counseling for older women include the following (Campbell, 2008; NCASA, 2006):

- General awareness of issues around addiction and the aging process
- Assessing and addressing environmental factors that may impact addiction, including issues of oppression, poverty, disability, and isolation
- Counseling from a nonconfrontational, supportive perspective
- Providing social and medical support
- Acting as a conduit to other services and community agencies while becoming involved in the client's world outside the counseling setting
- Protecting clients from abuse from family, or assisting in building stronger relationships with healthy, supportive family members
- Allowing the duration and frequency of counseling to evolve as necessary. For example, clients may need more frequent contact

at the outset (more than the traditional once per week session), then less frequent contact as conditions improve.

- Maintaining contact with clients who seem to be making little or no progress
- Case management services to increase access to housing, financial, and nutrition support
- Single-gender groups, as older women are likely to defer to male wishes in group counseling settings
- Clinical focus on issues around loss, grief, and loneliness

TREATMENT OUTCOMES

Older women experiencing addiction face specific barriers to entering treatment, as described previously. However, they tend to experience success following treatment, perhaps because of some of the same socialized gender traits that inhibited entering treatment in the first place. As we mentioned, older women tend to feel particular stigma regarding their addiction, and are often reluctant and ashamed to enter treatment. However, older women are also more likely to complete treatment and to maintain abstinence for up to five years after treatment (Satre et al., 2007). This may be because gender expectations have again been met for these women; thus, sobriety is supported by social expectations. Since length of stay in treatment is one of the strongest indicators for long-term abstinence, the fact that women tend to complete treatment more frequently than men bodes well for the health and psychological benefits that come from recovery.

Studies have determined that among older women and men who do not achieve abstinence after treatment, women have reduced their drinking more than men. Since a reduction of heavy drinking can bring health benefits, this is still a positive outcome for older women. One negative finding has been that older adults are less likely to make use of 12-Step meetings or other support groups in the community. As noted previously, social support and connection are particularly important for older women in recovery. Therefore, ongoing involvement in community-based recovery communities could be of benefit (Satre et al., 2007). Counselors can encourage and support older women clients in accessing these groups, and can include alternatives to traditional AA groups, such as Women for Sobriety.

CONCLUSION

Little clinical or research attention has been given to older women who struggle with addiction. Social stereotypes of the aging may inhibit these women from seeking treatment, or may allow clinicians, friends, and family to dismiss symptoms. Though older women are not among the most likely to develop an addiction, it would be professionally negligent to ignore the needs of this population. Alcohol use, prescription drug use, and gambling are among the areas of greatest concern. Specific treatment considerations for older women may increase treatment success.

Case Study

As Sheila ages, her substance use-related problems age along with her. After the death of her husband shortly after his retirement, Sheila finds herself feeling quite alone. Her children are both grown and established in their own lives. She no longer has a workplace to go to. While she engages in some community involvement, including church and volunteer work, she finds herself alone most of the time. After a lifetime surrounded by family, Sheila struggles with intense loneliness and isolation. She feels her identity has shifted so dramatically, she barely knows herself anymore. She begins drinking a cocktail in the evening to cheer herself up and to fend off the creeping sense of sadness she feels at the end of the day. She also obtains another pain medication from a doctor who fails to investigate her medical history fully. Fearful of a significant relapse, Sheila finds a local Women for Sobriety group that facilitates her ongoing recovery and gives her a sense of community.

At this point in her life Sheila may be reluctant to seek counseling for her relapsing addiction due to feelings of shame and stigma. Older women often feel they should "be over it" with regard to addictive behaviors, or have not experienced addiction before in their lives and are confused by their own actions. More than likely, if Sheila were to seek professional help at this time, she would go first to her doctor to discuss her symptoms, and perhaps later to a counselor for further assistance. However, older women often feel out of place in traditional group counseling as offered by most outpatient addiction treatment facilities. They may not feel their life stage concerns are echoed by other members of the group, and may feel out of place as the oldest member. Furthermore, older women struggling with addiction often have milder symptoms than younger addicts, and fewer life consequences. Traditional therapies may feel too "hardcore" for someone like Sheila. Sheila would benefit from community support (like Women for Sobriety) for her addiction, as well as activities that can help her reestablish a positive identity now that her family is no longer the center of her life. It is also possible that Sheila may benefit from financial counseling to assist her in establishing a budget that can see her through her remaining years.

DISCUSSION QUESTIONS

1. What are some preconceived notions you hold about people over the age of 60? What kind of role models have you had in your own life with regard to aging? How do you feel about your own aging process?

2. Often younger counselors have difficulty developing empathy for older clients. What are some actions you might take to increase your own empathic understanding for older clients, or what are some ways you can encourage empathy in your fellow counselors?

3. Often, older clients are more comfortable going to doctors or other medical professionals rather than counselors to address their addiction issues. Discuss current social norms and attitudes that may contribute to this situation. What societal attitudes contribute to older clients seeking medical care before counseling? What barriers exist to inhibit older clients from seeking counseling in the first place?

REFERENCES

Ackard, D. M., Fulkerson, J. A., & Neumark-Sztainer, D. (2007). Prevelence and utility of DSM-IV eating disorder diagnostic criteria among youth. *International Journal of Eating Disorders, 40,* 409–417.

Alcoholics Anonymous (AA). (2001). *The big book* (4th ed.). Retrieved July 8, 2008, from http://www.aa.org/bigbookonline/en_tableofcnt.cfm

Alleyne, V., & Rheineck, J. E. (2008). People of color and addictions. In D. Capuzzi & M. Stauffer (Eds.), *Foundations of addiction counseling* (pp. 348–365). Boston: Pearson Education.

Allison, S. E., von Wahlde, L., Shockley, T., & Gabbard, G. O. (2006). The development of the self in the era of the Internet and role-playing fantasy games. *American Journal of Psychiatry, 163,* 381–385.

Amen, D. G. (1998). *Change your brain, change your life.* New York: Times Books.

American Academy of Child and Adolescent Psychiatry (AACAP). (2008). Retrieved October 8, 2008, from www.aacap.org

American Lung Association (2008). CDC study shows youth smoking figures have stagnated. Retrieved on March 8, 2009 from: http://www.lungusa.org/site/apps/nlnet/content3.aspx?=dvLUK9O0E&b=4785835&c=5611169

American Psychiatric Association (APA). (2000). *Diagnostic and statistical manual of mental disorders* (4th ed., text rev.). Washington, DC: Author.

American Psychological Association (APA). (2007). *Report of the APA task force on the sexualization of girls.* Washington, DC: APA.

American Society of Addiction Medicine (ASAM). Retrieved September 15, 2008, from www.asam.org/patientplacmentcriteria.html

American Yoga Association (AYA). (n.d.). What is yoga? Retrieved July 9, 2008, from http://www.americanyogaassociation.org/general.html#WhatisYoga

Angove, R., & Fothergill, A. (2003). Women and alcohol: Misrepresented and misunderstood. *Journal of Psychiatric and Mental Health Nursing, 10*, 213–219.

Apodaca, T. R., & Miller, W. R. (2003). A meta-analysis of the effectiveness of bibliotherapy for alcohol problems. Journal of Clinical Psychology, 59, 289–304.

Arias, E. (2007, March 28). United States Life Tables, 2003. *National Vital Statistics Report, 54*(14), 1–40.

Astramovich, R. L., & Harris, K. R. (2007). Promoting self-advocacy among minority students in school counseling. *Journal of Counseling and Development*, 85, 269–276.

Back, S. E., Sonne, S. C., Killeen, T., Dansky, B. S., & Brady, K. T. (2003). Comparative profiles of women with PTSD and comorbid cocaine or alcohol dependence. American Journal of Drug and Alcohol Abuse, 29, 169–189.

Baldwin, J. A., Johnson, R. M., Gotz, N. K., Wayment, H. A., & Elwell, K. (2006). Perspectives of college students and their primary health care providers on substance abuse screening and intervention. *Journal of American College Health, 55*, 115–119.

Beard, K. W. (2005). Internet addiction: A review of current assessment techniques and potential assessment questions. *CyberPsychology and Behavior, 8*, 7–14.

Blake, S. M., Amaro, H., Schwartz, P. M., & Flinchbaugh, L. J. (2001). A review of substance abuse prevention interventions for young adolescent girls. *Journal of Early Adolescence, 21*, 294–324.

Bradford, J. W., & Petrie, T. A. (2008). Sociocultural Factors and the Development of Disordered Eating: A Longitudinal Analysis of Competing Hypotheses. *Journal of Counseling Psychology, 55*(2), 246–262.

Brecher, E. M. (1972). *The consumer's union report on licit and illicit drugs.* Retrieved July 20, 2007, from http://www.druglibrary.org/SCHAFFER/library/studies/cu/cu8.html

Brennan, P. L., Schutte, K. K., & Moos, R.H. (2005). Pain and the use of alcohol to manage pain: Prevalence and 3-year outcomes among older problem and non-problem drinkers. *Addiction, 100*, 777–786.

Bride, B. E. (2001). Single-gender treatment of substance abuse: Effect on treatment retention and completion. *Social Work Research, 25*, 223–232.

Briggs, C. A., & Pehrsson, D. E. (2008). Use of bibliotherapy in the treatment of grief and loss: A guide to current counseling practices. *Adultspan Journal, 7*, 32–42.

Brown University. (2006, February). Frail, elderly patients and unnecessary drug use. *The Brown University Geriatric Psychopharmacology Update*, 3–4.

Burrow-Sanchez, J. J. (2006). Understanding adolescent substance abuse: Prevalence, risk factors, and clinical implications. *Journal of Counseling and Development, 84*, 283–290.

Camilleri, V. (2000). Music therapy groups: A path to social-emotional growth and academic success. *Educational Horizons, 78*, 184–189.

Campbell, J. W. (2008). *Addictions across the life span.* (D. Capuzzi, & M. D. Stauffer, Eds.). Boston: Pearson Education, Inc.

Campbell, N. D. (2000). *Using women: Gender, drug policy, and social justice.* New York: Routledge.

Centers for Disease Control and Prevention (CDC). (n.d.). Smoking & tobacco use. Retrieved February 6, 2008, from http://www.cdc.gov/tobacco/index.htm

Chen, X., Tyler, K. A., Whitbeck, L. B., & Hoyt, D. R. (2004). Early sexual abuse, street adversity, and drug use among female homeless and runaway adolescents in the Midwest. *Journal of Drug Issues, 34,* 1–22.

Chi, F. W., Sterling, S., & Weisner, C. (2006). Adolescents with co-occurring substance use and mental conditions in a private managed care health plan: Prevalence, patient characteristics and treatment initiation and engagement. *American Journal on Addictions, 15,* 67–79.

Clark, D. B., De Bellis, M. D., Lynch, K. G., Cornelius, J. R., & Martin, C. S. (2003). Physical and sexual abuse, depression and alcohol use disorders in adolescents: Onsets and outcomes. *Drug and Alcohol Dependence, 69,* 51–60.

Collins, P. H. (2000). *Black feminist thought: Knowledge, consciousness, and the politics of empowerment* (2nd ed.). New York: Routledge.

Colton, P. A., Olmsted, M. P., & Rodin, G. M. (2007). Eating disturbances in a school population of preteen girls: Assessment and screening. *International Journal of Eating Disorders, 40,* 435–440.

Cook, L. S., Epperson, L., & Gariti, P. (2005). Determining the need for gender-specific chemical dependence treatment: Assessment of treatment variables. *American Journal on Addictions, 14,* 328–338.

Cornelius, J. R., & Clark, D. B. (2008). Depressive disorders and adolescent substance use disorders. In Y. Kaminer & O. G. Bukstein (Eds.), *Adolescent substance abuse: Psychiatric comorbidity and high-risk behaviors* (pp. 221–242). New York: Routledge.

Courbasson, C. M. A., de Sorkin, A. A., Dullerud, B., & Van Wyk, L. (2007). Acupuncture treatment for women with concurrent substance use and anxiety/depression: An effective alternative therapy? *Family Community Health, 30,* 112–120.

Covington, S. (2008). *Helping women recover: A program for treating addiction* (rev. ed.). San Francisco: Jossey-Bass.

Covington, S., & Surrey, J. (1997). The relational model of women's psychological development: Implications for substance abuse. In S. Wilsnack & R. Wilsnack (Eds.), *Gender and alcohol: Individual and social perspectives.* (pp. 335–351) New Brunswick, NJ: Rutgers Center of Alcohol Studies.

Crawford, M., & Unger, R. (2004). *Women and gender: A feminist psychology* (4th ed.). Boston: McGraw-Hill.

Dansky, B. S., Byrne, C. A., & Brady, K. T. (1999). Intimate violence and post-traumatic stress disorder among individuals with cocaine dependence. *American Journal of Drug and Alcohol Abuse, 25,* 257–268.

DATA. (2005). New research suggests a relationship between intimate partner violence and crack or marijuana use. *Brown University Digest of Addiction Theory and Application, 7,* 6.

DATA. (2006, November). Alcohol problems contribute to physical violence, psychological aggression. *Brown University Digest of Addiction Theory and Application, 25,* 4–5.

DATA. (2002). Problem gambling: Gambling patterns and problems differ by gender. *Brown University Digest of Addiction Theory and Application, 21,* 1–7.

DATA. (2007, February). Study: Smoking primes teen brain for addiction. *Brown University Digest of Addiction Theory and Application, 26,* 8.

DATA. (2007, July). More teen girls than boys abusing prescription drugs. *Brown University Digest of Addiction Theory and Application, 26,* 8.

Denning, P., Little, J., & Glickman, A. (2004). *Over the influence: The harm reduction guide for managing drugs and alcohol.* New York: Guilford Press.

Devaud, L. L., Risinger, F. O., & Selvage, D. (2006). Impact of the hormonal milieu on the neurobiology of alcohol dependence and withdrawal. *Journal of General Psychology, 133,* 337–356.

Deykin, E. Y., & Buka, S. L. (1997). Prevalence and risk factors for posttraumatic stress disorder among chemically dependent adolescents. *American Journal of Psychiatry, 154,* 752–757.

DiClemente, C. C. (2003). *Addiction and change: How addictions develop and addicted people recover.* New York: Guilford Press.

Drug and Alcohol Services Information System (DASIS). (2006). *Facilities offering special programs or groups for women.* Retrieved November 17, 2006, from http://oas.samhsa.gov/2k6/womenTx/womenTX.htm

Drug Policy Alliance. (2001, November). *Policy issues concerning women offenders and their children.* Retrieved September 11, 2008, from Lindesmith Library: http://www.drugpolicy.org/library/owen_women_offenders2.cfm

Drug War Facts. (n.d.). *Annual causes of death in the United States.* Retrieved July 26, 2007, from http://www.drugwarfacts.org/causes.htm

Drug War Facts. (2005). *Race, prison, and the drug laws.* Retrieved October 29, 2008, from http://www.drugwarfacts.org/racepris.htm

Drysdale, M., & Rye, B. (2006). *Taking sides: Clashing views in adolescence.* Dubuque, IA: McGraw Hill.

Eaves, C. (2004). Heroin use among female adolescents: The role of partner influence in path of initiation and route of administration. *American Journal of Drug and Alcohol Abuse, 30,* 21–38.

Edwards, J. M., Halpern, C. T., & Wechsberg, W. M. (2006). Correlates of exchanging sex for drugs or money among women who use crack cocaine. *AIDS Education and Prevention, 18,* 420–429.

Eisenthal, S., & Udin, H. (1972). Psychological factors associated with drug and alcohol usage among Neighborhood Youth Corps enrollees. *Developmental Psychology, 7,* 119–123.

Engels, R. C. M. E., Scholte, R. H. J., van Lieshout C. F. M., deKemp, R., & Overbeek, G. (2006). Should adolescents be allowed to drink alcohol? Yes. In M. Drysdale & B. J. Rye (Eds.), *Taking sides* (pp. 20–26). Dubuque, IA: McGraw Hill.

Enns, C. Z. (2003). Contemporary adaptations of traditional approaches to the counseling of women. In M. Kopala & M. A. Keitel (Eds.), *Handbook of counseling women* (pp. 3–21). Thousand Oaks, CA: Sage.

Erickson, L., Molina, C. A., Ladd, G. T., Pietrzak, R. H., & Petry, N. M. (2005). Problem and pathological gambling are associated with poorer mental and physical health in older adults. *International Journal of Geriatric Psychiatry, 20*, 754–759.

Erk, R. R. (2008). *Counseling treatment for children and adolescents with DSM-IV-TR disorders* (2nd ed.). Columbus, OH: Pearson.

Ewald, R. (2003). Sexual addiction. *AllPsych Journal* (online version). Retrieved July 27, 2007, from http://allpsych.com/journal/sexaddiction.html

Favazza, A. R., & Simeon, D. (1995), Self-mutilation. In E. Hollander & D. J. Stein (Eds.), *Impulsivity and aggression* (pp. 185–200). Sussex, England: Wiley.

Fendrich, M., Hubbell, A., & Lurigio, A. J. (2006). Providers' perceptions of gender-specific drug treatment. *Journal of Drug Issues, 36*, 667–686.

Finnegan, D. G. (2001). Clinical issues with lesbians. In *U.S. Department of Health and Human Services, Substance Abuse and Mental Health Treatment Services (SAMHSA): A provider's introduction to substance abuse treatment for lesbian, gay, bisexual, and transgender individuals* (pp. 73–77). Washington, DC: U.S. Department of Health and Human Services.

Fiorentine, R., & Hillhouse, M. P. (1999). Drug treatment effectiveness and client-counselor empathy: Exploring the effects of gender and ethnic congruency. *Journal of Drug Issues, 29*, 59–74.

Foote, J., Wilkens, C., & Vavagiakis, P. (2004). A national survey of alcohol screening and referral in college health centers. *Journal of American College Health, 52*, 149–157.

Fowle, N. (2008, July 3). *Drug addiction: A public health issue, not a law enforcement problem.* Petoskey, MI: Petoskey News-Review.

Freedman, E. B. (2002). *No turning back: The history of feminism and the future of women.* New York: Ballantine Books.

Gallant, W., Holoko, M., & Siegel, S. (1997). The use of music in counseling addictive clients. *Journal of Alcohol and Drug Education, 42*, 42–52.

Galvani, S. (2004). Responsible disinhibition: Alcohol, men and violence to women. *Addiction Research and Theory, 12*, 357–371.

Gilligan, C., Ward, J. V., & Taylor, J. M. (1988). *Mapping the moral domain.* Boston: Harvard University Press.

Godfrey, J. R. (2006). Toward optimal health: Eva Selhub, M.D., discusses mind-body medicine for women. *Journal of Women's Health, 15*, 1111–1115.

Golub, A., & Johnson, B. D. (2001). Variation in youthful risks of progression from alcohol and tobacco to marijuana and to hard drugs across generations. *American Journal of Public Health, 91*, 225–232.

Gordon, S. M. (2002). *Women and addiction: Gender issues in abuse and treatment* (Report CG031857). Wernersville, PA: Caron Foundation. (ERIC Document Reproduction Service ED466897)

Gray, M. (1998). *Drug crazy.* New York: Random House.

Green, C. A. (2006). Gender and use of substance abuse treatment services. *Alcohol Research and Health, 29,* 55–62.

Greenfield, S. F. (2002). Women and alcohol use disorders. *Harvard Review of Psychiatry, 10,* 76–85.

Grose, T. K. (2007, March 26/April 2). Abuse as a disease, not a crime. *U.S. News and World Report,* p. 59.

Guthrie, B. J., & Flinchbaugh, L. J. (2001). Gender-specific substance prevention programming: Going beyond just focusing on girls. *Journal of Early Adolescence, 21,* 354–372.

Guyon, L., Brochu, S., Parent, I., & Desjardins, L. (1999). At-risk behaviors with regard to HIV and addiction among women in prison. *Women and Health, 29,* 49–66.

Hall, P. (2006). Understanding sexual addiction. *Therapy Today, 17,* 30–34.

Hanna, C. A., Hanna, F. J., Giordano, F. G., & Tollerud, T. (1998). Meeting the needs of women in counseling: Implications of a review of the literature. *Journal of Humanistic Education and Development, 36,* 160–170.

Hapke, U., Schumann, A., Rumpf, H.-J., John, U., & Meyer, C. (2006). Post-traumatic stress disorder: The role of trauma, pre-existing psychiatric disorders, and gender. *European Archives of Psychiatry and Clinical Neuroscience, 256,* 299–306.

Harley, D. A., & Bishop, M. (2008). Persons with disabilities and addictions. In D. Capuzzi & M. Stauffer (Eds.), *Foundations of addiction counseling* (pp. 366–386). Boston: Pearson Education.

Harned, M. S., Najavits, L. M., & Weiss, R. D. (2006). Self-harm and suicidal behavior in women with comorbid PTSD and substance dependence. *American Journal on Addictions, 15,* 392–395.

Harrison, P. A., Fulkerson, J. A., & Beebe, T. J. (1997). Multiple substance use among adolescent physical and sexual abuse victims. *Child Abuse and Neglect, 21,* 529–539.

Hartz, L., & Thick, L. (2005). Art therapy strategies to raise self-esteem in female juvenile offenders: A comparison of art psychotherapy and art as therapy approaches. *Art Therapy, 22,* 70–80.

Haseltine, F. P. (2000). Gender differences in addiction and recovery. *Journal of Women's Health and Gender-Based Medicine, 9,* 579–583.

Hegamin, A., Anglin, G., & Farabee, D. (2001). Gender differences in the perception of drug user treatment: Assessing drug user treatment for youthful offenders. *Substance Use and Misuse, 36,* 2159–2170.

Hernandez, D., & Leong, P. L. (2009). Feminism's future: Young feminists of color take the mic. In E. Disch (Ed.), *Reconstructing gender: A multicultural anthology* (5th ed., pp. 639–642). Boston: McGraw Hill.

Hoaken, P. N. S., & Pihl, R. O. (2000). The effects of alcohol intoxication on aggressive responses in men and women. *Alcohol and Alcoholism, 35,* 471–477.

Holder, H. D. (2006). Racial and gender differences in substance abuse: What should communities do about them? In W. R. Miller & K. M. Carroll (Eds.), *Rethinking substance abuse: What the science shows, and what we should do about it* (pp. 153–165). New York: Guilford Press.

Hood, A. B., & Johnson, R. W. (2007). *Assessment in counseling: A guide to the use of psychological assessment procedures* (4th ed.). Alexandria, VA: American Counseling Association.

hooks, b. (2000). *Feminist theory: From margin to center* (2nd ed.). Cambridge, MA: South End Press.

Horay, B. J. (2006). Moving towards gray: Art therapy and ambivalence in substance abuse treatment. *Art Therapy, 23,* 14–22.

Howard, D. E., & Wang, M. Q. (2005). Psychosocial correlates of U.S. adolescents who report a history of forced sexual intercourse. *Journal of Adolescent Health, 36,* 372–379.

Huchting, K., Lac, A., & LaBrie, J. W. (2007). An application of the theory of planned behavior to sorority alcohol consumption. *Addictive Behaviors, 33,* 538–551.

Husler, G., & Plancherel, B. (2006). A gender specific model of substance use. *Addiction Research and Theory, 14,* 399–412.

Hussong, A. M. (2000). The settings of adolescent alcohol and drug use. *Journal of Youth and Adolescence, 29,* 107–119.

Joint United Nations Programme on HIV/AIDS, Global Coalition on Women and AIDS (GCWA). (n.d.). *Preventing HIV infection in girls and young women.* Retrieved January 27, 2008, from data.unaids.org/GCWA/GCWA_BG_prevention_en.pdf

Jordan, J. V., Kaplan, A. G., Miller, J. B., Stiver, I. P., & Surrey, J. L. (1991). *Women's growth in connection.* New York: Guilford Press.

Jordan, K. M. (2000). Substance abuse among gay, lesbian, bisexual, transgender, and questioning adolescents. *School Psychology Review, 29,* 201–206.

Kaskutas, L. A., Zhang, L., French, M. T., & Witbrodt, J. (2005). Women's programs versus mixed-gender day treatment: Results from a randomized study. *Addiction, 100,* 60–69.

Kerr, B. A. (1994). *Smart girls two: A new psychology of girls, women and giftedness.* Dayton, OH: Psychology Press.

Kilbourne, J. (2004). "The more you subtract the more you add": Cutting girls down to size. In T. Kasser & A. D. Kanner (Eds.), *Psychology and consumer culture: The struggle for a good life in a materialistic world* (pp. 251–270). Washington, DC: American Psychological Association.

Ko, C., Yen, J., Chen, C., Chen, S., Wu, K., & Yen, C. (2006). Tridimensional personality of adolescents with Internet addiction and substance use experience. *Canadian Journal of Psychiatry, 51,* 887–894.

Koehn, C. V., & Hardy, C. (2006). Substance dependence and depression in women. *Guidance and Counseling, 21,* 274–282.

Kuhn, C., Swartzwelder, S., & Wilson, W. (2008). *Buzzed: The straight facts about the most used and abused drugs from alcohol to ecstasy.* New York: W.W. Norton & Company.

Kulis, S., Nieri, T., Yabiku, S., Stromwall, L. K., & Marsiglia, F. F. (2007). Promoting reduced and discontinued substance use among adolescent substance users: Effectiveness of a universal prevention program. *Prevention Science, 8,* 35–49.

Landheim, A. S., Bakken, K., & Vaglum, P. (2003). Gender differences in the prevalence of symptom disorders and personality disorders among polysubstance abusers and pure alcoholics. *European Addiction Research, 9,* 8–17.

Leonard, K. E. (2005). Editorial. *Addiction, 100,* 422–425.

Leslie, D. R., Perina, B. A., & Maqueda, M. C. (2001). Clinical issues with transgender individuals. In *U.S. Department of Health and Human Services, Substance Abuse and Mental Health Treatment Services (SAMHSA): A provider's introduction to substance abuse treatment for lesbian, gay, bisexual, and transgender individuals* (pp. 91–98). Washington, DC: U.S. Department of Health and Human Services.

Libby, A. M., & Riggs, P. D. (2008). Integrated substance use and mental health services for adolescents: Challenges and opportunities. In Y. Kaminer & O. G. Bukstein (Eds.), *Adolescent substance abuse: Psychiatric comorbidity and high-risk behaviors* (pp. 435–452). New York: Haworth Press.

Ling, D. C., Wong, W. C., Holroyd, E. A., & Gray, S. A. (2007). Silent killers of the night: An exploration of psychological health and suicidality among female street sex workers. *Journal of Sex and Marital Therapy, 33,* 281–299.

Lips, H. M. (2006). *A new psychology of women: Gender, culture, and ethnicity* (3rd ed.). Boston: McGraw-Hill.

Lisansky-Gomberg, E. S. (1989). Suicide risk among women with alcohol problems. *American Journal of Public Health, 79,* 1363–1365.

Litt, J., & McNeil, M. (1994). *Troubling children: Studies of children and social problems* (J. Best, Ed.). Hawthorne, NY: Aldine Transaction.

Lynch, W. J., Roth, M. E., & Carroll, M. E. (2002). Biological basis of sex differences in drug abuse: Preclinical and clinical studies. *Psychopharmacology, 164,* 121–137.

Lysaught, E., & Wodarski, J. S. (1996). Model: A dual focused intervention for depression and addiction. *Journal of Child and Adolescent Substance Abuse, 5,* 55–72.

Maisto, S. A., Pollock, N. K., Cornelius, J. R., Lynch, K. G., & Martin, C. S. (2003). Alcohol relapse as a function of relapse definition in a clinical sample of adolescents. *Addictive Behaviors, 28,* 449–459.

March of Dimes. (n.d.). *Drinking alcohol during pregnancy.* Retrieved January 8, 2006, from http://www.marchofdimes.com/professionals/14332_1170. asp

Marcus, M. D., & Kalarchian, M. A. (2003). Binge eating in children and adolescents. *International Journal of Eating Disorders, 34,* S47–S57.

Marquenie, L. A., Schade, A., van Balkom, A. J., Comijs, H. C., de Graaf, R., Vollebergh, W., et al. (2007). Origin of the comorbidity of anxiety disorders and alcohol dependence: Findings of a general population study. *European Addiction Research, 13*, 39–49.

Marsh, J. C., D'Aunno, T. A., & Smith, B. D. (2000). Increasing access and providing social services to improve drug abuse treatment for women with children. *Addiction, 95*, 1237–1247.

Matthews, C. R., & Lorah, P. (2005). An examination of addiction treatment completion by gender and ethnicity. *Journal of Addictions and Offender Counseling, 25*, 114–125.

McCance-Katz, E. F., Carroll, K. M., & Rounsaville, B. J. (1999). Gender differences in treatment-seeking cocaine abusers: Implications for treatment and prognosis. *American Journal on Addictions, 8*, 300–311.

McNeese, C. A., & DiNitto, D. M. (2005). *Chemical dependency: A systems approach* (3rd ed.). Boston: Allyn & Bacon.

McVinney, D. (2001). Clinical issues with bisexuals. In *U.S. Department of Health and Human Services, Substance Abuse and Mental Health Treatment Services (SAMHSA): A provider's introduction to substance abuse treatment for lesbian, gay, bisexual, and transgender individuals* (pp. 87–90). Washington, DC: U.S. Department of Health and Human Services.

Miller, A. (1981). *The drama of the gifted child: The search for the true self.* Frankfurt, Germany: Basic Books.

Miller, W. R., & Rollnick, S. (2002). *Motivational interviewing: Preparing people for change* (2nd ed.). New York: Guilford Press.

Monti, P. M., Tevyaw, T. O., & Borsari, B. (2004/2005). Drinking among young adults. *Alcohol Research and Health, 28*, 236–244.

Moore, L., & MacKinnon, D. (2001). Preadolescent girls and the presentation of the self: A dramaturgical perspective. *Alberta Journal of Educational Research, 47*, 309–324.

Moos, R. H., Schutte, K., Brennan, P., & Moos, B. S. (2004). Ten-year patterns of alcohol comsumption and drinking problems among older women and men. *Addiction, 99*, 829–838.

Moufakkir, O., (2006). An analysis of elderly gamers' trip characteristics and gambling behavior: Comparing the elderly with their younger counterparts. *UNLV Gaming Research & Review Journal, 10*(2), 63–75.

Mulia, N. (2002, December). Ironies in the pursuit of well-being: the perspectives of low-income, substance-using women on service institutions. *Contemporary Drug Problems.* Retrieved on March 8, 2009 from: http://www.accessmlibrary.com/coms2/summary_0286-10052331_ITM.

Najavits, L. M., Sullivan, T. P., Schmitz, M., Weiss, R. D., & Lee, C. S. (2004). Treatment utilization by women with PTSD and substance dependence. *American Journal on Addictions, 13*, 215–224.

Najavits, L. M., Weiss, R. D., Shaw, S. R., & Muenz, L. R. (1998). "Seeking safety": Outcome of a new cognitive-behavioral psychotherapy for women with posttraumatic stress disorder and substance dependence. *Journal of Traumatic Stress, 11*, 437–456.

National Center on Addiction and Substance Abuse (NCASA). (2006). *Women under the influence*. Baltimore: Johns Hopkins University Press.

National Institute on Drug Abuse (NIDA). (2005). *Research report: Prescription drugs abuse and addition*. Rockville, MD: National Institute on Drug Abuse.

National Survey on Drug Use and Health (NSDUH). (2005). Department of Health and Human Services, Substance Abuse and Mental Health Services Administration, Office of Applied Studies. Retrieved July 17, 2007, from http://www.oas.samhsa.gov/NSDUH/2k5NSDUH/2k5results.htm#3.3

NCASA. (2005). *Women under the influence*. Baltimore, MD: St. John's University Press.

Nelson-Zlupko, L., Kauffman, E., & Dore, M. M. (1995). Gender differences in drug addiction and treatment: Implications for social work intervention with substance-abusing women. *Social Work, 40*, 45–54.

NeSmith, C. L., Wilcoxon, S. A., & Satcher, J. F. (2000). Male leadership in an addicted women's group: An empirical approach. *Journal of Addictions and Offender Counseling, 20*, 75–83.

Nolen-Hoeksema, S., & Hilt, L. (2006). Possible contributors to the gender differences in alcohol use and problems. *Journal of General Psychology, 133*, 357–374.

Oggins, J., & Eichenbaum, J. (2002). Engaging transgender substance users in substance use treatment. *International Journal of Transgenderism, 6* [Online]. Retrieved July 8, 2008, from www.symposion.com/ijt/ijtvo06no02_03.htm

Olson, J. (2007, June 22). When it's no longer a game. *Pioneer Press*, St. Paul, MN: p. 1A.

Ozechowski, T. J., & Liddle, H. A. (2000). Family-based therapy for adolescent drug abuse: Knowns and unknowns. *Clinical Child and Family Psychology Review, 3*, 269–298.

Pardeck, J. T. (1991). Using books to prevent and treat adolescent chemical dependency. *Adolescence, 26*, 201–208.

Parks, C. A., Hesselbrock, M. N., Hesselbrock, V. M., & Segal, B. (2003). Factors affecting entry into substance abuse treatment: Gender differences among alcohol-dependent Alaska natives. *Social Work Research, 27*, 151–161.

Peebles-Wilkins, W. (2006). Let's pay attention to girls and drugs. *Children and Schools, 28*, 131–132.

Pipher, M. (1994). *Reviving Ophelia: Saving the selves of adolescent girls*. New York: Riverhead Books.

Pitcher, K. C. (2006). The staging of agency in *Girls Gone Wild*. *Critical Studies in Media Communication, 23*, 200–218.

Potenza, M. N., Steinberg, M. A., McLaughlin, S. D., Wu, R., Rounsaville, B. J., & O'Malley, S. S. (2001). Gender-related differences in the characteristics of problem gamblers using a gambling helpline. *American Journal of Psychiatry, 158*, 1500–1505.

Power, C. A. (2005). Food and sex addiction: Helping the clinician recognize and treat the interaction. *Sexual Addiction and Compulsivity, 12*, 219–234.

Problem gambling shown to affect all ages. (1994). *Alcoholism & Druge Abuse Weekly, 6*(16), 2–3.

Purington, A., & Whitlock, J. (2004, August). *Research facts and findings: Self-injury facts sheet.* ACT for Youth Upstate Center for Excellence. Publication of Cornell University, University of Rochester, and New York State Center for School Safety. Retrieved October 9, 2008, from www.actforyouth.net

Rahman, Q., & Clarke, C. D. (2005). Sex differences in neurocognitive functioning among abstinent recreational cocaine users. *Psychopharmacology, 181,* 374–380.

Rape, Abuse and Incest National Network (RAINN). (n.d.). *Statistics.* Retrieved January 15, 2006, from http://www.rainn.org/statistics.

Reinarman, C., & Levine, H. G. (1995). *Images of issues: Typifying contemporary social problems* (J. Best, Ed.). Piscataway, NJ: Aldine Transaction.

Riordan, R. J., & Wilson, L. S. (1989). Bibliotherapy: Does it work? *Journal of Counseling and Development, 67,* 506–508.

Risser, J. M. H., Timpson, S. C., McCurdy, S. A., Ross, M. W., & Williams, M. L. (2006). Psychological correlates of trading sex for money among African American crack cocaine smokers. *American Journal of Drug and Alcohol Abuse, 32,* 645–653.

Robertshawe, P. (2007). A comparative trial of yoga and relaxation to reduce stress and anxiety. *Journal of the Australian Traditional-Medicine Society, 13,* 225.

Roeloffs, C. A., Fink, A., Unutzer, J., Tang, L., & Wells, K. B. (2001). Problematic substance use, depressive symptoms, and gender in primary care. *Psychiatric Services, 52,* 1251–1253.

Rosen, R. (2007). Epilogue: Beyond backlash. In S. M. Shaw & J. Lee (Eds.), *Women's voices feminist visions: Classic and contemporary readings* (3rd ed.). New York: McGraw-Hill, 732–738.

Ross, L. E., & Toner, B. (2003). Sexism and women's mental health. *Women and Environments International Magazine, 60/61,* 34.

Ruder, D. B. (2008, September/October). A work in progress: The teen brain. *Harvard Magazine,* 8–10.

Satre, D. D., Blow, F. C., Chi, F. W., & Weisner, C. (2007). Gender differences in seven-year alcohol and drug treatment outcomes among older adults. *The American Journal on Addictions, 16,* 216–221.

Schinke, S. P., Fang, L., & Cole, K. C. A. (2008). Substance use among early adolescent girls: Risk and protective factors. *Journal of Adolescent Health, 43,* 191–194.

Schneider, J. P., Sealy, J., Montgomery, J., & Irons, R. R. (2005). Ritualization and reinforcement: Keys to understanding mixed addiction involving sex and drugs. *Sexual Addiction and Compulsivity, 12,* 121–148.

Schnoll, S. H., & Weaver, M. F. (1998). Pharmacology: Gender-specific considerations in the use of psychoactive medications. In C. L. Wetherington & A. B. Roman (Eds.), *Drug addiction research and the health of women* (pp. 223–228). Rockville, MD: National Institute on Drug Abuse.

Silverman, J. G., Raj, A., Mucci, L. A., & Hathaway, J. E. (2001). Dating violence against adolescent girls and associated substance use, unhealthy weight control, sexual risk behavior, pregnancy, and suicidality. *Journal of the American Medical Association, 286,* 572–579.

Simpson, J. S., & Hawke, W. A. (1970). Self-mutilation: Case of a 13-year-old girl. *Pediatrics, 45,* 1008–1011.

Singer, M. I., Bussey, J., Song, L.-Y., & Lunghofer, L. (1995). The psychosocial issues of women serving time in jail. *Social Work, 40,* 103–113.

Smart, R. G., & Fejer, D. (1972). Drug use among adolescents and their parents: Closing the generation gap in mood modification. *Journal of Abnormal Psychology, 79,* 153–160.

Sonne, S. C., Back, S. E., Zuniga, C. D., Randall, C. L., & Brady, K. T. (2003). Gender differences in individuals with comorbid alcohol dependence and post-traumatic stress disorder. *American Journal on Addictions, 12,* 412–423.

Spitzer, R. L. (1981). The diagnostic status of homosexuality in DSM-III: A reformulation of the issues. *American Journal of Psychiatry, 138,* 210–215.

Stern, L. (1991). Disavowing the self in female adolescence. In C. Gilligan, A. G. Rogers, & D. L. Tolman (Eds.), *Women, girls and psychotherapy: Reframing resistance* (pp. 105–117). New York: Harrington Park Press.

Stevens, P., & Smith, R. L. (2009). *Substance abuse counseling: Theory and practice* (4th ed.). Upper Saddle River, NJ: Pearson Education.

Stevenson, J. S., & Masters, J. A. (2005). Predictors of alcohol misuse and abuse in older women. *Journal of Nursing Scholarship, 37,*(4), 329–335.

Stewart, S. H., Morris, E., Mellings, T., & Komar, J. (2006). Relations of social anxiety variables to drinking motives, drinking quantity and frequency, and alcohol-related problems in undergraduates. *Journal of Mental Health, 15,* 671–682.

Stice, E., Presnell, K., & Spangler, D. (2002). Risk factors for binge eating onset in adolescent girls: A 2-year prospective investigation. *Health Psychology, 21,* 131–138.

Stitt, G. B., Giacopassi, D., & Nichols, M. (2003). Gambling among older adults: A comparative analysis.*Experiential Aging Research, 29,* 189–203.

Straussner, S. L. A., & Attia, P. R. (2002). Women's addiction and treatment through a historical lens. In S. L. A. Straussner & S. Brown (Eds.), *The handbook of addiction treatment for women* (pp. 3–25). San Francisco: Jossey-Bass.

Stukin, S. (n.d.). Asana columns: Freedom from addiction. *Yoga Journal.* Retrieved July 9, 2008, from http://www.yogajournal.com/practice/679

Su, S. S., Hoffmann, J. P., Gerstein, D. R., & Johnson, R. A. (1997). The effect of home environment on adolescent substance use and depressive symptoms. *Journal of Drug Issues, 27,* 851–877.

Substance Abuse and Mental Health Services Administration (SAMHSA). 1998). *Substance abuse among older adults: Treatment improvement protocol series #26.* Rockville, MD: U.S. Department of Health and Human Services.

Substance Abuse and Mental Health Services Administration (SAMHSA). 2007 report. Retrieved from http://www.oas.samhsa.gov, March 8, 2009.

Suicide Prevention Council. (n.d.). *About suicide: Facts and figures.* Retrieved October 8, 2008, from Feeling Blue: Suicide Prevention Council: http://feelingblue.org/about-suicide/facts-figures

Svirko, E., & Hawton, K. (2007). Self-injurious behavior and eating disorders: The extent and nature of the association. *Suicide and Life-Threatening Behavior, 37,* 409–421.

Tanskanen, A., Tuomilehto, J., Viinamaki, H., Vartiainen, E., & Lehtonen, J. (2000). Smoking and the risk of suicide. *Acta Psychiatrica Scandinavica, 101,* 243–245.

Tarter, R. E. (2002). Etiology of adolescent substance abuse: A developmental perspective. *American Journal on Addictions, 11,* 171–191.

Templeton, R. (2007). She who believes in freedom: Young women defy the prison industrial complex. In S. M. Shaw & J. Lee (Eds.), *Women's voices feminist visions: Classic and contemporary readings* (3rd ed.). New York: McGraw-Hill, 254–277.

Thompson, C. L., & Henderson, D. A. (2007). *Counseling children* (7th ed.). Belmont, CA: Thompson/Brooks-Cole.

Tiggemann, M., Gardiner, M., & Slater, A. (2000). I would rather be size 10 than have straight A's: A focus group study of adolescent girls' wish to be thinner. *Journal of Adolescence, 23,* 645–659.

Toporek, R. L., Lewis, J. A., & Crethar, H. C. (in press). Promoting systemic change through the advocacy competencies. *Journal of Counseling and Development.*

Tracy, E. M., & Martin, T. C. (2007). Children's roles in the social networks of women in substance abuse treatment. *Journal of Substance Abuse Treatment, 32,* 81–88.

Turner, M. (2008). Substance use and abuse by the elderly: Current and future trends in identification, assessment, and treatment. *Winona State University Capstone Presentation* (pp. 1–5). Winona: WSU.

U.S. Department of Health and Human Services (USDHHS). (2005). *Alcohol: A women's health issue.* NIH Publication 04-4956.

U.S. Department of Justice (USDOJ). (2007). *Bureau of Justice statistics.* Retrieved October 29, 2008, from http://www.ojp.usdoj.gov/bjs/welcome.html

Veach, L. J., Remley, T. P., Kippers, S. M., & Sorg, J. D. (2000). Retention predictors related to intensive outpatient programs for substance use disorders. *American Journal of Drug and Alcohol Abuse, 26,* 417–428.

Velasquez, M. M., & Stotts, A. L. (2003). The nature, course, and treatment of substance abuse among women. *Journal of Prevention and Treatment of Drug Abuse, 1,* 113–148.

Vernon, A., & Clemente, R. (2005). *Assessment and intervention with children and adolescents: Developmental and multicultural approaches.* Alexandria, VA: American Counseling Association.

Verona, E., Reed II, A., Curtin, J. J., & Pole, M. (2007). Gender differences in emotional and overt/covert aggressive responses to stress. *Aggressive Behavior, 33*, 261–271.

Wade, J. C. (1994). Substance abuse: Implications for counseling African American men. *Journal of Mental Health Counseling, 16*, 415–433.

Walker, G. C., Scott, P. S., & Koppersmith, G. (1998). The impact of child sexual abuse on addiction severity: An analysis of trauma processing. *Journal of Psychosocial Nursing and Mental Heath Services, 36*, 10–19.

Wallace, J. M., Bachman, J. G., O'Malley, P. M., Schulenberg, J. E., Cooper, S. M., & Johnston, L. D. (2003). Gender and ethnic differences in smoking, drinking, and illicit drug use among American 8th, 10th, and 12th grade students, 1976–2000. *Addiction, 98*, 225–234.

Wastell, C. A. (1996). Feminist developmental theory: Implications for counseling. *Journal of Counseling and Development, 74*, 575–581.

Webster, J. M., Rosen, P. J., McDonald, H. S., Staton-Tindall, M., Garrity, T. F., & Leukefeld, C. G. (2007). Mental health as a mediator of gender differences in employment barriers among drug abusers. *American Journal of Drug and Alcohol Abuse, 33*, 259–265.

Wehren, A., & De Lisi, R. (1983). The development of gender understanding: Judgments and explanations. *Child Development, 54*, 1568–1578.

Weisner, C. (2005). Substance misuse: What place for women-only treatment programs? *Addiction, 100*, 7–8.

What were Godfrey's Cordial and Dalby's Carminative? (1970). *Pediatrics, 45*, 1011.

White, I. R., Altmann, D. R., & Nanchahal, K. (2002). Alcohol consumption and mortality: Modelling risks for men and women at different ages. *British Medical Journal, 325*, 191–197.

Wilke, D. J. (2004). Predicting suicide ideation for substance abusers: The role of self-esteem, abstinence, and attendance at 12-Step meetings. *Addiction Research and Theory, 12*, 231–240.

Wilmshurst, L. (2005). *Essentials of child psychopathology*. Hoboken, NJ: Wiley.

Wilsnack, R. W., & Wilsnack, S. C. (1978). Sex roles and drinking among adolescent girls. *Journal of Studies on Alcohol, 39*, 1855–1874.

Wilson, J. M., & Donnermeyer, J. F. (2006). Urbanity, rurality, and adolescent substance use. *Criminal Justice Review, 31*, 337–356.

Women for Sobriety (WFS). (1993). "New Life" acceptance program: 13 statements. Retrieved June 26, 2008, from http://www.womenforsobriety.org/

Women's Christian Temperance Union (WCTU). (n.d.). *History.* Retrieved August 28, 2007, from http://www.wctu.org/history.html

World Health Organization (WHO). (n.d.). *Traditional medicine fact sheet.* Retrieved July 7, 2008, from http://www.who.int/topics/traditional_medicine/en/

Wright, P. B., Stewart, K. E., Fischer, E. P., Carlson, R. G., Falck, R., Wang, J., Leukefeld, C. G., & Booth, B. M. (2007). HIV risk behaviors among rural stimulant users: Variation by gender and race/ethnicity. *AIDS Education and Prevention, 19*, 137–150.

Young, A. M., Boyd, C., & Hubbell, A. (2000). Prostitution, drug use, and coping with psychological distress. *Journal of Drug Issues, 30,* 789–800.

Young, D. (2002). Study finds inappropriate medication use by community-dwelling elderly. *American Journal of Health-System Pharmacy, 59,* 228–230.

Zinn, H. (2003). *A people's history of the United States.* New York: HarperCollins.

INDEX

CPSIA information can be obtained
at www.ICGtesting.com
Printed in the USA
FFOW03n1851210618
47192693-49905FF